# Anything
# for
# Amelia

*A true story of the challenges endured by two gay men
who had the desire to adopt a child.*

Andrew C. Branham

**Anything for Amelia**
Copyright ©2015 Andrew C. Branham

ISBN 978-1506-900-26-1 PRINT
ISBN 978-1506-900-27-8 EBOOK

LCCN 2015949048

September 2015

Published and Distributed by
First Edition Design Publishing, Inc.
P.O. Box 20217, Sarasota, FL 34276-3217
www.firsteditiondesignpublishing.com

Library of Congress Cataloging-in-Publication Data
Branham, Andrew C.
    Anything for amelia / written by Andrew C. Branham.
    p. cm.
    ISBN 978-1506-900-02-5 pbk, 978-1506-900-03-2 digital

1. Family & Relationships / Adoption & Fostering. 2. Gay Studies. 3. Biography & Autobiography/ Lgbt.

B8214

*Forgive, O Lord, my little jokes on Thee And I'll forgive Thy great big one on me.*

- Robert Frost

A very special thank you to:
Lil
Tracy
Michele
Jeanne
Marnee and Rob
Jay and Lisa
DJ (David) McCann
Faye and DJ
All of our family and friends

## Author's Notes

Most of the names and places in this book have been changed to ensure privacy and to preserve the dignity of others.

This book was written from my perspective at the time of the events and based on my journal. This was done purposefully so that the reader could connect with how we were feeling at any given time.

This book is dedicated to all of the adoptive families, all of the adopted children, all of the waiting families, and all of the birth mothers who made the ultimate sacrifice of love.

# Chapter One

*There has always been a simple saying that "Everything happens for a reason." I believe this is the ultimate truth, and for 206 of the most challenging days of my life, I leaned on this to help me to take "one day at a time."*

It was an extraordinary, warm spring day in the East Bay of Northern California when our lives changed forever. I stood on the top steps of our three-story townhome in Livermore, dropped to my knees, and prayed. I knew the call was coming at any moment, and this gay agnostic/Catholic was taking one last opportunity to ask God for some help and guidance. I prayed that whatever decision that was coming was the right one, since my partner and I both believe that everything happens for a reason. I knew I had to accept whatever decision came.

Seconds later, the call we had been waiting for and dreaming about, came. I was stunned, ecstatic, overjoyed. My eyes watered and I stood paralyzed at a loss for words. When I hung up the phone, I thanked God for answering my prayers. My mind was racing, and I could not even manage to move. Finally I got myself together and called my partner DJ, who was at work at the time. He didn't answer. I decided that this was too important to wait, so I jumped in my Chevy Volt and drove to his workplace, all the while trying to think about what I was going to say. Just thinking about telling him made my eyes well up with joy.

It was a glorious day in the Bay Area, with bright blue skies, pleasant temperatures, and the view of the marine layer far off in the distance toward San Francisco. Livermore lies on the outskirts of the valley and is surrounded by rolling green hills, mountains, and wine vineyards. DJ's work was only a few miles from the house, so I arrived quickly and stepped inside. Every piece of sporting equipment known to mankind filled this big box franchise. The store was busy, and he had a very long line of customers to attend to. *Damn it*, I thought to myself. He noticed that I had walked in, and we made urgent eye contact. He shrugged and gestured to his long line of customers, but I stormed over and cut to the front of the line. Trying not to cry in public, I said, "Babe, we are matched! We're going to be daddies!"

He looked stunned, but he had no time to react before a frustrated customer gave him the look of death. His eyes lit up like the bright star on top of the most glorious Christmas tree. "I will call you as soon as I can," he stuttered as customers pushed by me to make their purchases.

Before I even arrived home, my phone rang, and of course it was DJ, who had taken an emergency break. I told him that I had just received the call that I had been matched with a young woman from Golden Valley, Arizona; with the code name Bette (adoption agencies give a birth mother a code name before you match to protect her privacy). At first he did not know what to say, and then he began to cry and said, "Oh my God, we are daddies." He was engulfed in emotion, jubilation, and joy.

At the time, the only thing I knew was that she was in Golden Valley, she was two months pregnant, the gender was unknown, and that she and the baby were healthy. The baby was due in November of 2014 and would be a C-section one week before the due date. We knew about her medical history, since we had read her profile the night before when we decided to submit my profile booklet to her and officially be in the adoption pool. Our adoption facilitator, Jill, had told us that she had spoken with Bette several times and that she was polite, warm, friendly, easy to talk to, and very outgoing. According to her medical files, she did not drink, did not smoke, did not do any drugs, and had no previous psychiatric issues. She was taking great care of herself by taking prenatal vitamins, eating well, and having regular visits to her OBGYN. She was not married but had a long-term rocky relationship with her boyfriend Doug. We knew that she was 24 years old, that this would be her sixth child, and that she had successfully placed two children for adoption with separate adoptive families in the past two years.

The matching process had happened quickly. Essentially Bette, the birth mother, had been presented to all of the agency's clients the night before. The process asks that you carefully review all the information (medical history, medical records, etc.) and decide if you want to be submitted to the birth mother. We had decided that she was a nice fit for us, and she was open to same sex couples. After discussing it with Jill, the adoption facilitator, we decided to submit our profile. Profiles are short packets of information about the adoptive parent or parents. They include information about the applicant, dozens of pictures, a "Dear Birth Mother Letter," and other relevant information. The birth mother then looks at all of the profiles that are submitted to her and decides on a family to match with.

For most "waiting families" the matching process is a very difficult, lengthy and emotional time. In fact, waiting times of twelve to eighteen months are not uncommon. It is a challenging time for most families. These families are engulfed by the fact that they must be chosen and each time they are not matched, they question why. Waiting families dream of having their first child, but are bound by the fact that they must wait to be chosen. For us, Sandi was the first time we had submitted our profile. Our expectations of being selected were low, we were emotional and nervous. Immediately after we submitted our profile DJ had already become optimistically-anxious, "Drew, this was just meant to be. I know it in my heart. I feel it. This is the one for us and we're going to be selected!" On the other-hand I was sure that we would not be selected and was keeping my hopes realistic, "Babe there are so many others that applied for this baby. Why would she select our profile? We're unmarried, gay and it's a single adoption. Let's be realistic." While our opinions differed drastically, our emotions and nerves were extremely high. DJ would call Jill every hour to see if there were any updates (much to her dismay).

Much to my surprise, at about 8pm that evening, I received a call from Jill. "Hi, Andrew, I have Bette, the birth mother, on the other line, and she would like to speak with you. If the conversation goes well, you will likely be matched with her. So please keep calm and just have a natural conversation with her. Are you ready? I'll connect her now."

Of course I was ready, and I indicated to Jill that I was eager to speak to Bette. There was a long hold and then Jill's voice returned and said that Bette was now on the line. It was a bit awkward at first, since it was somewhat difficult to hear her over the sound of several kids in the background. She seemed slightly reluctant to talk, answering my questions in terse replies: "yes," "no," "sure," "ok." Eventually she asked if I was comfortable with the process being an open adoption, with sending pictures on a monthly basis, and with in-person visits at least once a year. She also said that she would be breastfeeding the baby when it was born and wanted to ensure that I was ok with that. I indicated that I was fine with all of the stipulations and I was very hopeful that she would choose me. Jill then ended the call and said that if it were a match, she would call me back that night or the next morning. I set my phone down, and that was the point that I started my praying on the stairs. I was expecting a long wait; at the earliest it would be the next morning, since it was already late. Much to my surprise, the phone rang just minutes later, and it was Jill. "Andrew, are you sitting down? Bette would like to speak with you." I was so caught off guard that I just stayed on my steps and mumbled that I was ready. Jill got us both on the line again and told me that Bette had something to say.

"Hi again, Andrew. My name is actually Sandi, and I would like to match with you for my adoption."

Jill then jumped in and asked me if I wanted to match as well. I quickly said, "Hi, Sandi, it is a pleasure to meet you, and we would be honored to match with you."

Again, Jill jumped in, congratulated us both on the match and indicated that more information would be emailed that night. We spoke for a few more minutes and then Jill ended the conversation. My emotions were pumping; I wanted to cry, laugh, and jump up and down. I wanted to call everyone I knew.

My initial thoughts about Sandi were that she was a little bit cold, difficult to speak to, and seemed very distracted by her children, but otherwise seemed like a fairly nice person. That night, Jill emailed me Sandi's contact information, full name, email address, cell phone number, the additional documents that I needed to sign, and Sandi's bank account information. She also suggested that I send something nice to Sandi as a kind gesture to start our long relationship as adoptive dad and birth mother. I called the only flower shop that was still open and ordered some flowers and chocolate-dipped strawberries to be delivered to Sandi's home the next day. I was also informed that Sandi's family was much different than what I was accustomed to. They were very poor, did not work, and lived under the poverty line. Hell, I had grown up in Lorain, Ohio, a melting pot of cultures and finances, and I could proudly say I was a very open person to any and all people. I was not worried about her being in a "different class" than DJ or myself.

I grew up the son of two hard-working and loving parents in a blue-collar town outside of Cleveland. My father was a teacher, and my mother stayed at home with my sister Kerri and me, so we were far from well-off, financially. My mother was a wonderful elementary school teacher who taught for 28 years. She took our early childhood years off so that she could be home with us. In reality, I still considered myself "Lorain;" I was still comfortable on someone's rickety front porch with a sofa on it, with multi-cultural food, and with a mixture of different people. I had long since given up drinking alcohol, but back when I did drink I preferred Olde English 800, Colt 45, or Schlitz 40s over fancy drinks or microbrews. In the interest of full disclosure, my high school and college years involved attending free-style rap parties in one of my close friend's basements. The Puerto Rican market that served random pig parts and the best rice and beans on Earth knew me by name, and it was my first stop every time I went home to visit. I am what one may call a Lorainite at heart, while wearing a business suit in my office.

Similarly, DJ grew up in the rural central lands of Florida. His family's modest home sat adjacent to an actual swamp. His father owned a sweeping-truck business, and his mother was a retail sales representative for a food broker. He was, and is, very lucky to have the parents he has because they are two of the most loving and accepting people I have ever met. They adored DJ and his sister and did everything they could for them. Growing up, they often struggled with money or even to put food on the table. His parents worked very hard, and they managed to get by paycheck to paycheck. The town, Lake Panassoffkee, was very small, and most people were considered rednecks.

It was a poor town where blue-collar workers lived day-to-day, and most people went to church on Sunday and the local bar most other days.

Every time I share the following story I get yelled at, but it paints a perfect picture of just how rural his home was. In his youth, DJ had a dog named Buddy that he absolutely loved and played with every day. He was his playmate and his best friend; a typical young boy and his dog relationship. Buddy was part waterdog and simply loved running into the water, the swamp, and the nearby low river. For fun, Buddy would chase birds and tease alligators while running up and down the shallow river under the hanging moss of the swamp trees. His parents knew the danger of Buddy's hobby of teasing gators, but they simply could not stop him. It was in his blood, and the damn dog just would not stay away from the river. Sadly, the inevitable happened one day, while Buddy was running along the riverbank chasing a bird. Thankfully DJ did not have to witness it, but the neighbors saw a 12-foot adult gator grab Buddy and devour him in a few bites. The whole family was devastated, and DJ was heartbroken. Sadly, DJ was also severely bullied throughout his youth and teen years for being small and obviously gay. Today, he would have been protected by new anti-bullying laws, but in the 1990s such protections did not exist. It made for a rough and tumultuous childhood and teenage years.

Many months before we matched with Sandi, DJ and I had made the decision to adopt. I would be adopting as a single parent, and DJ would adopt after we were married. He was still in college studying addiction medicine, and we did not think juggling marriage, school, and an adoption would be in his best interest at this time. Thus, I would be adopting myself, we would marry shortly after the baby was born, and he would then legally adopt. Just like all families seeking to adopt, we went through all the possible avenues. We had our own personal website with all of our information in an attempt to find a birth mother on our own. It included a letter to potential birth mothers, photos, our contact info, and biographies about our families and us. I am a marketer by profession, so I also did a lot of digital marketing on my own. I used Google AdWords as my main method of marketing so that any time someone searched for anything about adoption our webpage popped up on the right hand side as a paid search. In addition, I had target banner ads on many of the most popular websites. We also set up a sponsored Facebook page, "Drew and DJ's Adoption" and got over a thousand "likes" in a very short period of time. In addition, we were active on many other website such as Adoptimist.com, where profiles are available for any birth mother to see.

At the same time we interviewed several adoption agencies, sat through day-long adoption agency conferences, and finally decided on a large national agency. We paid the large up-front adoption fees and immediately started the process of getting ready to get into the pool of potential parents. The advantages of working with this large agency were that it worked with thousands of birth mothers and had the largest marketing budget in the industry. In fact, basically any time you did an adoption search on the Internet, their site was nearly always the first to come up. We worked closely with them as they began to build our profile page. They placed us in the African-American program because they said that it would help us get matched more quickly, and we had no race or sex preference. They told us that they mainly did heterosexual couples but had just opened up their agency to same sex couples. It was a good match, and we rounded up several hundred images of ourselves to send to their digital team. The agency seemed well-organized and was always quick to respond to our needs.

Meanwhile, as the agency was preparing our information to be placed in the "waiting families" pool, we had many other hurdles to overcome. The largest of these hurdles was the infamous home study. For any adoption—private, open, closed, international or foster—a home study must be completed. The process can be long and sometimes painful. In essence, a licensed social worker agency had to ensure that that my home was fit for an infant and that I was fit to be a parent. For most, the home study takes many months to complete and sometimes as long as a year. Anyone who knows me, however, knows that I am extremely impatient. I was bound and determined to finish this process in record time. You could not be matched with a birth mother until your home study was complete. Since I was adopting as a single parent, only my home and myself were required to do the study. This tedious but necessary process involves three visits to the home by a social worker, a very through medical exam with updated shots and records, a criminal and federal background check involving being fingerprinted, filling out a plethora of paperwork, and obtaining child abuse clearances from every state that I had ever lived in. DJ and I attended several parenting classes and learned adult and child first aid and CPR. I had to have eight people write personal character references for me. In addition, I had to baby-proof my house, which involved purchasing gun safes, fire extinguishers, more smoke and carbon monoxide detectors, and wall outlet guards. I also had to move all cleaners, soaps, solvents, and anything not natural to places where kids could not reach. Despite all of these requirements, I was determined to get it all done as quickly as I could.

I actually achieved my goal of completing the home study in record time. Our agency stated that it was the fastest turnaround for a home study that they had ever witnessed. In roughly six weeks I had the signed and official home study into the agency's hands. This major hurdle was out of the way.

Despite this, things began to unravel very quickly. While the agency proclaimed itself ready for same sex adoptions, we were dismayed to learn they were fairly clueless about the realities of gay adoption. Our first clue was when they called to tell us that our adoption page and profile were up and ready to be viewed by birth mothers. It had me as the father and DJ as the mother. Though they promised it would be a simple fix, this ended up being the undoing of our relationship with the agency. As days turned to weeks and every part of our profile had a mother and a father, they began to make up excuses for these issues. Since DJ was not in the adoption, he could only be listed as my partner. They actually tried to convince us it would be fine just calling us a mother and father. We continued to press them and were then told the issue was much larger and would take them time to fix. Meanwhile, our profile was basically worthless, and we were wasting valuable time. After many back and forth phone calls and emails we finally had enough and demanded our money back. Fortunately, the agency did not fight this. They apologized, returned our funds, and wished us the best of luck. Sadly for us, we were back to square one.

Fortunately, it did not take us long to figure out our next step. We had been following a private adoption facilitator who lived in our area and had a very nice webpage and process. The reviews on her business were all very good, and most patrons stated that they were matched very quickly and had successful adoptions via her services. Along with all the positive comments, nearly everyone stated that the facilitator and owner, Jill, could be terse, cranky, and very hard to work with at times. We called Jill several times and had many lengthy conversations with her. She impressed us with her attention to detail and her commitment to the open adoption process. The way her program worked was that when she had a new birth mother, she sent a group email out to all of her prospective parents. The email had a code name for the mom, all of the available information, the medical records, the due date, and the expected full cost, including the birth mother's living expenses. In California, as in most states, the adoptive family is required by law to pay all reasonable living expenses for the birth mother, including rent, food, car insurance, laundry, utility bills, clothing, phone bills, and spending money. Each alert that Jill sent out included the estimated birth mother living expenses and projected a total cost. After long discussions and input from our family, we always watched her alerts when they came out and read them in detail. We always ended up passing because many of the birth mothers drank alcohol, smoked, and/or did hard drugs. We had done our homework and knew we did not want to get involved with a mother who did these things for fear of fetal alcohol syndrome or drug-related complications. A few of the other options had serious histories of mental illness. One mother was bipolar and schizophrenic; her boyfriend was bipolar and schizophrenic; her parents were bipolar and schizophrenic; and the grandparents were as well. While we were open to any sex and any race, we were not prepared for the lifetime of mental issues that would likely be inherited.

On Wednesday, April 30th of 2014, an alert came through on Bette. We reviewed all the information and thought about it until the very last minute. We consulted friends and family, prayed, and finally decided that this was our opportunity. Jill told us that Bette was a wonderful person who had a history of completing successful adoptions. She ensured us that she knew of no skeletons in Bette's closet. We paid the small fee to be submitted, and our profile booklet was sent to Bette along with many other hopeful adoptive families in waiting. We felt our chances were slim to none, since many straight couples had applied as well. What were the odds that a birth mother would choose us, a non-married gay couple, over the many straight couples who applied? However, we also felt that we stood out as a unique option for birth mothers due to our relationship. As stated earlier, we believe that everything happens for a reason, and low and behold I was chosen by Bette to be the father of her infant. Little did I know that that fateful day would change our lives forever. Into our lives walked Sandi Peters, and in turn we walked right into the lion's den with fresh steaks tied to our necks.

# Chapter Two

I had always wanted to be a father and to have a traditional, albeit gay, family. I had very close relationships with my two young nieces, whom I love with all my heart. I have always enjoyed children, and it was a personal goal of mine to have a family of my own. My clock was ticking, since I was 38 years old and I had begun to think the time was now or never. For the past 13 years, my "baby" had been my super-friendly and loving Tonkinese cat, Boomer, named after Ronald Reagan. Hell, I actually almost got beat up by some skinheads in San Diego when I had foolishly purchased a caged-in cat stroller. While strolling him down the beach boardwalk, people kept coming up and trying to see my "baby," only to be shocked to find the world's cutest cat. The skinheads did not see the humor and began following and harassing me. I guess that is what I got for thinking a gay man could stroll a cat along the beach without any repercussions.

DJ already had a lot of experience with babies, toddlers, and young children since he has a very large and close family he adores. In addition, all of his high school and college friends were at the point in life where they were all having babies, and his very close sister had also just given birth to a beautiful baby boy. We had recently gone on two very luxurious vacations, one to Bora Bora and one to an exclusive resort in the Riviera Maya. We had just relocated for my job from Pittsburgh, Pennsylvania, to California and had found the perfect family home. Suddenly we realized that we had traveled the world and done our fair share of partying. We were tired of that, and our party days were long since history. It was time to really settle down, get married at some point, and start our family. It was at this point that I officially decided to begin the process of adoption. Once DJ and I set our minds to something, you can bet it gets done and gets done quickly. We were now "all in," as they say in the game of Texas Hold-Em, and ready to take on this beautiful challenge and wonderful process.

I guess you can call us suckers, but things started out relatively smoothly with Sandi and her family. We had a couple of phone conversations with her, which were very short and frequently interrupted by her kids. She actually told us that she preferred text messaging to phone calls and that is how she wanted to communicate moving forward. At the time, we really did not think anything of it. We were fine with that approach for now since it took away some of the awkwardness that comes along with having conversations with people you hardly know. Thus we decided to comply with Sandi's request, and we used text messaging as our primary source of communication. One of the first things we noticed was that because Sandi was not working, her boyfriend was not working, and her kids were not in school, she had a hell of a lot of free time. Free time translated to lots and lots and lots and lots of text messages. For several days our phones never stopped receiving text messages from her. We were both extremely busy people. DJ was engulfed in school as a full time student in addiction medicine and I was the Director of Marketing for a $3 billion dollar food company. Despite this, our birth mother could not conceive of the fact that anyone could have a life outside of watching TV all day long. If we didn't respond within a minute of Sandi's text, she would start typing, "hey," "hey," "hey," "y no text back," "Andrew??" and "hey!" She would continue this behavior non-stop until DJ or I responded to her. This was one of our very first indicators that something was a little bit off with her. We chalked it up to her different lifestyle and tried to be as patient as possible with her.

Sadly, this behavior did not stop; in fact, it only grew more and more intense with each passing day. Additionally, we were worried she hadn't received the flowers and chocolate-dipped strawberries that we had sent because we never heard from her, so we finally asked if she had received them. Her response was yet another warning sign. "Ya" she stated, with no "thank you" or any other sign of appreciation. We also sent her and her family a gift card to a local restaurant so that they could enjoy a nice meal for Mother's Day. Once again, we never received anything from her except "Ya I got it. Next time can you make it for more 'cause I have a big family?" We received no thanks, no appreciation, and no gratitude. Nevertheless, Sandi insisted on bombarding our phones with texts. In one of her first attempts at manipulation and scamming she spent an entire evening blowing up our phones regarding how Doug had left her and the family to go out drinking. According to Sandi, he was a terrible alcoholic and had left them for good to drink and was never coming back. She said she had no money for anything including food for her, the children, or the baby in her womb. Obviously we cared, so after consulting with our attorney we offered to send her some money via the Walmart Money Store so she could buy some groceries. She accepted the money and, as usual, provided no "thank you" or any appreciation. The very next day we did not hear from her, so I called her to see what was going on. The very same night I sent her money, Doug had come back home, and apparently he had only been out for a short time, despite the fact that she had said he was never coming back. Sandi just said, "Oh ya, he does this all the time, but he always comes back lol." To pour salt on the wound, she did not use the money for groceries but rather to buy herself a nice dinner at the local buffet restaurant. She displayed absolutely no guilt or shame and made us feel as though we were in a new episode of *The Twilight Zone*.

As recommended by the adoption agency and several books we had read, we felt that there would be no better time for our first visit to see Sandi in Golden Valley so that we could begin the process of bonding with her family. Bonding with the birth mother and family is the single most important part of open adoption. By bonding with the family and gaining mutual trust, you vastly improve your chances of not having the adoption disrupted (i.e. unmatching with the birth mother). So after receiving more text messages from Sandi in two weeks than we had received in two years, we decided to make the trip with the hopes of establishing a strong bond and creating new rules of engagement. We were hoping that if we explained to Sandi how busy we were that she would significantly cut back on the barrage of texts and start using phone calls instead. The agency had told us that another family had made a "no texting" rule with her in a prior adoption after they could no longer tolerate her texting diarrhea.

We had traveled pretty much all over the world, but we had never heard of Golden Valley, Arizona. There was no easy way to get there from San Francisco except an expensive flight into the Golden Valley Regional Airport; a cheap flight to Las Vegas, a rental car, and a two-hour drive; or a nine-hour drive from Livermore. We chose the Vegas option and departed in the middle of May 2014 for our first visit with Sandi and her family. As part of the plan, we were allowed to attend Sandi's second ultrasound and ask the doctor any questions. Sandi insisted that we rent an expensive van to tote her entire family around while we were there. She never asked; she just ordered. We did not want to push back too soon, so we relented and got the expensive van. Sandi had given birth to five children already, even though she was only 24 years old. She kept her first three, Camille (5), Duncan (4) and Carrie (3), and had successfully placed two children for adoption. One family lived in our area, and they had requested that Sandi attempt to find a birth family near them so the siblings could interact and have a relationship. We were excited about this possibility. We wondered what this other family was like and what their relationship with Sandi was like. We wanted to talk to them desperately, but we did not have any way of obtaining their contact information except by asking Sandi. We felt that it was too early in the process to ask Sandi for this critical information, so we decided to wait.

After a short flight, we arrived in Las Vegas and were quickly in our rental car and bound for Golden Valley, Arizona. To be frank, there was nothing to see but dead land, desert, and dry mountains. As we approached we noticed the beautiful Hualapai Mountains that overlooked Golden Valley. Towering over all the death and desert of Golden Valley was this lush, green, and temperate mountain with towering pine trees reaching toward the clouds. Beneath the Hualapais was a dead and dying city with nearly nothing to offer other than strip malls, a Walmart, and a few grocery stores. For most people, reaching the mountains was difficult because of the long, twisting, and turning single lane road that led to the top. For many, including Sandi, their cars were not able to make the ascent. I remember thinking how ironic it was to have something as beautiful as the Hualapais so close but so far away.

As the adoption process went on, I would think about that analogy nearly every day.

We were nervous meeting Sandi and her family for the first time. We had seen pictures on Facebook of their home, and it looked quite different than what we were used to. Sheets were used as window treatments, the floor was covered in dirt, there were cigarette butts on the floor (despite her saying she did not smoke), and a zoo of animals that also occupied their home, including pitbulls, cats, kittens, puppies, and whatever else the animals dragged in. In the front of their home was a very old station wagon with garbage filling up the entire back. While the pictures of the kids she texted us were adorable, we also noticed a consistent theme of them being extremely dirty and un-groomed. We honestly could not have cared less that they were poor (in fact we wanted to help), but the images of filth and squalor really made us concerned. To make matters worse, Sandi had just texted us to tell us her boyfriend was angry and sad because she had killed his newest kitten by slamming its head in the door. She never made it clear if it was accidental or intentional. We only knew they had been fighting and that the poor animal had met its tragic fate at the front door. We were both animal lovers, and this broke our hearts, as well as Doug's. She was sending us very strong signals that she had done this on purpose and had even laughed about it. We concluded that we were probably overthinking this, though. No sane individual could purposefully kill their partner's beloved kitten, could they? She would later text us to say that she had purchased Doug a new kitten as a surprise replacement. We wondered where she got the money.

In Golden Valley, Sandi did not want us to go to their house for the first visit, so we decided to meet them at our modest hotel a few miles away. She texted us and said that they were very nervous about meeting us in person. We told them not to be worried and that we were two of the easiest people to talk to. A few minutes later there was a knock on the door of room 309. It was Sandi and family and, once again, our lives were about to change forever. They came into the hotel room, and we briefly hugged and said our awkward hellos. Sandi was of average height, had dark, red hair pulled back into a ponytail, was overweight, and had a permanent scowl on her face. Her facial expressions rarely ever changed, and she had rotting yellow teeth. Doug was tall and lanky with a shaved head, several tattoos including words across both hands on the knuckles, and had teeth that were so rotten that they were missing or black. I was not sure how it was even possible for teeth to be so decayed that they were black, but I assumed it was a combination of drug abuse and simple hygiene neglect. In a way, he looked like a very rough version of Kevin Bacon.

Sandi and Doug had on some ratty outfits and smelled of strong body odor, and their three kids were covered in dirt from head to toe. Carrie was the youngest at three years old. She was very small for her age, had sandy blonde hair, a cute face, and clothing covered in food and stains. Her face was covered in scrapes, scratches, and bruises. Duncan was four years old, with short bright red hair, pale skin, bright blue eyes, and was very cute. He too was covered in dirt and food, and his hands were black with mud and dirt. Camille was the oldest child at age five, and she had natural beauty with a striking face, reddish-brown hair, and a tall and thin body. All of the kids' clothing was too small or too large and was covered in dirt, food stains, or holes.

Though we were taken aback by their appearance, we struck up a nice conversation, and before twenty minutes had passed we were talking like long-time friends. We had one official piece of business to do from the agency, which was to get Doug to sign his waiver of parental rights, an official court document that essentially took all of Doug's parental rights away. We also had to get Sandi to sign an "Intent to Adopt" agreement, which was just a legal letter stating her intention to give us the baby 72 hours after she delivered. Feeling like we were walking on eggshells, we let them know about the documents. Sandi signed her letter immediately with no hesitation, and Doug had no issue signing his either. We managed to get both documents signed, notarized, and overnight mailed to our attorney before we left Golden Valley.

We had promised them that we would take them swimming at the hotel pool, so the kids changed into their bathing suits and we walked to the pool. Immediately we noticed that Sandi wanted nothing to do with any part of playing with the kids. She sat in a chair, scowling, and cursed at the kids for doing absolutely nothing wrong, "Get the fuck away from the side. Don't fucking run, God damn it. Oh, I am going to kill your little asses." The kids were excited since they rarely got the opportunity to swim and were simply being a little wild. Doug came into the pool and actually seemed like a loving and caring father. He played with them, blew up their floats, kept his eyes on them, and did fatherly things. Sandi sat in the chair cussing, and she had a mean scowl on her face the entire time. DJ and I quickly bonded with the kids, and before we knew it not only were they clean from the pool water, but they were crawling all over us, laughing and playing. DJ bonded very closely with Carrie, the youngest, and I bonded with Duncan. We both bonded with Camille, although she was a little bit more socially awkward than the others. In all honesty we had a blast playing with the kids, catching them as they jumped in, pulling them along, playing shark, or just being silly. Doug seemed to be having fun too, although Sandi sat in the corner ordering Doug and everyone around and cussing, her expression never changing.

When the time came to get out of the pool, Duncan did not want to leave my side. All three kids started crying and did not want to get out. Doug was understanding and explained to them why they had to get out. Sandi took a slightly different approach, yelling "Get yer God damn little asses out of the pool right fuckin' now or I am gonna beat all yer asses!" as she yanked on their arms. She smacked Carrie very hard on the head to the point that we were both concerned. Carrie was crying; no child deserved to be hit like that. DJ and I stared at each other in disbelief.

Back in room 309, the family grabbed their things, changed into dry clothing, and headed back to their house to change for dinner. It was widely accepted that the adoptive family (me) should treat the birth mother and family to meals during these visits. Hence, Sandi and Doug were extremely excited to choose the most expensive steakhouse in all of Golden Valley for our first meal together. Since they were gone, we took the opportunity to also clean up and get ready. I wish we could have captured this moment because this would be the first and only time where we had a high regard for Sandi and Doug. We were thrilled that we bonded with the family, especially the children. After this meeting, we had no doubt that everything was going to work out and the adoption would be smooth sailing. They were nice people, even if Sandi was a little rough around the edges. Sandi seemed difficult, but we had been assured she would give us the baby. We simply needed to put ourselves in Sandi's shoes and try to understand the difficulties she was facing.

Because their car was not capable of making it very far and had no insurance or headlights, we had no choice but to pick up Sandi's family at their house on Golden Valley Road. They often drove their car despite the issues and lack of insurance, but would avoid doing so when other options were available. As we pulled up, we noticed that their house was surrounded by abandoned homes. We found their house and pulled up to the back door. Their white house was very small and appeared to be just one or two rooms from the outside, with towels and sheets covering the windows. The windows were so dirty that they didn't even look like glass. Garbage and debris littered the entire property from the front porch to the side yard and all the way into the backyard. Mattresses, box springs, toys, clothing items, trash bags, food, meat, cans, dead animals, and bottles were all spread out in their small property. The trash combined with 101-degree temperatures made for an awful stink, and I had to hold my breath to avoid gagging. We did not go inside; however, Doug asked me to get the car seats out of their white Corolla wagon. I have seen some nasty things in my life, and I have smelled some foul things, but at this point I was pretty sure I was near the cusp of Hell. The car was completely full of rotting food and garbage. You could not see out of any window with the exception of the driver's window due to dirt, debris, and piled-up garbage. The smell was bad enough to make a proctologist squirm. I somehow managed to get the seats out when I noticed several dead animal carcasses on the seats and floor. I did not realize Doug was behind me, and I jumped at the sight of the dead animals. Doug caught on to my astonishment and said, "Ha, I see ya found some of my cat's prized possessions. Yeah, she brings 'em almost daily. Snakes, mice, rats, birds, lizards… you name it, she brings 'em here. After a while you just say 'fuck it' and leave them here. It ain't hurtin' nobody." Disgusted, I made my way over to the garden hose to rinse my hands—only to find a half-eaten snake inside the tip.

Worrying that I would never be clean again, we loaded up the car and headed to a steakhouse.

When we arrived at Golden Valley Steakhouse, DJ nearly bowled everyone over in order to get to the bathroom to wash up, and I quickly followed. We were shown to our table, and DJ and I were surrounded by all the kids. Duncan and Camille were fairly well-behaved, but Carrie was a nightmare. She screamed, cried, put her fingers and hands in peoples' food and drinks, got out of her high chair, and poured out the salt and pepper, all while Sandi cussed at her. They showed no modesty as they literally ordered nearly everything on the menu, including the most expensive steaks they had. In addition, despite the kids being small, they ordered a dish for each of them. We took a few pictures, had a fairly good conversation with Doug (Sandi complained the entire time), played with the kids, paid the bill, and headed back to drop them off. We agreed to meet for breakfast the next morning at IHOP, and then we would go meet our beautiful baby for the first time via ultrasound. We were exhausted; we both took showers and fell asleep almost instantly.

I have always been described as being ADD, high-strung, etc. Basically I am your typical sales and marketing professional, and DJ is pretty much the same way. I did not want to sit through a long breakfast prior to meeting my baby for the first time; I wanted it to be quick so that we could be off to the doctor as quickly as possible. Needless to say, the moving white garbage wagon was late to show up at IHOP. When it did arrive, the adorable kids came running out to hug us, sadly still dirty, unbathed, and wearing the same clothes as the day before. Right behind them was their cursing ginger mother, screaming at the kids and Doug. We greeted them and immediately smelled the intense smell of cigarettes all over Sandi. Her hair, clothing, and skin all smelled of smoke, yet she had proclaimed that she was a non-smoker to both us and on the medical sheets. The time for a confrontation was not now, so we decided to hold off on the topic until another time. The service was slow and bad, so we ended up having a very long breakfast and just enough time to get to the doctor's appointment. All throughout breakfast Duncan was stuck to my side and Carrie to DJ's.

We packed into my rented van and drive off to the Golden Valley Regional Medical Center, where we would get the very first glimpse of our baby. Nerves were a little high because this would be our first time seeing the baby and ensuring that she or he was healthy. Sandi was going to allow DJ and I to go into the ultrasound room. The smoking issue had really frightened us, as we had read up on the dangers and implications of smoking to a baby in utero. The doctor was far behind schedule, so we all had to wait in the waiting room for about 30 minutes. Due to the lack of hygiene, a particular smell emanated throughout the waiting room, similar to the smell of an unemptied dumpster in the hot sun. The kids played in the kids; area while Doug sat listening to Sandi bitch and cuss at him for nothing. She would scowl and send an occasional yell to the kids just so everyone was aware of who was in charge.

Finally we were called to the back. DJ and Sandi went in first, while Doug and I remained in the waiting room. It was very early in the pregnancy, so the chances of us finding out the sex of the baby were slim at this point. We were anxious to find out the sex of the baby so we could start purchasing gender-specific toys and clothes. DJ was in for about fifteen minutes before he came out grinning ear to ear. I thought for sure he knew something. "It is your turn now Babe. It is so amazing," he said with a big smile. I went into the ultrasound room and saw Sandi on the exam table with the doctor sitting down by the ultrasound machine. They were doing measurements, taking photos of the baby's face, and looking at the placenta and other vital parts. The ultrasound technician was very kind and walked me through every part: "What you are seeing here, Andrew, is your baby's femur, and now you are seeing the spine..." I was damn near certain that I saw a penis between the legs, and holy shit was it large for a tiny baby! Confidently I pointed to it and said, "Guess I'm having a boy!" The ultrasound tech smiled and said, "Honey, if that big thing was a penis you would have big problems. That's the umbilical cord. But nice try." We all shared a laugh as she continued her exam.

The baby was on its side, and they could not get a clear shot of the genitals. The lab tech pushed and pushed and probed and probed trying to get the baby to turn over on its back. But the baby was not willing to cooperate that day; stubborn like the mom. The technician stated that she was sorry but the gender was undetermined and we would have to wait a month for the next exam. She then took a picture of the placenta, and I noticed her put a comment on it. I asked her if everything was ok with the placenta, thinking back to the smell of smoke on Sandi. She replied, "The placenta looks ok, but I just want the doctor to look at it." My heart started to race. I did not like the way that the tech had said that. Lastly, she took several shots of the baby's face and printed them out. Sandi was actually being kind and said, "Take them; it's your baby. Just send me a copy." That made me feel better, and I left with a smile on my face.

After the doctor's appointment we took the group to a family fun center about thirty miles away in Laughlin, Nevada, where they played games, go karts, mini golf, and ate pizza. For most of the time, Doug was having alcohol withdrawal and made himself comfortable in the men's room to vomit and dry heave. He had told us that he had quit drinking the day before and was now having some unpleasant side effects. Sandi was apparently not happy that her kids were actually having fun and enjoying themselves. She sat by herself with her arms crossed, a scowl on her face and kept asking when we were going to do something that she could enjoy. "This is boring! There's nothin' here for me to do." Despite her foul mood, DJ thought now was the perfect time to bring up the smoking.

"Sandi," he began, "we want you to be honest with us about something. Are you smoking cigarettes?"

Surprisingly, Sandi came clean with us. She indicated that she had indeed quit when she filled out the medical disclosure but that she had started smoking again recently, about a pack per day. We very much vocalized our displeasure and told her what could happen to the baby as a result, including preterm labor, lung and asthma issues, placenta issues, and low birth weight. Sandi brushed it off and said she had smoked through all six of her pregnancies and all of her kids were fine. We begged her to stop and even drove everyone to an e-cigarette store to buy her everything she needed to quit. She said she would try. DJ and I were furious with her for lying to us and for her selfishness in putting the baby and all of her kids at risk. Inside, we fumed (pun intended), but outside we could not show our emotions. We knew it wouldn't do any good to upset her.

Sandi had complained that she did not have any maternity clothes or food, so I decided to take the family shopping after I got the ok from my adoption attorney. There were only two stores in town, JC Penney and Walmart, and neither had maternity items. So we stopped at McDonald's for the free Wi-Fi and allowed her to order things off the Internet. Meanwhile she stuffed down a full order of 20-piece nuggets and began talking about how she did not believe in prenatal care; particularly vitamins. Up to this point, she had been telling us that she was taking prenatal vitamins every day. I started to wonder if anything she had put on the disclosure was true. "How long have you not been taking them?" I asked. She quickly responded that she actually never took any because they make her constipated. Thus we uncovered yet another lie, as we had mailed her some expensive vitamins that would not cause constipation and she had told us she was taking them every day. Now she was saying she refused to take any with the same excuse as her smoking—"I didn't never take any vitamins, and all my kids are fine." We begged her to take them, "Sandi, it is really important that you take the vitamins. It would really make us happy if you took them," DJ said. She promised us that she would try from this point forward.

After one last family dinner with the clan and a quick trip to Safeway to fill up their refrigerator, we had spent pretty much all of our energy. We had a long drive back to Vegas, where we had to return the rental car and catch our flight home. We all did our hugs, said goodbye and that we had a nice visit, and tried to give the kids, who were clinging on to us, some last minute love and attention. Doug gave us a very nice "thank you" and showed his appreciation in a very nice way, but the only thing we got from our selfless friend Sandi was, "Next time you need to stay longer. We didn't even have time to do more shopping and stuff." All three children cried extremely hard as we pulled away.

# Chapter Three

We assumed that the visit to Golden Valley would calm Sandi down and stop the marathon text sessions, especially now that they had food, clothing, and all the necessities. Sadly, and to our surprise, it actually made things worse. Sandi felt closer to us and thus felt more entitlement. She asked for gift cards to restaurants because she was starving, and, being the suckers we were, we sent them. She asked for gift cards to the grocery store because she was completely out of food, and we gave in. If we didn't send her something she asked for, she would get angry and stop talking to us. One thing we would not cave in on was cash, but she constantly asked us for cash via Walmart or an advance to be given from her weekly living expenses. Our attorney and Jill told her to not talk to us about money or ask us anything related to money, but she would not stop. She was relentless and caused all of us to wonder what she would do next. The general rule was that everything needed to be documented by our attorney and that money could only be for true living expenses like food, shelter, medications, hygiene, laundry, and transportation. No matter what happened, we stuck to these rules so as not to do anything that disrupted the adoption. We followed these laws exactly as written at all times.

One day, we received a barrage of texts followed by a phone call from Sandi. She was in full panic mode, and it was hard to make sense of what she was saying. She told us that Doug and his brother-in-law were fist fighting in the front yard and that the police had been called, as had Child Protective Services. She also informed us that the brother-in-law had threatened her and her family's lives. She was on the phone crying and begging for me to get her a hotel room to get her family away from this violence. Of course we were not going to allow anyone to hurt Sandi, any of the kids, or our baby, so we immediately called the adoption attorney and asked if it was okay to get them a hotel room for a night or two. It was indeed legal in order to prevent physical harm, so we spent a few hours trying to find a hotel that would take a credit card over the phone. We found a cheap hotel in a safe neighborhood and sent them on their way. Sandi said Doug was drunk, so he was not allowed to come to the hotel.

About an hour later they called us and said that they needed a pizza for the family and that Doug was back. Was Sandi that clueless or that dumb to think that we would be ok with Doug being there when we had just purchased a hotel room to get her away from him? Was it simply that she just did not care and was shoving it in our faces? Regardless...we felt suckered again! Now she had moved from manipulation to straight up lying to our faces. You may be thinking, *Wow, Drew and DJ are idiots.* That may be true in a sense, but we actually have a heart and true emotions. Despite Sandi's behavior, at this point we actually cared about the whole family, generally liked them, and did not want to see anything bad happen to them. Dumb? No. Manipulated? Damn straight.

To add fuel to the fire, I decided to call the doctor's office to ensure everything was ok with the ultrasound after the odd behavior by the technician. Because I had a medical authorization release signed by Sandi, I could talk directly to the doctor. To my shock, the doctor had some concerns about the placenta and had referred Sandi to a specialist in Golden Valley. He told me there were some areas of her placenta that were not functioning properly and not providing enough blood or oxygen to the baby. He said it was very minor now and not dangerous, but it could become a bigger issue as the pregnancy progressed. Interestingly, he asked me if Sandi smoked cigarettes. I mentioned that she did, and he told me that was the likely cause of the placenta abnormalities. He told me that if she stopped smoking the placenta would likely be ok and actually return to a completely normal state. I shared the news with DJ, and it sent us both into a panic. How in the hell were we going to stop this narcissistic woman from smoking her beloved cigarettes? She lied, didn't think rationally, manipulated others, and didn't really care for anyone but herself.

We called Sandi and told her what the doctor had said. She said that she would quit immediately and start using the vaporizer cigarette that we had purchased for her. There was nothing for us to worry about, she declared; as of that day she would be cigarette free!

Besides the drove of daily texts and daily drama, things quieted down for a few days. Sandi and Doug would break up a few times a week, so we had learned to not even play that game with them. He always left, came back, and she forgave him after giving him hell for 12 or 13 hours. To avoid too many trips to the lovely city of Golden Valley, we planned our next meeting to be them driving to California. We reserved them a rental car, got them a hotel for three nights in our town, and had everything planned perfectly. Doug used his debit card to rent the car, and we placed the exact amount of money he needed into his account. But a few hours before they were supposed to depart Golden Valley for San Francisco the phone rang. It was Jill, the adoption facilitator. She told us that Doug had gone to the bank to withdraw some of his own money and that the bank had decided to shred his card because he had a negative balance prior to this day. *Why was he withdrawing funds?* we wondered. This meant they were no longer able to rent the car because they needed a debit or credit card to do so. As a result of failing her written driving test many times, Sandi did not have her license, so she could not rent a car either. Now Doug had no debit card and was unable to rent the reserved car, and the hotel we had reserved in the East Bay was non-refundable. Sandi was having a full-fledged nervous breakdown, and she and Doug were fighting like Archie and Edith Bunker.

To make matters worse, DJ and I were both having an extremely busy day. I had to present at a board meeting, and DJ had a very important final exam. We had told Sandi that we would not be available for most of the day. She ignored those warnings and began the biggest streak of calls and text messages that Jill, DJ, and I had ever experienced. She text messaged me about one hundred times in one hour and did the same to DJ. She repeatedly called Jill about rental car issues and continued to tell her that there was nothing she could do. DJ was walking into his final exam when she texted him "911... emergency. Please pick up" and then started repeatedly calling him. He thought something was wrong with the baby, so he actually stepped out of his final exam to see what was going on. When she told him it was a rental car issue, he sternly explained to her that he was in a final exam and could not talk for the next two hours. She then tried my phone again about ten times, but I refused to answer. Despite DJ's stern words to her, she started repeatedly dialing him and really breaking his concentration on the test. Sandi went so far as to scream, "I don't give a fuck about yer school or work. This is important." We were both furious and could not believe her self-centered behavior. DJ had been pushed too far by Sandi's comments and he erupted at her, "Sandi! I am turning my damn phone off and I am temporarily blocking you. It is not ok for you to disregard my school like you did. So do not…I repeat do not call or text me again until after school."

I finally got out of work and decided to call Jill, who filled me in on the situation. I then called Sandi, who after all of this was acting completely normal. I asked her what she wanted me to do. She turned on the tears and asked me to rent the car in our names. I declined and told her that if she wanted to do that, she would need to find a family member in Golden Valley that could bring their license and then add Doug on as a driver. After three hours of Sandi drama, a few hundred text messages, and a half dozen calls, her grandpa pulled through and was able to get them the car. We received no thanks for our help or for giving them the opportunity to spend time with us. What did we get? "This car is too small," she groaned. But they were on their way to Livermore….. oh, joy!

Over the past two weeks, DJ and I had both been checking in with Sandi about her smoking. She had been so proud to say that she had quit outright and was no longer smoking at all. We were very happy and, for some unexplainable reason, we had actually believed her. As they made the long nine-hour drive from Golden Valley to Livermore, we got constant updates on their progress. Duncan had to pee every thirty minutes, and Sandi and Doug fought the entire trip. I could not even imagine what those poor kids were subjected to during the long drive. They were supposed to arrive at their hotel at 8pm, but all the fighting and peeing caused their estimated arrival time to move to 2am. When they finally arrived, we told them good night and said we would see them in the morning. I had to work half of the day and planned on meeting them after lunch. DJ was off and had planned on letting them sleep in and would meet them in downtown Pleasanton for a nice brunch.

I wrongly assumed it would be a drama–free day since DJ would be with them and could keep everything under control. That idea came to an abrupt end when Sandi finished her massive breakfast at the restaurant and then stepped outside, went into her purse, and pulled out her menthol cigarettes. DJ was stunned and did not know what to say. He confronted her while simultaneously texting me, "Sandi what in the hell are you doing? You told us that you completely quit smoking. Don't you care about the baby? How in the world can you do this? I don't even know what to say Sandi!" He continued to discuss the situation with Sandi and he did not attempt to cover up the fact that he was extremely angry.

I was furious when I found out she had been lying, and I really let her have it via text message. "How can you be so selfish?" I demanded. "How could you lie like this right to our faces? Do you even care about the baby?" She immediately turned on the drama and collapsed against a flagpole, sobbing. She texted me and asked if I wanted her to go home. I told her that I did not want her to go home, but I told her that I was very disappointed in her and that if I saw her smoking I would rip the cigarette out of her mouth, take the pack out of her purse, and smash it. Great start to visit number one to Livermore.

Sandi sulked in her room at the Motel 6 for several hours pretending to be mad at us and trying to use her master manipulation skills. We realized this visit wasn't going to work. She could either pack up and drive the nine hours back to Golden Valley, or she could apologize for lying and we could potentially have an enjoyable visit. She chose the latter (for the only time that I can ever remember) and apologized, swearing she would no longer smoke cigarettes. She asked us to buy her more coils and liquids that go along with the e-cigarette, which we happily agreed to. Since we truly did care about her kids and Doug, we decided to not waste the night and to take them to Fisherman's Wharf for dinner and some fun.

Anyone who knows San Francisco knows that summer is the coldest time of the year. We had told them to bring warm clothes and dress for the weather. They showed up at our door in flip-flops, shorts, and t-shirts. We started the short drive to the city, and immediately Sandi began complaining.

"Oh my God, how long is this drive?"

"Where is all this fucking traffic coming from?"

"Why is it so cold here?"

"Andrew, you are making me carsick."

"Carrie, if you fucking stand up in that car seat one more fucking time I am going to whip your ass!"

Sandi turned around in the car and smacked Carrie right in the face, leaving a red mark. I was stunned and could not believe anyone could hit a child like that. She was literally ruining a once in a lifetime opportunity for her kids to see San Francisco. Doug calmly told her to shut up, which of course sets her off on him: "Doug, don't fucking do this. Don't you dare fucking talk to me like that, or you will really regret it later. Just wait until we get back to the hotel. Oh, you are so fucking dead!"

We made it to Fisherman's Wharf and had to park a few blocks away. We had taken two cars so we could fit everyone in comfortably. We parked in separate places, and immediately Sandi began to complain about the two-block walk. "Can we get a fucking cab? I'm four months pregnant; I can't be expected to walk like this. Jesus." Thankfully, the kids were used to her poor behavior and immediately started to have fun despite being cold. They were enamored with all the shops, food stalls, and magic shops. They did a lot of window-shopping, and we stopped to get them fried funnel cake sticks and crepes, which they very much enjoyed. I looked around and noticed all the tourists and locals enjoying themselves, having a blast and taking in the carnival-like atmosphere. The air was filled with the fragrant smells of fried mini donuts, ice cream, cotton candy, corn dogs, and of course the famous San Francisco clam chowder in bread bowls. I turned back and looked at Sandi, and she had the usual scowl on her face as she shouted at someone on her phone. Someone was supposed to check on their family of pets, which were ruthlessly tied up on leashes in the 100-degree heat, but the person had not shown up. Thus Sandi was screaming and swearing at some poor soul and trying to find an alternative arrangement.

We decided to just ignore her and ensure that the kids had a nice night. We took them to the various interesting shops, gave them several rides on the classic merry-go-round, and took them to see the famous sea lions that had invaded the docks years ago. We purchased Finn and Jake hats from the kids' show *Adventure Time* from a novelty store, and immediately Duncan became a new person. He and DJ were having a blast pretending to be on an *Adventure Time* adventure. Everywhere he went he was in his cute fighting stance, and he had a new sense of bravery, raising his imaginary sword to all who got in his way. It reminded me again why I loved children and how great of a father DJ would be. Any kid would be lucky to have him as a loving father. He would encourage Duncan to use his imagination, "Alright Duncan…are you ready? Now we are approaching the dungeons. Can you help us fight our way out? Let's go!"

Doug was pretty much on his own and not paying attention, since he knew he would be in big trouble with Sandi when they got back to the hotel. We took the escalator up to the top tier of the midway and got a table at Bubba Gump Shrimp at the request of Sandi. She said she had always dreamed of eating there, and we knew she loved anything fried, especially bay shrimp.

She complained viciously about the wait, the "terrible service," that her Dr. Pepper "wasn't right," and about the time it took to get her appetizer. The food came out, and in a very rare occurrence she actually claimed that it was "ok." She went on to devour several dozen various fried shrimp. As soon as she was done, she demanded, "Where in the hell is the waiter? Can we get our bill and go?"

We departed the restaurant and started the insurmountable task of walking two blocks with a lovely mother who was four months pregnant. Doug thanked us countless times for treating them to a nice night and apologized for Sandi's behavior. "She's always like this," he explained sadly. On the way back to the car she insisted that she would ride in the car with Doug. He opposed the idea because he was not used to driving in this big city and did not know his way around. An enormous public fight then ensued in the middle of Fisherman's Wharf with Doug actually holding his ground. He told Sandi that he would not drive and that she needed to ride home with DJ. Sandi literally went into a tantrum of curse words and hand gestures and then began walking away by herself in the opposite direction. She claimed he was dead when they got back and that he would seriously regret this. Poor DJ had to follow her like a puppy as she continued her tirade down the Embarcadero. She barely talked to DJ on the way home but rather was on her phone texting someone in a rant. He would try to make conversation with her and she simply did not respond. "Ok then…guess I'll turn the radio on," DJ joked. Doug later told me on the ride home that she did all of that so she could bum a cigarette from someone without us seeing. She did not give a damn about her family being safe; the whole show had just been to get the chance to have a cigarette. Once again, we got no thanks from her for giving her family a night of fun on our own dime. Our view of Sandi was quickly changing, and she was rapidly becoming a nightmare instead of the close personal friend we had hoped she would be.

Thankfully, when we met back at the house they quickly got in the car and headed back to their motel. We could see Sandi screaming at Doug as the car pulled away down our quiet street. DJ and I were exhausted, and as soon as we walked in our house we went right to sleep with bad memories of Sandi fresh in our minds.

After some counseling from friends and family, we were quickly reenergized for the next day, when we planned to show them all around San Francisco. Our family and friends quickly reminded us of our real mission, which was to appease Sandi, bond, and make it until November 12th, when we would be blessed with our loving bundle of joy. We had to keep reminding ourselves of that on a daily basis. We had to take it "one day at a time," as they say in 12-step programs. So we loaded our cars and headed to the city, this time with fewer complaints from Sandi since there was no traffic.

They really wanted to see Chinatown, so that was our first stop for the day. Chinatown in San Francisco is a sensory overload, with live Asian music playing, lanterns hanging from above, shops with rare items, restaurants displaying whole ducks hanging upside-down in their windows, and curious Eastern medicinal shops. The smells range from amazingly appealing to so vile you feel like vomiting. Sandi complained about potential starvation because she had not eaten in two hours, so we were compelled to find the first restaurant that we came upon. It was a nice dim sum place in the heart of Chinatown that was well known for great food. Everyone was excited as we entered the unique Chinese place full of rare Asian decor and artifacts and were seated at the grand table with a top that spun around to facilitate sharing dishes. We ordered off the picture menu, and everyone chowed down to enjoy the steamed pork buns, calamari, noodles, roasted chicken skewers, pot stickers, and more. The kids were having a blast playing with the mini umbrellas and chopsticks, and Doug was loving the food. But Sandi could not have been more miserable or unhappy. She was eating like someone who had not eaten in weeks, but between mouthfuls she complained about how gross and disgusting it was. "Let's just get the bill and get out of here," she demanded with an angry scowl on her face. We all ignored her and finished our meals, trying to not let her ruin the experience for all of us. Doug was in Chinese food heaven, the kids were having fun, and we decided that's what mattered to us.

To appease Sandi, we got the check shortly thereafter and made our way through the exciting and mysterious streets and alleys of Chinatown. The kids' eyes were the size of saucers as they saw all of the toys, gadgets, swords, and fireworks. They did not know where to look first and were very excited. We made the usual trip to the fortune cookie factory in a small, dark alley so the kids could watch and sample. Here was a rare instance where Sandi was happy and seemed to enjoy herself. We all ate the fresh cookies, took pictures, and Sandi even purchased some cookies to take home. On the way out we all stopped and got tapioca bubble tea, which they had never tried. For some reason, I was in the mood to annoy Sandi due to her behavior, so I ordered a fresh durian shake (a Southeast Asian fruit notorious for its offensive aroma). She was seriously pissed about the smell and wanted me to throw it away, but I refused. In fact, the kids all tasted it, and we had fun with it. People walking by were saying, "What in the world is that awful smell?" It was a rare opportunity to pick at Sandi and have a little fun doing it.

DJ's first thought was always about the kids and he wanted to ensure that they were having fun, so he bought them a few boxes of Chinese snaps, little fireworks that explode when they hit the ground. That may have been the highlight of the many moments of fun that Duncan,

Carrie, and Camille had. "Hey let's try sneak up on Drew and see if we can scare him with some of these," DJ snickered. All three of the kids and DJ simultaneously launched handfuls of the snaps at my feet. I pretended to be startled and screamed. We finished off our time in Chinatown by visiting the Eastern medicinal shops with their rows and rows of dried fish, sea cucumbers, starfish, weird fruits, and vegetables, and things that we could not even identify. The kids just laughed and had a great time while holding their noses shut. DJ continued having fun with the kids by insisting that they smell or touch "gross" items. Sandi, of course, was angry due to the smells and did not see the fun in it. She yelled at Doug and paid no attention as Carrie ran into the middle of the street with oncoming cars and loud buses. A Good Samaritan grabbed Carrie in the nick of time and brought her over to Sandi. She showed absolutely no concern but instead gave her a hard open-hand smack on the face and swore at her. My heart melted a little bit that day, as it was abundantly clear that Sandi did not care about her kids or Doug, but rather only cared about herself. She gave Doug a harsh verbal assault and blamed him for the entire incident. Under his breath, DJ whispered, "Well maybe you should have been paying attention."

For the sake of our sanity and for Doug and the kids, we continued our day in San Francisco. Despite it being no place to take a child, Sandi demanded that we go to the Haight so that she could get a picture by the Haight-Ashbury sign. Again, because they had not listened to my weather advice, everyone was freezing. Doug was fine, but Sandi and the kids were having a hard time. We stopped at the Goodwill and got everyone sweatshirts and hoodies. As we strolled up and down the Haight, being offered drugs of every kind, smelling the aroma of weed, opium, and human urine – Sandi was able to get her coveted picture. We were worried that the kids were being exposed to things they were too young to see, but Sandi upped the ante by demanding that we go into the bad side of Golden Gate Park and visit the historic "hippie hill." There we sat as a horde of hippies stuck in 1979 smoked pot, hit large water bongs, danced like only people on LSD could, and played drums. We sat patiently on the hill waiting to leave as Sandi looked on in amusement. The kids were not on their best behavior, and Carrie grabbed a large piece of dirt and flung it at my head, covering my hair and body in soil. Kids will be kids, and I understand that, but Sandi grabbed her extremely hard, spanked her bottom, and insisted that she apologize to me. Carrie refused and was pretty much in the doghouse for the remainder of the day.

We left the Haight, and our last stop was Golden Gate Bridge. Again we had two cars, so we rode in groups. I was blessed being with Sandi while Doug, DJ, and the kids went into the other car. It was a fairly long ride to the bridge, and I took Sandi through the extremely nice part of town, through the redwoods, and through the Presidio, none of which interested her. We arrived at Golden Gate Bridge and saw the amazing views of the Pacific Ocean and the gateway to the west. Sandi was unimpressed. She repeatedly called DJ to ask why they hadn't arrived yet. Due to traffic and other factors, DJ, Doug, and the kids had ended up parking on the opposite side of the bridge. We had a difficult time finding one another, and Sandi quickly grew angry. They were trying to find us in a very busy place on a very busy day. We finally found them on the observation deck, where we took some pictures and Sandi put on some fake scowl/smiles. As soon as the pictures were over, Sandi exploded on Doug. It was an all-out attack, and they fought like cats and dogs in the middle of the thousands of tourists. It was quite an embarrassment. Finally, she cussed him out and told him that he would get the silent treatment for the remainder of the day. "Just wait until we get back to the hotel," she threatened once again.

On the car ride home, I rode with Doug and the kids and DJ drove Sandi. I hoped this would give them some one-on-one time to bond. I had a very long and intense conversation with Doug and tried to find out why Sandi acted the way she did. Doug went into detail about how she had had a rough upbringing, how her family did not really talk to her, and how this had made her a sad and angry person. I actually felt some sympathy for her, and for a brief moment I began to think maybe I was just missing her good parts. Then Doug began discussing how she controlled every aspect of his life, didn't allow him to get a job, and was always treating him and the kids like dirt. He explained that every time he got a job, Sandi would show up all day, call repeatedly, and would bring in the kids until the management could no longer take it and would fire him. This had happened at every one of his jobs. Doug told me that he really liked us and wanted to be honest with us as long as we did not snitch him out to Sandi. He told me she was still smoking and had never stopped, nor had she taken any of the prenatal vitamins as she had promised. Finally he admitted that she really did not need money when she came asking for emergency funds. He told me that he felt bad for us but there was nothing he could do to stop her. He warned me to be vigilant and to ask a lot of questions before we sent anything. He also told me if we got him a cheap prepaid phone we could call him and ask him about anything if we wanted to. For the time being, this really helped DJ and I to trust Doug. The last thing he told me was that Sandi loved us, thought of us as family, and just was not used to someone actually caring about her. He said she had every intention of placing the baby with us, and he promised there would be no games or issues at the hospital. These words meant a lot to me and really helped to settle my fears.

In the other car DJ was having a fairly deep conversation with Sandi. He told her that, at the end of the process, all we wanted was for the open adoption to be a success. He explained our end goal of wanting to be one big, happy family. He explained to her, "Everything should be about the baby. We want you and Doug to be a part of its life. Everything we do should be about that. Plain and simple." He talked to her about the lying and how we had felt that she sometimes tried to manipulate us. She seemed to have some genuine concern and said, "I didn't never lie to you guys. I won't lie. We want the same thing and we love all of ya!" DJ was very excited as he thought he really had made an impact on Sandi and the entire situation. He was proud and he truly believed her at this point.

It was late and everyone was tired, so they packed up at our house and went back to the hotel. Doug insisted on eating the leftover shrimp from Bubba Gump, which was unrefrigerated from the day before. We warned him about food safety and told him that I was an expert in this area. He ignored our warnings, and let us just say he was not doing so well the next morning. Exhausted, DJ and I lay in bed and reflected on the day and our emotional confusion about Sandi. Did she actually have a heart and emotions? Was her behavior just a front? Or was she really the soulless and heartless queen of manipulation we had come to know?

"You know Babe, maybe she just doesn't know how to open her heart. Maybe nobody has ever really loved her. Clearly she has issues but maybe there is something we're missing. We have to keep trying to connect with her. After all, she is going to a part of our lives forever. It's an open adoption and we want it to work." DJ said this with a look of genuine care in his eyes. I could appreciate what he was saying, "I know Hon, we'll just keep trying. Eventually she'll come around. We all want the same thing and that is to have a lasting relationship with her. Let's just try even harder."

The next morning came, and we met them at a crepe restaurant for breakfast. The kids were restless and wanted to swim at our pool as we promised them. Sandi tried every trick up her sleeve to get us to extend their trip. This was not possible, as DJ had school and I had work. Everyone enjoyed their food, with the exception of Doug, who spent the entire time in the bathroom vomiting from the spoiled shrimp. They needed to get on the road, and we needed them to get on the road for our own sanity, but we wanted to keep our swimming promise to the kids. It was an extremely hot day in Livermore, nearing 105 degrees, so everyone except Sandi went swimming. We had a blast with the kids, playing, jumping, throwing, and playing catch. Sandi sat in the shade with a scowl on her face. Several other kids tried to come up and play with Camille but she had never interacted with any children her age and refused to speak. Sadly, one of the children called her autistic to her face just to be mean. Thankfully she did not know what that meant, but her lack of social interaction was quite evident and sad. DJ was clearly offended by the child and politely said, "Hey, Camille doesn't want to play right now. Go back to your Mom."

Doug was still as sick as a dog and really wanted to get the drive started. So they packed up their belongings, loaded the car, and we all said our goodbyes and did our hugs. Sandi made one more attempt to try and stay an extra night but we did not succumb. They were on their way home, and we were as confused as ever.

As was usually the case, the drama never ended with Sandi. We began getting a flood of text messages at about 8pm saying that Doug was so sick from the food poisoning that he could no longer drive. He was pulling over every five minutes to vomit. She demanded that we pay for a hotel, since they did not have a single dollar other than gas money. I found them a very cheap hotel in the middle of Bakersfield, California, for $29 total. Thus ended our weekend, and the last and only time we ever had the entire family come up again.

# Chapter Four

After their visit, DJ and I were able to get back to our normal lives for a few weeks. We knew we had to continue to make visits to Golden Valley to bond with the family and ensure that everything was going smoothly. Our next trip was not planned until the weekend of July 4th, so we actually had time to take care of some things at home and focus on work and school. Our planned side project was to get the nursery started so we were not scrambling at the last minute. Many adoption books and agencies will tell you not to do this. They state that you never want to get ahead of yourselves in an adoption since things can change quickly due to disruptions, health issues, or the birth mother changing her mind. Doing things prematurely, they advised, could result in a permanent reminder in your home of an adoption gone terribly wrong.

This type of thinking was not in DJ's and my DNA. We saw the glass half full, and we were extremely confident that we would either finish the adoption with Sandi or find another birth mother if we had to. Hence, the plan was to get started on the nursery right away and focus on neutral colors. It was actually something we were looking forward to. In addition, we planned on building our baby registry for friends and family at Babies "R" Us.

Before we got started, Sandi had an appointment with her OBGYN in Golden Valley, which we were unable to attend. It was on a Wednesday, and we knew her appointment was in the late afternoon, so we decided to leave her alone for the day and call her that evening to see how the appointment went. Of course throughout the day we still received twenty or so text messages from her regarding various subjects. Despite not knowing the sex of our baby, we had already chosen names for both a boy and a girl. Our girl name was Amelia, and our boy name was Silas. We honestly did not have a preference on the sex; one day we wanted a boy because we loved the clothing options, but the next day we found ourselves wanting a sweet little girl. Our final conclusion was just that we wanted a healthy baby.

Around 6pm that night I was at the gym working out and noticed Sandi was calling. It was rare to get a call from her, but I did not want to stop my workout, so I decided to call her back at a later time. She began repeatedly calling me and then sent a text message saying, "Emergency, please call me now." The gym was just a few blocks from our house, so I ran home in a panic to I could call her and talk in private. DJ was at work, so I texted him that something was wrong and that I would call him as soon as I got off the phone with Sandi. I immediately dialed her number, and I was surprised that she didn't sound upset in any way when she answered. "Hey, Andrew, you know I had my appointment today with my OBYGN. He said everything looked good with the baby, and he was also able to tell the sex. You guys are going to have a little boy!" *Wow*, I thought, *that sure happened quickly.* The ultrasound was not clear on the last visit but the primary OBGYN had been able to make a gender determination. I told her how happy and excited we were to know our baby would be little Silas Branham. She told us that her doctor had looked at the ultrasound picture, run some tests, and had determined it was definitely a boy. I called DJ, and he was thrilled as well: Silas Edward (after my father) Branham! We were both brought to tears with the amazing news.

As soon as DJ got home, it was time to tell our friends and family about Silas, as we were not good at keeping secrets. We thought we would make it a little fun and make our announcement on Facebook. Our post included a cartoon picture of two dads with a baby boy sitting between them and stated, "It's official: we are having a baby boy! Silas Edward." All night long we got supportive comments, private messages, and tips on how to father baby boys. We had upwards of one hundred "likes" and comments. We also posted the news on our adoption Facebook page, where roughly 1200 people saw the post. We also made the important phone calls to our family members. While they were all excited, they began questioning how the OBGYN could know the sex when the specialist ultrasound technician and doctor could not. DJ's sister had just had a baby boy and thought that it was odd to have conflicting information. My sister was a doctor of audiology, a mother of two, and had studied medicine in-depth. She too questioned Sandi's news. We were not skeptical at all because we felt there would be absolutely no reason for someone to lie about the sex of the baby; doing so would not accomplish anything. So we put our trust in Sandi and believed her report. Since we were going back to Golden Valley for the next ultrasound, we would get validation from the doctor.

A few hours after Sandi shared the news, she began texting us about a dire situation regarding food. She stated that all of her food was gone, she had nothing to eat, and everyone was starving. We emailed her links to food banks and soup kitchens in Golden Valley, but this did not satisfy her. She was repeatedly texting both of us and would not let up. Was it coincidence that she delivered what she assumed was great news and then suddenly was asking for money? We reiterated that we couldn't talk to her about money and that she needed to go to Jill, the adoption facilitator. She did not like that answer at all and said, "Really? Real fucking nice, Andrew. You are going to fucking let us starve?" Once again, I explained to Sandi that we could not talk about money and that everything had to go through Jill and the attorney to ensure that everything was legal. We asked her what had happened to her weekly funds, and she stated that she had to pay her cable bill to get it turned back on, including a reconnection fee. The bill was $200 and took up all of her funds. She did not have a single penny. So in summary, rather than buying food, drinks, water, gas, or hygiene products to support her family, she had paid a $200 cable bill and was now without anything to eat. I held my ground, much to her dismay and fury. Not only did this make us angry, but it also forced us to question what kind of mother would make such a bad family decision.

The next morning Jill called and said that Sandi had been texting her since the previous night and asking her, "Y no text back?" "What is wrong?" "Hey!" and "I need money." Despite being told 100 times that Jill's hours of operation were 9am to 5pm, Sandi completely disregarded that and messaged her at all hours of the day and night. We explained to Jill that Sandi had spent all of her money on the cable bill and now had nothing to eat. We consulted with our attorney, and we concluded there was nothing we could do other than send her a gift card for groceries. Once again, Sandi won, and we had a $100 Safeway gift card emailed to her. I knew that nothing good could have possibly come from this.

We were still fuming about the continuous onslaught of extra expenses, and we finally came up with a viable plan. We talked to the WIC office in Golden Valley and arranged an appointment for Sandi. Once she went to the appointment she would receive free groceries twice a month, as well as food stamps in the amount of $600 a month. Combined, Sandi and her family should have an abundance of food for at least the next year. We felt that we had, at the very least, solved the food problem for the duration of the adoption. Sandi pushed back about going to the appointment, but we insisted, and she finally agreed to go. Immediately she received both the WIC benefits and the food stamp benefits. As was always the case, we did not receive any thanks from Sandi.

Not too soon after the food crisis was solved (or at least we thought), Sandi text messaged me about 20 times one morning stating that she needed help getting Camille's birth certificate so that she could enroll her in kindergarten. She said she needed my help since she did not have a computer and then provided me with all of the information. I went to the website and found that one of the parents had to show up in person at the office, which was three blocks away from her house and on the same street on which she lived. I explained this to Sandi, and she was absolutely furious. She ranted about how she was too busy for this "bullshit" and that it was ridiculous that she had to go in person. "Jesus, can't you just do this for me? I am just asking for one damn favor," she exclaimed. When I failed to respond, she turned to DJ for help. He was much more blunt to her, "Sandi, there's nothing I can do from here. Walk down the street three blocks and you can get it right there." Sandi was not happy and snapped at DJ as well, "Oh my fucking God. I can't ask you for shit!"

Later that same day, she text messaged me to inform me that she had changed her mind about school due to the birth certificate and now was going to home-school Camille. I reminded her about the importance of social interaction and asked how she would do that without a computer. She did not care whatsoever; she seemed to only be concerned about not having to take the time to get the birth certificate three blocks down the road. Her last text to me on the subject was, "Wat? Home-schooling is better 'cause Camille does not like to be away from me. I have Internet on my phone so I will just use that." I was astonished; this woman was so lazy that she was going to home-school her oldest daughter on an Android phone because she did not want to drive three blocks. Again, we wondered what kind of person Sandi really was. Who would do such a thing and not have any guilt at all? The only good news that we received a few weeks later was that the school had decided to send Sandi's family a personal computer since they were under the poverty line. While we doubted that Sandi could school her child when she never received schooling herself, we at least felt better that she would have a chance with a computer.

Now that we seriously doubted Sandi's character, it was time to begin doing some rough investigation of our own. Sandi did not get along with Jill at all. In fact, she was outright mean to her and abused her verbally on a daily basis. In one of her rants, she exclaimed, "Jill is a fucking bitch. Elaine, the agent from my last adoption, understands me better and don't treat me like I am 10 years old." Wisely, I gently asked Sandi if I could talk to Elaine to help smooth things out, and she gave me Elaine's number. I also talked her into giving me the names and number of the family in San Francisco who had adopted her last baby girl. They were John and Kim, and they lived right outside of San Francisco. I was very excited that they lived so close to Livermore and we could possibly have a relationship with them. I envisioned our baby having regular play dates with his sister. I was also happy that I had received these phone numbers so that we could get a better idea of what we were actually dealing with in regard to Sandi.

That very night I made my first phone call to John and Kim. Kim answered the phone and was overjoyed to hear from us. John and Kim were thrilled when they found out we lived nearby. They seemed like wonderful and kind people, and they were very easy to talk to. John worked for a major animated film production company as an animator, and Kim worked as a cosmetologist with her own business. DJ was with me at the time, so we put the call on speaker so he could ask questions as well. During our first conversation, John and Kim were a bit reserved about talking badly about Sandi. We were able to find out that they had adopted their beautiful little daughter at the very last moment at the hospital in Golden Valley. They had not gone through the waiting process with Sandi at all. In fact, the previous couple who had matched with Sandi had become so upset and furious by her behavior and manipulation at the hospital that they walked away from her and never looked back. John and Kim became the lucky ones who simply had to drive to Golden Valley, get an attorney, and have Sandi sign the consent to adopt papers after the 72-hour waiting period required by law. Their three days were not without drama. In fact, they had not agreed to Sandi breast-feeding the baby, but she had done so anyway. During the last day of the 72-hour waiting period, Sandi had also started wavering on whether she wanted to place the baby for adoption at all. She would tell the family that she was ready to sign, the social worker would start her drive to Golden Valley, and then Sandi would change her mind. This happened several times before she actually kept her word. There were also last-minute attempts to collect money from the family that never took place due to adoption laws. Sandi insisted on taking the baby out of the hospital to show her off to her family, who really could not care any less about the baby. They were angry about the adoption and did not want to have to see the baby that they felt was being taken away from them. She reluctantly gave them the baby to have for the day. John and Kim went back to the hotel with their new baby girl and began to bond. That night, around 2am, Sandi called them repeatedly until they answered. She demanded they bring the baby back to her house immediately. They pushed back and said the baby was sleeping and asked her if she really wanted to wake her up. Sandi insisted on waking her up and bringing her to the house at that very moment so she could see her. In the end, with high levels of drama and lots of uncertain moments, Sandi signed the consent papers, and the baby girl was officially John and Kim's. Arizona law required that the adopting family stay in Arizona until the adoption cleared the ICPC (Interstate Compact on the Placement of Children), which usually took about 10 days. John and Kim wanted no more of Sandi's antics, so they packed up and moved to a hotel in Phoenix, which was at least three hours away and farther than Sandi's car could drive. They stayed there until the ICPC cleared and then flew back to California. They made a rule with Sandi that they would block her ability to text and would only take phone calls from her. Evidently that method worked, and to this day they very rarely heard from Sandi. They offered Sandi one visit per year for 30 minutes in a hotel lobby. Once the 30 minutes were over they would take Sandi's family to lunch and then leave. Their sweet baby girl, Emma, was apparently smart, well behaved, healthy, loving, and extremely far above normal on the intelligence scale. It was important and refreshing for DJ and me to know that a baby could come from Sandi, be loved and nurtured properly, and become a normal, intelligent, and loving child. We decided to bank on nurture versus nature.

I then proceeded to call Sandi's former adoption facilitator, Elaine. Prior to this phone call I would have said our stress levels were about as high as Mitt Romney on election night, if not higher. After speaking with Elaine I would have said our stress levels doubled at the very least. Our heads felt like nuclear cooling reactors that were about to melt down. The first thing out of Elaine's mouth was, "Oh my God, please tell me that Sandi is not your birth mom!" It was fair to say this was not the best way to start the conversation. We spent nearly an hour on the phone, and we were ready to just cry. Elaine explained that Sandi had been the worst client she had ever had in over 20 years of business. She said she was narcissistic, self-centered, and "an evil, wretched bitch." Elaine told us that after Sandi's last adoption she had begged the other agencies (including the one we had used) to ban her from the process in the future. There was a "scam board" that many of the facilitators used, and Elaine wanted Sandi placed on this for fraud, manipulation, and "baby selling." She claimed that she had told Jill everything that had happened in the past few adoptions, but Jill had not disclosed any of this to us. In Sandi's past two adoptions, two couples had walked away due to Sandi's manipulation, texting, and behavior. The first family that actually adopted her first child after the previous family walked away had similar horrific stories of dealing with her.

In one story, she told us, the adoptive couple was there while Sandi was in labor. A complication came up with the delivery, and the doctor told Sandi that she had to have a C-section or they could lose the baby. Without any regard for the unborn baby or the couple waiting, she told the doctor "absolutely not, 'cause it will hurt. You aren't doing anything that is going to cause me more pain." She told the doctor that he could not do the C-section. The stunned adopting couple sat outside of the room helplessly as they cried and prayed. Finally the doctor became extremely angry with Sandi and shouted at her. He begged her to forget about herself for a moment and allow him to do the C-section to save the baby. Reluctantly, Sandi signed the papers, delivered a healthy baby girl, and eventually signed the consent for the adoption. As the couple was leaving, the doctor came up to them and said (verbatim), "Get as far away from this woman as you can and never look back. Please listen to me." And that is exactly what they did. They took the baby, got in their car, and never looked back. We would actually get the exact story later from the adoption agency firsthand.

Despite this terrible story, Elaine was not finished. She had one more piece of advice for us. She said, and I quote, "Be prepared for *anything* at the hospital. I don't want to scare you, because you made it this far and you need to keep going. There is a light at the end of this dark tunnel. But I want you to know that she will make up one more manipulative scheme up during the delivery... and it will be really bad." She said she expected Sandi to make a big push for money after the delivery and that she would use the consent papers as ammunition. She said that Sandi would likely call another adoption agency and tell us that they would give her $10,000 for a new, healthy baby. She would use that as manipulation into getting us to buy our baby back. Elaine said that she would say something like, "I know I took a lot of advances from my postpartum funds, but I want it all back! Every penny, plus two extra months. So if you want me to sign these papers I need cash." Elaine said that her tactics were very illegal but that there was not much we could do about it and that we should be prepared for the worst-case scenario. She advised us to try and pay off Doug when the baby was due in order to get Sandi to sign. We consulted our attorney, and this was very illegal and risky, so we ruled it out. We had done everything by the book and did not want a foolish decision to ruin our adoption. She told us to just be mentally prepared for probably what would be the worst 72 hours of our lives. Great—just great!

We were very irritated that Jill had withheld this information from us. As a matter of fact, we confronted her about it via phone and email, outlining all the fraud that Sandi had already committed. Jill played ignorant and said she knew nothing about Sandi or she would never have matched her with us. We mentioned Elaine to Jill and she pretty much had to reverse course. She insisted that she only knew that Sandi was difficult and did not know any further details. We asked her, "Well Jill, if you knew she was difficult, why did you tell us that she seemed like a nice person on the date we matched?" Jill really did not have any response. Now it was time to reintroduce the subject of the fraud and how we could get out of this match while still keeping the $17,500 that we paid the agency. The contract stated that the funds could be reapplied to a new match if the birth mother or agency misrepresented or was involved in fraud. Clearly both of these boxes were checked. Jill made up a dozen reasons why this was not fraud and that if we unmatched with Sandi we would only get our money back if she was rematched. Who the hell in their right mind would match with Sandi at this point? She would have to disclose all of this information, and nobody would match with her. So despite there being tons of new birth mothers whom Jill had waiting, we could not match with them unless we paid another large sum of cash. We were stuck with Sandi. We had no choice other than to play it out until the delivery of the baby. It was going to be stressful, difficult, and challenging every day, but we had no choice other than suing Jill, which we considered but decided against. We still believed that maybe God had brought us together for some unknown reason that would be exposed later. Maybe we were supposed to save this baby from a life of neglect, filth, and no love. Maybe, just maybe, the reasons would become clearer as the days and months passed. However, every time we saw a couple matched with a perfect birth mom or baby our hearts split open just a little bit more. Jill was a great adoption facilitator and a very hard and dedicated worker. We would never know what information she had or did not have. Nonetheless, we were irritated.

# Chapter Five

Everyone seems to have an opinion about what love is or what love is about. I know what love is: I experience it every day with my partner DJ. People have always doubted our relationship because we have a sizable age difference. Age means absolutely nothing to us, and we are as happy and committed as a couple could be. True love is precious, a once in a lifetime opportunity for eternal happiness. It is delicate like the petal of an orchid stretching toward the light in a vibrant jungle. In my view, love is an endless river with no shores, a lifetime of adventure, sadness, surprise, intimacy, and happiness. Love is forever, and nothing can negate that. So for us, we held it together so we could continue down our endless river together and with our baby. There would be no turning back, even against the toughest of currents. Yes, we had monumental amounts of stress in our lives, but our love for each other never once wavered.

Each new day was like living in a nightmare, and the stress showed up at our work, school, and in our relationship. Thankfully my work was very understanding and knew what we were going through. I had a very time-consuming job running a marketing department at a very large national company. My co-workers were amazing: they checked in on me, asked for updates, donated toys and clothing, and even planned a baby shower for us. DJ's college was as understanding as possible and allowed him to have a few absences without any repercussions. At home, the stress got to us, but we never allowed it to get between us as a couple. We had done some pre-adoption therapy that prepared us for some of what was coming, though nobody could have predicted Sandi. Yes, there were some Sandi-related arguments, and some days we felt like we were living in a boxing ring, but for the most part we handled our relationship very well. At the end of each day we were exhausted both mentally and physically. For stress relief I would run for miles at a time, exercise, and watch TV and movies after work. My real stress relief, however, came when I decided to start this book. Writing was an outlet for me, and I loved it. DJ started using exercise as a stress outlet, but he also turned to junk food. Gas station chips, donuts, and pastries were his salvation. He also spent hours talking to his friends and family, which was a healthier way to vent. For me, the stress would have been too much to share with my sister and parents. I gave them minimal details but kept them in the loop as much as I felt was necessary. It was simply better this way for my family. Both of our families were anxiously awaiting the arrival of our son with open arms.

As the saying goes, if you can't beat them, join them—and that was going to be our new approach. Obviously Sandi had the upper hand, so we simply decided we would play the game with her. Any argument that ensued always landed us in the hot seat with her. She was the dealer; we were simply playing blackjack at her table. We decided we would pretend that we loved her, make additional visits, keep bonding with Doug and the kids, and do our best to manage the money situation legally without breaking our bank. We often had the attorney send gift cards, food cards, or grocery cards to the family just to be kind. Sandi would say things like, "Can you just send cash? These cards are not helpful at all. We need cash!" The hardest part was that we tried to find sympathy for Sandi, but she just made it so hard. Any time we would find empathy for her, she would do something so outrageous that our empathy turned to hate. We also truly loved her children, and they loved us. The fact was that we had bonded with them and loved them, caring deeply for them and constantly worrying about their living environment and upbringing. We wished there was some way we could rewrite their future so they wouldn't be trapped by their upbringing and Sandi's physical and emotional abuse. When we would part ways after a visit or even a Skype calls, the kids would cry their eyes out, breaking our hearts. We wanted to turn something negative into something positive, so we directed our energy into making these beautiful children find some sense of love and affection, fun, and happiness, even if it was only temporary.

For the past few weeks, Sandi had gone back into her devilish ways of using manipulation to extort funds from us. She would make up outlandish lies and stories to try and get us to send her money or gift cards outside of her normal living expenses. She would claim that she had terrible morning sickness and needed $50 for over-the-counter medications. She would say her breasts hurt because she did not have a properly-fitting maternity bra, even though she was hardly showing at this point. She would claim infestation of insects or rodents, but she could not produce a picture or an estimate from an exterminator. She would try to use the starvation ploy against us, but we knew her refrigerator was loaded with wholesome foods from her food stamps and WIC benefits. She would call us in tears saying she had not eaten in days, but Doug would tell us that she was lying. She would research adoption laws and try to find loopholes through which she could force us to send her something. Sandi was not educated, but she was street smart and not dumb by any stretch of the imagination. She found one of our glaring weaknesses: her health. It started small with things like nausea, swollen feet, and pains in her back and then it progressed to her texting us about preterm labor, bleeding and spotting, pains in her abdomen, or contractions. At first we fell into the trap and called doctors, OBGYNs, and anyone who would listen to us. She did this for attention, compassion, and drama. We knew this because she would never go to the doctor, would be perfectly fine an hour later, and Doug would confirm that nothing was wrong. We were able to manage these texts and calls at first, but that only worked for so long.

Another way she tried to manipulate us was to start telling us that she despised her current home and wanted us to relocate the family to a new one. Jill had already told us that paying for this would be illegal. She continued to push, saying that the house was unfit to live in and demanding we find her a new home. The texts and calls never stopped. "Why can't you just do it? All the other families did it for us with the other adoptions. Why do you have to be so mean?" We finally had to be very harsh and firm with her and told her, "Sandi, we CAN NOT relocate you. It is illegal for us to that. So please drop it. The only way an adoptive family can do a relocation is if something happens to the house that makes it unlivable." That was a conversation that I would end up regretting more than words can say.

The constant daily stress with Sandi was seriously killing us, and we knew that, given the growing adoption expenses, there was no way we could afford a well-deserved vacation. We also knew that given the time we had to take off for the birth and bonding, neither DJ's school nor my work would allow us to take a vacation. We knew we had to visit as part of the bonding process, and we were overdue for a trip to Golden Valley. Going back to our motto of making the children's life a little better, even if only for a little while, we came up with the grand plan of treating them to a weekend at the children's hotel Circus Circus in Las Vegas. It did not take them long to accept this idea and get very excited. They could not wait for this weekend and would text us every day saying how excited they were, how they could barely wait, and how the kids would not stop talking about it. It was going to be expensive and time-consuming, but we were more than happy to do it for the kids.

To keep our sanity, we came out two days earlier than we told them and spent two wonderful nights at the Mandalay Bay Hotel. Since we could not do a real vacation, this was the best we could come up with. We did some gambling, ate at two fine seafood restaurants, explored the strip, and kicked back at the amazing pool before we packed up. Because their car could not make it from Golden Valley and no buses ran that route, we actually had to drive two hours to Golden Valley and pick them up. Then we had to drive two hours back to Las Vegas. It was obvious that the kids were excited, but Sandi began her complaining immediately about the long car ride through the desert. It was a busy weekend and the hotels were swamped, so you can imagine her reaction to waiting for parking and check-in when we arrived. She was NOT happy at all. The scowl had returned, the yelling and cussing at the kids was back, and Doug was constantly being berated. In her opinion, the hotel was "too busy" and "too kid friendly." She did not give a damn that this trip was for the kids; all she cared about was herself. She complained in the elevator, complained down the hall, and complained about her room we had purchased for her and her family. It was too small, too dark, there was no view, etc. Next door a man and his wife had a brief argument, and she turned it into an elaborate story about him kicking and pounding on the door and screaming, none of which really happened. She demanded a new room because she felt unsafe and wanted an upgrade. We informed her that the hotel was sold out and she would have to live with it. The family wanted thirty minutes to relax before going to the Adventure Dome, so we parted ways. We were going to meet in the lobby in thirty minutes and head out for some fun. When they arrived, Sandi was in full bitch mode and was making life miserable for everyone in her family. She had forgotten her purse and refused to go get it. I volunteered, took the key, and went up to grab it. To my astonishment, when I entered the room there was an actual cloud of cigarette smoke, and cigarette butts and ashes filled the toilet. The whole room reeked of cigarettes and smoke, yet she was telling us she was a non-smoker. I was irate and had to control my anger so as not to ruin the day. Again I was thinking of the kids and tried to take some deep breaths to calm myself. I figured that I would talk to her later and try to find a way to gently bring up the subject without causing a big fight. I was at a loss for words, wounded inside knowing she was harming my unborn son even though she knew the effects smoking would have on him, not to mention the harm it would cause the rest of her family. Nevertheless, I had to put on my fake happy face and go down there and wine and dine Sandi. At this point we really started to find ourselves hating her, unable to understand how anyone could be so selfish, cold, and manipulative.

Pretending that everything was fine and plastering on fake smiles, we were very intent on making sure the kids had a nice vacation. We walked through the midway, and the kids got to see all of the exciting activities that surrounded them. They were on a beeline for the Adventure Dome, a huge indoor theme park designed for families with children. Just as we approached the entrance to the park, Sandi grabbed the kids and yelled, "Just stop for damn minute!" She had decided she was "dying of thirst and starving" despite all of us having already had lunch and drinks. She could have very easily just allowed the kids to go inside, where there was a plethora of food options. But instead she took her sweet time deciding what she wanted to eat—and whatever it was, I knew we would be paying for it. She ordered herself some fried food and a drink and we thought we would be on our way. Once again we were wrong. The kids were going crazy with excitement, but Sandi needed to have a sit-down meal and relax because her feet already hurt, or so she told us. So we sat there at the table for a solid 45 minutes before we could leave and head to the park.

It was not cheap at all, but I wanted everyone to have a good time, so I purchased ride bracelets for everyone that allowed all of us to go on as many rides as we wanted. The kids' eyes were as big as saucers as we walked into the smells of peanuts and popcorn, cotton candy and the sights of clowns walking around, hundreds of midway games, fun rides, and big roller coasters. It was too much to take in for these sheltered children, so we had to pick the rides for them at first. The very first ride we took them on was a plane ride that flew in a circle and the kids could use the controls to move their plane up and down. We were in line for the ride when Carrie just started peeing her pants for no reason. Sandi smacked her, cussed at her, made a big scene, and then proceeded to have a public fight with Doug. Meanwhile, Carrie was on the ground playing in the pee, splashing it around with her hands and stepping in it with her bare feet (she had removed her shoes). Her clothes were soaked in urine and her hands and feet were covered in it. Any normal parent would take their kids up to the hotel room, clean them up, and change their clothes, but not Sandi! She was having nothing to do with going all the way back up to her hotel room. Instead, she hit Carrie several times on the back of her head and on her hands and then patted her dry with a paper towel. Carrie ran right up to poor DJ and, with her urine-soaked hand, sweetly grabbed his hand to hold. I could see the look on DJ's face, but he did a great job of playing it cool. They went on the ride and had a blast, demanding to go on it again. We explained that the entire place was full of rides and we would move on to the next one. As usual, Duncan would not leave my side, and he wanted me to carry him on my shoulders, which I happily did. Again, poor DJ got the short end of the stick when Carrie demanded that DJ give her a ride. He was already unnerved by the urine on his hands and now he had to place a urine-soaked toddler on his neck! Oh, the things we do as adoptive parents to ensure things go smoothly. I really felt sorry for both Carrie and DJ. She would later have a second accident as we were waiting on Doug and DJ to get off a roller coaster, and again Sandi did nothing about it other than yell at the poor child. The final thing we did was take a walk through the midway and let the kids play some of the carnival games. They had a blast, and Doug and Duncan even won a stuffed toy from the show *South Park*.

We ended up spending a full day at the park, and the kids had the time of their lives. They had an amazing time, and even Doug had a blast. DJ and I enjoyed ourselves as well, and it was so exciting to see the kids having fun and feeling normal for a day. Sandi looked miserable, scowling and yelling at the kids. It was almost as if she were jealous that the kids were having fun. Most parents would make that sacrifice to see their loved ones have a unique opportunity, but not Sandi; she was not having any of the fun and did her best to make everyone else miserable all day.

We all took a break back at our rooms, then showered and got ready to go out for the evening. Sandi, Doug, and the kids wanted a tour of the strip to see the lights, water shows, and free entertainment. We drove up and down the strip in my rented van, and the kids "ooh"ed and "aah"ed at the overstimulating display of lights, colors, and sounds. We got out to watch the Bellagio water show and to see some of the crazy street entertainers. As usual, everyone had a brilliant time, with Sandi being the exception: "How far do we have to walk? When are we eating? This shit is tacky." and so on. We got back into the car, and the kids wanted to see the large Ferris wheel that dominated the skyline behind South Las Vegas Drive. The plan was to actually ride it until Sandi heard someone say it took about 45 minutes to go around. The kids wanted to go desperately, but Sandi shot down the idea very quickly. "Fuck that, I ain't goin' on no stupid wheel for 45 minutes. Screw that," she said. "Pleeaaasee Mommy?" one of the kids begged. "Shut the hell up," Sandi remarked.

DJ and I had made a dinner reservation at a famous Italian restaurant off the beaten path and known for its nostalgic decor. It looked like a dive from the outside, had not been remodeled in years, and resembled a restaurant out of a 1990s Italian gangster movie. Pictures of famous people lined the walls along with decades of memorabilia, and a 90-year-old Italian man walked around playing live accordion music. My family had been dining here for decades as well, and it was a fun place to go with excellent food. We were there on time, but our table was not quite ready as they were having a problem getting a drunken couple out of our private room. Sandi stomped her feet and whined like a little girl. Meanwhile the rest of us played, goofed off, looked at the pictures, and just had some carefree fun. Within ten minutes our table was ready and we were seated. Most of the kids had never heard of much of the food, so we helped them order. Believe it or not, Sandi was thrilled with her meal, and so was the entire family. They raved about the food, the endless garlic bread, and even Sandi raved about the portion sizes. We actually had a quality dinner with the entire family without any complaining. We had good conversation, good food, the kids had fun, and we ended the night on a positive note.

In the morning we had to take DJ to the airport, as he was leaving one day before me due to school. I was staying to drive them to Golden Valley and to attend the second ultrasound. Before leaving, DJ treated the kids to some more fun in the midway and showed them a lot of the love and affection they so desperately needed. In another very selfless and kind moment of generosity, DJ also took Doug to the casino and allowed him to play the slots for a while. Doug had never had this opportunity due to financial constraints, and he really, truly enjoyed the moment. I think he felt free for the moment—free from Sandi, free from money worries, and free to just be himself for an hour. We purposefully kept Sandi away from him by getting her a snack to eat with the kids. Doug hit a few big wins and then of course put it all back in the machine. The point was that he had fun, and it was a wonderful act of kindness and generosity that I witnessed DJ display. Despite Sandi's lies, manipulation, and evil ways, DJ still had it in his heart to give the kids and Doug a special moment. Doug had a heart; it was torn up, shredded, pureed, and stomped on by Sandi, but it was clearly still there. He often times displayed affection and love for the kids and always claimed he would do anything for them.

Regardless of Sandi's behavior during the trip, we could not help but feel a sense of pity for her. We continued to wonder what had driven such a young woman to be so angry and hateful all of the time. We realized that she held deep pain from something in her past that we would never fully understand. We truly felt empathy toward her at times and wanted to help her if we could. We still had hopes that we would someday connect with her and she would open up to our love. We could only begin to imagine what her life must have been like in her past to make her so angry and cold in the present.

We all packed up the van, dropped DJ off at the airport (the kids cried again), and headed back to Golden Valley. The entire trip I thought, *Oh my God, I still have to make this drive one more time to get back to the Las Vegas airport.* Everyone in the car slept all the way back except Doug, and it really gave us a chance to talk openly and honestly and also to bond. We talked about everything, and he apologized for Sandi's antics, games, manipulation, and for the way she treated us. He seemed sincere. He told me more about her horrible childhood being raised by a drunk and drug addicted mother and her history of sexual and physical abuse. She had sisters and a brother who lived in Golden Valley, but they had pretty much banished her from the family and rarely did anything with her. He said she used to use intravenous drugs, drink, party, and smoke marijuana until her first child was born. She then stopped cold turkey. He also told me that she had spent three years in juvenile prison for constantly running away. For a moment, all of her games and manipulation went out the window, and I felt a deep sense of sadness and compassion for her. I wanted to try harder to like and understand her. That being said, I could not understand why she would inflict the same abuse on her own kids. I wondered how she could be so emotionless toward the kids and never show them any affection. How could she kill a cat, extort money from people, and essentially sell infants for a living, knowing the terrible effects such behavior could have on a person? I was completely confused and full of mixed emotions. I thought, *Maybe, I can learn to like or even love this woman.* DJ and I both wanted a kind and loving birth family to be close to. We hoped to have a long-lasting relationship with them and to celebrate holidays and birthdays together. We thought maybe someday we could even meet them for a vacation at my family's condo in south Florida. Sadly, that bond had not yet occurred, and we had a like/hate relationship with Sandi and her family at this point. We loved the kids, we pretty much loved Doug—but Sandi was a hard pill to swallow.

As the saying goes, things can change in an instant. The very next morning I picked them up for an early OBGYN appointment and an ultrasound. Of course, Sandi would never allow Doug to be alone, so the entire family came to the appointment. I was excited to see my son again and to see how he had grown and developed since the last ultrasound. Doug was going to watch the kids while Sandi and I went back for the exam. The doctor called me in and said they were ready for us. He was a very kind man, cracking jokes and answering any questions we had. That was sometimes rare for doctors these days, so I really appreciated it. He started out the exam by looking at the baby's heart, spine, and vital organs and making measurements. He happily said that the baby looked very normal and happy.

Then came the crucial exam of the placenta, and he got a worried look on his face, quieted down, and started taking a lot of pictures and measurement. As I did last time, I asked, "Is everything ok, Doctor"?

"I think so," he replied, "but there are still some abnormalities in the placenta. There are some non-functioning areas that may not be getting enough blood or oxygen. This is not my area of expertise, so we will need to send Sandi to a specialist in town. It is probably something that will go away naturally, but it's worth checking out. Quitting smoking would be a really big help for this, Sandi."

I asked a few more questions, and he gave vague and safe answers. "You know, Doctor," I continued, "all I'm concerned about is the health of my son."

The doctor looked a little confused and said, "Oh, so you think it's a boy?"

At this point I was confused, so I told him that Sandi had told us that the sex had been determined. Sandi began to squirm and look scared. The doctor looked at me, lowered his glasses, and told me that at no point had he made any suggestions about the sex, nor had anyone else in his office. He stated that they did not know at this point, though we might be able to find out in a few minutes. Sandi, caught red handed in a bold and blatant lie, calmly said, "Oh, I said it was a boy because I've had six kids. I can tell by the way he is sitting. That's why I told you that." The doctor then remarked that she could make her predictions but there was no medical evidence that could determine a gender.

Inside I was filled with anger. Why would she lie about this? Why did she do this? We had already announced to all of our family that it was Silas Branham. We announced to the world on our adoption webpage with thousands of followers. To be frank, DJ and I did not care either way what the sex was, and we would be happy with either a girl or boy. The audacity, however, for her to make up such a horrific lie without even thinking of the impact it would have on us was disgusting. It was plain mean.

I was trying to keep it together and not show my anger. It's not good for the adoptive family and birth mother to fight. It becomes dangerous ground, and the adoptive family begins walking on thin ice. At any moment she could get mad at us, disrupt the adoption, walk away, and find another sucker family. So I held my anger in, even though it took every ounce of willpower I had.

The doctor continued the exam and said he was now going to see if he could determine the gender. The baby was on its side and pointed in the wrong direction, and the umbilical cord was also in the way. He used every trick in the book to get the baby to roll over, but we got absolutely no cooperation. We could already see that the baby had Sandi's stubbornness. After another fifteen minutes of trying, he concluded that we could not determine the sex today and would have to wait another two to four weeks.

I am sure Sandi knew I was angry, but I tried my best not to show it. She never apologized or even said a word about it. I had promised them that I would get them some groceries before I departed, so I stopped at the local Safeway store and ran in to do some quick shopping. I filled up my cart with $200 worth of healthy and wholesome foods that should last them over a week. I purchased a lot of fresh meats, vegetables, and fruits in the hope that Sandi and family would eat a little bit healthier. Immediately after this I dropped them off at home, gave my hugs, said goodbye to the kids, and quickly left to catch my flight. On the way to the airport I had to call DJ and tell him that she had lied and we did not know if the baby was Silas Branham or Amelia Branham. He too was stunned, angry, confused, and blindsided by Sandi's ridiculous games. We were not sad, because we just wanted a healthy baby, but we hated being lied to, and we were worried about our baby's health given the placenta. That flight home was long and lonely as all I could think about was our unborn baby. Would he or she be ok? We decided we would not make any announcements about the sex until we knew for sure. We just told our families not to send any presents yet. What an end to a crazy trip.

# Chapter Six

B ack to our normal routine in Livermore, we attempted to have as little contact with Sandi as possible. Due to the hundreds of texts we both received from her on a daily basis, we reached out to Jill and asked for some professional advice. She told us to simply cut Sandi off cold turkey and take a mental break. She promised that if we did this Sandi would back down and learn that we wouldn't partake in her constant texting. We decided that we would give it a try and would take a weekend off from her craziness. We both told her that we would be busy for the weekend and that we would most likely not be available. She did not respond back. It took about two hours before the barrage of text messages began. "Hey, something is wrong with my house." "Hey y no text back." "Hey!" "Hey!" "Hey!" "Andrew!!" "Hey!" "Why no text back?" "What the fuck?" "Really Andrew?" "Hey!" This continued on both my phone and DJ's phone for hours. We received hundreds of texts in just a few hours' time and then she began repeatedly calling both of our phones. She had completely lost control of herself and she continued nonstop for hours. It was ruining our weekend, and we could not keep ignoring her. She was so mad that she started sending texts saying, "I am done. I am done with you guys. That's it. Don't talk to me ever again." In her threatening way, she was telling us that she would unmatch with us if we did not call her immediately. Once again, we had no choice. We could listen to Jill and not text or call her back and lose our child, or we could cave in and talk to Sandi. Of course we chose to do the latter.

We explained to Sandi that we had been busy and that we were not near our phones. She quickly calmed down and shifted gears toward money. She needed emergency funds for medication and hygiene products. We asked what it was she needed, and she replied, "Stuff." We reminded her again that we could not talk about money, which as usual really pissed her off. "We are sorry, Sandi, but you have to call Jill about all money issues," we told her. We did not hear from her for a while because at the same time she was calling and texting Jill. She had no luck getting through and turned her attention back to us. We told her there was nothing we could do. She decided to give us the silent treatment as punishment and did not talk to us for the remainder of the weekend, which we secretly loved.

When we heard from her again, it was for her to tell us, "I can't do this anymore! I need you to move me to a new fucking house." We repeated that she had to go through Jill for any money issues. "She always says no," Sandi replied. "I hate Jill." We explained that Jill was only doing her job, that she cared about Sandi, and that we had to do things within the law. We explained to her that she had lived in her current house for many months without issue and that relocation was expensive. Once again she snapped back that both of her previous adoptive families had relocated her. We finally had to be extremely firm with her and told her that we would not be relocating her; we did not have the money, it was not legal, and if she wanted to move she would have to save up the money herself. We also suggested Doug could get a job. Sandi was livid with us and said some not-so-nice things before returning to the welcomed silent treatment for the rest of the day.

Early the next day I was at work and DJ was at school. The texts started again and came in bundles of five. "OMG, it rained last night and our roof is leaking. It is like a waterfall in here." We told her to call her landlord, but she said she was a slumlord who wouldn't return any of her calls. When the rain stopped Doug informed us that the leak was very small and was no big deal. Sandi would not stop texting and calling, making it seem as if a water main had broken in the middle of her house. We continued to copy and repeat the texts that told her we were not moving her and she had to talk to Jill about money.

The next wave of texts started coming in with links to Craigslist ads of houses for rent in Golden Valley. "Look at this awesome home I found… and it's only $650 a month!" she wrote. Our current agreed-upon living expense budget was $500 for rent. We reminded her again that we were not moving her, that she should not waste her time sending us these links, and that the legal agreement for rent was $500 per month. This did not stop her. "Andrew, will you please contact this landlord? He has a place that is perfect!" I reiterated that we were not moving her and then had Jill call her to reinforce this point. Sandi was furious, but we knew it was what we had to do. We both immediately received "I'm pissed off at you" texts, and she stated that she was just going to move herself then. We warned her not to do anything until she had all the money saved so she did not get stuck being homeless. It went in one ear and out the other. When Sandi got an idea in her head nobody could stop her—not Doug, not Jill, and certainly not us. She claimed her landlord owed her money and that she had $500. We did not buy into this for a minute and foresaw catastrophe. We consulted with both Jill and the attorney, and both told us that we could not control her and that we just had to allow her to do whatever it was that she was doing. They told us just to discourage her and remind her how expensive relocation was.

As all of this was going on Sandi had her first follow-up appointment with the specialist, and we requested gender identification during this appointment. The doctor allowed me to call in on Facetime for the appointment while DJ was at school. Surprisingly, Sandi did not push back and had no issues with me attending the ultrasound in this way. The doctor immediately examined the placenta and noted the irregularities. He made many notes, took many measurements, and ran several tests. His early analysis was that there were some minor issues with the placenta but nothing to be concerned about at this point. He said that she would need bi-weekly ultrasounds moving forward in order to monitor the issues. He assured us that the baby was growing normally at this point, but he sternly told Sandi that if she would quit smoking cigarettes and watch her diet that it would help dramatically.

The doctor finished making his regular measurements and then asked if we wanted to know the gender of the baby. We both said that we did, and he began his gender determination exam. "Well, this looks very clear to me. Sandi, you said you thought it was a boy? Well, you can see the hips, the legs, and if you look right about here you will see these two lines. Those would be labia. Your baby is going to be a beautiful little girl."

My reaction was happiness as thoughts of tea parties, princesses, and rainbows began running through my mind. So after all of this, it was official: our daughter would be Amelia Laurie Branham. Sandi, knowing that she had lied, quickly asked me if I was mad or disappointed. I told her and the doctor that I was thrilled and that I was just happy that the baby was healthy. Sandi then proclaimed that she was concerned about the baby now and that smoking was no longer an option. She promised that she would stop and that this time there would be no games. She would never smoke another cigarette.

I immediately called DJ and gave him the news. He cried with joy. "Amelia," he said. "We are going to be the proud daddies of a baby girl!" We had fun turning our attention from cars, trucks, superheroes, and sports to princesses, dress-up, playing house, and buying baby girl clothing. Of course we also had to reverse course with all of our friends and family, whom we had told that our baby was a boy. First we made the calls to our immediate family, and everyone was very excited. Many told us that they always thought a little girl would be best for us. My two young nieces were both laughing (they thought it was funny that boys were having a baby girl), but they were overjoyed at the idea of a baby cousin to pamper. We then made it official by posting a Facebook update explaining the situation and announcing Amelia Laurie to our Facebook friends. We managed to get dozens of comments and hundreds of "likes" on our post. Everyone was excited for us and started offering ideas about how to raise a baby girl. We welcomed the advice and looked forward to getting the nursery completed and doing some clothes shopping. Every day we dreamed of holding Amelia in our arms.

But as was always the case, Sandi did not stay quiet for long. She continued to press us about her need to move and for us to relocate her. Even Jill had become tired of it and was now ignoring all her emails regarding the subject. Then, at 8am one Monday morning, everything changed. Sandi had done her research, and she had somehow found a loophole in the adoption law. She discovered that if her home was deemed unlivable that the adoptive family had to find a new and safe place for the family to live. Thus, at 8:01am I got the text from Sandi reading, "OMG we have black mold everywhere in the ceiling where the roof was leaking. That's why I'm always sic. We got to get out now. The whole family is in the yard!" Of course I immediately called her, and she was sure that her home had become a breeding ground for black mold. She told me she had pictures and that the landlord had come over and confirmed it. I told her to please send the pictures along with any other documentation that she had confirming the mold to Jill, the attorney, and to me. She sent one picture of a hole in the ceiling with a tiny black mark near it and a sketchy note supposedly from the landlord saying that she indeed had black mold. She then proceeded to send a copy of the text of the law to all of us and said that she needed a hotel immediately until we could find her a new home.

DJ and I were as mad as we had ever been toward Sandi. She had orchestrated this entire thing, convinced the landlord to corroborate the story (we later found out she told the landlord she could keep the remaining deposit), and was now putting us in a no-win situation. The lawyer told us that we really had no choice and that if we did not comply, we could be putting the family at risk for illness and Sandi would have an excuse to disrupt the adoption and find another family. Even though the fraud was completely transparent, Sandi had calculated everything perfectly. There was nothing we could do.

You would think in this situation that Sandi and Doug would be scrambling to find a new home in their price range. They were not. They were happily relaxing in their room at the Golden Valley Motel 6, swimming in the pool, and eating pizza. They were not making any effort to find a new home since they knew we had to pay the hotel fees until a new home was found. Sandi even went so far as to tell Jill and myself that it was not her job to find the home. We were the people who had the resources to find it and she was going to sit on her fat ass until we did so. "Oh my God, you want a pregnant women to do this?" she said to us. "You do it. It is your responsibility! Find me a damn house!" We wondered why Doug was not trying to help. Usually he was rational and would make an effort to help. Now he seemed to be assisting Sandi in the scam. We felt hurt as now Doug seemed to be part of the problem rather than a solution. We did not really know how to feel about him any longer.

Thus began the tedious, torturous, and nearly impossible task of finding a new home for a family with no credit, no money, a criminal record, several animals, disheveled appearances, and three children. In addition, we discovered that they were notoriously known in the Golden Valley rental circle for moving into homes, destroying them, and then moving out. Several places that I called hung up on me when I mentioned their names. To make matters worse, the churches of the community had once helped them out by providing a household's worth of furniture for them at no cost only to have them sell it all for cash the very next day. So almost everyone in the community knew their names and the things that they had done and wanted nothing to do with my rental inquiries. Sandi was not helpful at all, and when we did find a potential place, she acted completely irritated that she had to go look at it. When she did go, she would have nothing but complaints about the place. Finally, we were fed up and told her she had three days to find a place herself. After those three days we would not be paying the hotel bill any longer. This woke her up to a point, but we still had to do all the legwork while she, Doug, and the family sat around at the hotel. Jill was also working very hard to help us find a place and spent nearly an entire day assisting me with the grunt work. I must say that Jill was very helpful during this time, and I sincerely appreciated all the help. When he was not in class or doing homework, DJ also searched Golden Valley for any available place. He was not happy as it was really dipping into his time that he had allotted for school work.

My bank account was dwindling fast with all of the unexpected expenses and trips that Sandi required. I had to take a second adoption loan out to keep my head above water since DJ was in school full time and not working. I was supporting two families plus the "Sandi factor." Taking debt was not optimal, but at that point we would have done anything for Amelia, and we knew our family and friends would help us as we got closer to the delivery date. We could not find any homes that would accept the family at their $500 price tag. As a result, I had to increase the budget and start looking for places that were slightly more expensive. I found a very nice, clean, and large mobile home in a nice neighborhood that had three bedrooms and two bathrooms. I spoke with the landlords, and they were very skeptical about renting to the family. They told me to have Sandi and Doug meet them at the house the very next morning. The rules they gave were that Sandi and Doug had to be on time; if they were one minute late they would not consider renting to them. While it may seem second nature to most folks, Jill was very concerned about how Sandi and Doug would appear when they showed up. She sent Sandi a very direct text that instructed her to have the entire family show up showered and in their nicest clothing, with the car cleaned inside and out. The owners' biggest concern was the children and the impact that they could have on the home. Jill also directed everyone to be on their best behavior with the landlords and to be generous, thankful, and polite.

Surprisingly, the entire family showed up, and everyone loved the home, including Sandi. They were thrilled with the size, layout, and the massive yard with a full garage and breezeway. It had a large fenced-in yard for their dogs and an enormous front porch. Shortly after the visit, the landlords called Jill and said that as much as they wanted to help them, they simply did not trust Doug and Sandi enough to rent to them, especially since neither was working. We were going to be back to the drawing board, and I could not handle that; we were running out of time. Sixteen years in sales/marketing had given me some bargaining skills, so I picked up the phone and called the landlords. I explained the situation to them and talked about how Sandi's family would be homeless if this did not work out. I gave them my attorney's phone number and told them that they could call her if it made them feel better, since she would be paying them directly each month for the rent. I also gave them my word that they would receive on-time payments all the way through January of 2015. I used some of my learned sales skills, and after about twenty minutes I had convinced them to allow the family to move in that very day. I was also able to negotiate the price down to $550, which was only $50 more per month than Sandi and Doug's current rent. The negatives were that I had to pay first and last month's rent, which meant yet another check from me in the amount of $1100. I also had to pay about $200 in utility transfer fees and hook-ups.

I informed Sandi that they had accepted and that they could begin moving in that day. Sandi was thrilled, of course, but then came the immediate complaining about how she was going to move all of her stuff. We should have known that this would be the next cycle of her drama-filled world. "I'm pregnant, I can't move. I need movers," she bellowed. At this point, I had had enough. I told her that she needed to get her family, brother-in-law, and lazy boyfriend Doug to begin moving the items load by load. They did not have any large items because they did not have any furniture. She was not getting any movers out of my wallet, and it should take them no more than a few trips to get their meager belongings. Sandi got angry and yelled, cried, and tried every trick in her arsenal. I was not budging on this one, and none of her manipulation worked. Finally, she said she just needed gas money so she could borrow someone's truck, and I had the attorney send her money for this.

Believe it or not, it took them three full days to move their sparse amount of household goods. In the meantime they just all slept on the floor of the new place while the animals, thankfully, stayed outside. She bitched the entire three days and never once thanked us for anything. We were now $45,000+ into this adoption, and the meter was still running. We still had a long way to go, and we knew more unexpected Sandi expenses were surely on their way. The old landlord was now calling Jill and myself complaining about the disaster that Sandi and her family had left behind. She claimed their place was unlivable and demanded restitution. Thankfully, it was not my problem, and we were not liable for any of the damage. Sadly, it was actually the last adoptive couple whose deposit was stolen and who were potentially liable for the damage. Wherever Sandi walked, she left a wake of destruction in her path, and she had no remorse for anyone who got in her way. To add insult to injury, we had also made her very last car payment for her on her beaten-up Toyota wagon a few weeks earlier. It was supposed to be our last payment as part of the agreement. To our astonishment, she had gone and taken a cash loan out and used the car as collateral. Now she was forced to make car payments again, and we knew we would have to pay these one way or another. We would also later find out through various sources that Sandi had used the black mold lie on the past two adoptive families, thus forcing them to relocate her as well.

At this point we only knew one thing: we needed a serious Sandi break, and we were bound and determined to get it.

# Chapter Seven

Finances were becoming a problem, and we had to watch every penny so we could continue to support Sandi and pay the legal fees, adoption fees, and our own expenses. This was very stressful, and we needed to get away for a few days. As if God was looking down on us, a large check for unclaimed escrow funds from 2006 came suddenly and without notice in the mail. We could have easily banked this money and used it for all the things we needed for the adoption. For once, however, we decided to do something just for ourselves, and we took off for a long weekend together in Big Sur, California, at a very nice, peaceful, and nature-oriented resort. We told Sandi that we were going to Mexico for the weekend and would not have cell phone service. It did not stop her from texting us, but we had a great excuse to ignore her. Her latest issue was that her cell phone had quit working and she could only use it while it was plugged in. We knew we needed to stay in contact with her for the next several months so not having a cell phone was a real issue. While in Big Sur, we talked to the attorney, and Jill arranged for Sandi to get a new phone at Walmart that was under the same carrier. They deposited the funds into her account.

Big Sur is one of the most glorious and stunning places in our entire nation. As you drive from San Francisco you are immersed in giant redwoods and landscape on your left and dramatic, rugged cliffs toward the Pacific on your right. The long, winding road nearly hovers over the ocean with an aerial view of the crystal clear blue-green water while passing over single-lane bridges that have been there for centuries. The steep cliffs overlooking the ocean have scattered, towering waterfalls where the water gracefully descends in the rocky shoreline. It provided an instant sense of peace that we had been seeking for a long time.

DJ and I really enjoyed our three day weekend and stayed Sandi-free for those days. We relaxed by the pool, pampered ourselves with five star food, went on hikes in the redwoods, ate lavish fresh breakfasts, and even got to have a romantic bonfire on the beach in a private cove. We hiked, read, swam, used the hotel's elaborate Japanese hot springs, and just spent time reconnecting with each other. We allowed ourselves to find our intimacy again, which really just involved cuddling up together, holding each other, and having long late-night talks. It was great, and the natural surroundings temporarily lifted our massive levels of stress. We really enjoyed ourselves, and when Sunday came we were saddened to have to face Sandi reality again on Monday. At the very least, the trip revived us for the time being and was much needed.

Monday came, and, as usual, Sandi's drama commenced. She was not only bitching about the phone issues, but she was also complaining that she had no food despite having just received her weekly funds, WIC, and her food stamps. While we were gone, instead of taking the money the attorney had sent to her for the new phone, she had pocketed the money, effectively stealing it. She then went to the Sprint store and took advantage of their new contracts, which didn't require credit checks. She knew that we were only paying $55 per month as per the adoption living expenses agreement. Without any thought she not only signed up for a phone for herself, but she got Doug one as well. She got the very best phone currently on the market for both of them and worked the cost of the phone into her contract. She left the store with two new phones, paid no money down, and had no idea what her monthly bill would be. She texted us, thrilled, to tell us that now she *and* Doug had smartphones and we could now stay in touch more often and even use Skype. We inquired about the bill, and she said she did not know the monthly fees. We reminded her that we were only paying $55 per month, but she ignored our reminder. DJ did some digging around on the Sprint website and found that at minimum her new bill would be $100 each per month, plus the cost of the phone and the pro-rated first month. We estimated that the first bill would be over $300. We gently reminded her one more time about the $55, and she again did not respond. We agreed that we would never pay any more than the agreed-upon fees, and we discussed this with Jill and the attorney. They agreed with us, and Jill reminded Sandi of this as well. She gave no response. We all decided to hold firm on the payments no matter what happened. We knew Sandi would end up defaulting on the bill and losing her service at some point. That being said, we just let it go for the time being, knowing that a hurricane would be forming in about a month. Once again, Sandi had chosen to get the world's best phones with no regard for the bill. She was once again choosing herself over the kids and her family.

She was also completely out of food and said that she was literally begging for anything to eat. She used her normal manipulation tactics to convince us to give her an advance out of her postpartum funds so that she could eat. As usual we talked to the attorney, and she said it was fine to give Sandi money from her postpartum funds as long as she knew what she was doing. It was all documented, and all the texts and emails were saved. Now she was eating into her only means of support after we were long gone. You may call us stupid for falling for this, but we actually did not mind her taking her postpartum funds. I would soon be on family and medical leave with no income once the baby was born, so any funds we could pay her now would essentially help us out down the road. The attorney sent her $100 for food.

Roughly two days of silence went by without any Sandi drama, and this concerned us dearly. We knew it was the calm before the storm. The texts started soon thereafter; this time it was a dental emergency. She had not one, not two, but three completely rotten and infected teeth, and her government insurance did not cover dental bills. She had gone to the urgent care center, and they had given her antibiotics and told her the teeth had to come out. The medical report was faxed to Jill and our attorney and showed the needed proof of her condition. This time she was not lying, but as usual she expected us to find a solution to her problem. Between DJ, Jill, and I, we called every dentist in town, but none of them did a sliding scale or helped the less fortunate. They referred us to a free clinic that was 200 miles away. That provided no help to us, as Sandi and Doug's car could not make it that far. Meanwhile, Sandi was unable to eat, refused to drink any nutritional shakes, and was losing weight, which was not good for a second trimester pregnancy. We found one kind dentist who said he would take a look at Sandi if she would take the time to see him. It took Jill, DJ, Doug, and I to convince her to go. Several hours later the report was faxed to Jill and me. Sandi indeed needed all three teeth extracted, and they were all infected. Thankfully she had been taking the antibiotics, and the dentist could do the procedure right there. Normally he would charge $1000 for three major extractions, but since Sandi did not have any income, he offered to do it for $300 total. DJ and I had no choice but to foot the emergency dental bill so that Sandi could eat and our baby would be ok. $300 more tacked on to our growing list of expenses. As usual, we never received any call, text, or email saying, "Thank you." Sandi just went on with her life as usual.

Now up to this point Sandi had done some terrible and manipulative things to us, and we were very aware of the abuse. But we just kept thinking about Amelia and how she would soon be in our arms. We knew Sandi was a terrible person, a despicable mother, and a lying, self-centered narcissist. She showed no love or affection toward her kids; they were not taken care of, they lived in filth, and Doug and Sandi cursed around them, used food money for things for themselves, and Sandi had murdered a cat. That was in addition to her also using us as her personal ATM, employing any method or lie that she could come up with. We thought we had seen it all.

DJ has one of the most amazing aunts that anyone could ever hope for. She was not just an aunt, but a mentor, friend, confidant, and DJ's personal hero. She had also accepted me as part of the family since day one. Prink, DJ's aunt, worked as a nurse, lived modestly, and was almost always helping people. She almost never thought of herself. She spent the bulk of her money paying for a surgery for a young child in Peru who had been in a terrible accident and needed reconstructive surgery. The child was a complete stranger to Prink, yet when she heard the story she rushed to her aid. She had brought her to the United States for the surgery, but international laws would not allow the child to stay. The child and the mother had to go back to Peru. In Prink's spare time she saved and raised money to try and get both the child and the mother back to the United States. Prink had converted her garage into an apartment for the two of them to live in. She was still working through all the red tape, but still dedicated finances and time to keep fighting this uphill battle. She was also a dedicated member and guitarist for a large Christian church in Tampa, Florida. She had no kids of her own and always treated DJ and his sister as if they were her own. She had personally helped DJ through some very tough times in his teenage years.

DJ talked to Prink often, so she was very aware of the current situation. She was frustrated with Sandi's manipulations, but she still cared enough to actually want to help. She always tried to find the beauty in everyone and everything. She did not have a ton of money, but she called DJ and said that she wanted to help. Knowing how Sandi was, she didn't want to send Sandi any money, so she came up with an amazing idea. Sandi was always having issues keeping food on the table, and Prink believed she had a solution that would last at least a month. She worked on her plan and then told DJ she was ready to execute it. She was going to order $400 worth of food, groceries, and living supplies from Sam's Club online, pay it, and have it designated for Sandi to pick up. This way, Sandi would have no more excuses about food, and they would have healthy food to eat for four to six weeks. DJ called Sandi to tell her the good news, but she was not appreciative or excited at all. "You mean I have to drive all the way to fucking Bullhead City to pick it up? Jesus!" she yelled. However, after a long discussion, she agreed to have a friend take her to pick up the food as long as we gave her gas money to get there.

DJ relayed the message to Prink, and she was happy that she could help. She took hours placing the order online and had it all ready for pick-up. Then a small glitch happened that set off a chain of events that would forever change the way we looked at Sandi. Sam's Club would take payment over the phone or online but the person who picked up the order was required to show their identification that matched the credit card at that time. Since Sandi was picking up the order and Prink was the holder of the credit card, this method would not work. There was no way Prink was sending Sandi $400 in cash, so she found another way. She ordered $400 of digital Sam's Club and Walmart gift cards and emailed them to Sandi so she could pick up the order. Sandi was very aware of the kind gesture that Prink was making and was also aware that she was not rich by any means. $400 was a huge amount of money for her. DJ called her to let her know that about the gift cards and that the order was ready for pick-up. Sandi indicated that she would get the ride and use the cards to go pick up the groceries. Hours went by. We didn't hear from Sandi, but we received an email that she had printed the gift cards. She was not responding to our texts, so we called Sam's Club, only to find out that the order had not been picked up. It was getting late, and we were very worried. Prink was nearly in tears at this point, wondering what was going on with her hard-earned $400. We called, texted, and emailed Sandi with no response. We texted and called Doug, but he didn't respond either. Finally, late that night, Sandi responded to DJ and said, "Oh sorry, I couldn't find a ride to Sam's!"

DJ was irate and about to have a meltdown and/or panic attack. "Ok, well then please just give us back the gift cards and we can get a refund," he said.

"No way," Sandi replied. "That's my fucking money, and I can use it however I want!"

I listened to DJ beg her for an hour not to do this to Prink. He pleaded with her and tried to talk sense into her for the entire night. It was all for naught! Sandi had stolen the money and there was little we could do about it. DJ was crying, Prink was crying, and I was like a nuclear bomb of anger that was about to explode. I tried talking sense into Sandi, but she did not respond to me. In a last ditch effort, Prink called Walmart to attempt to deactivate the cards. They insisted that they could not do that; however, there was still one card that had not been printed. They were able to refund that card back to her, but it was only a small portion. Sandi had the rest of the cards and was not planning to return them under any circumstances. Prink was so angry that she did not talk to DJ for over a week. She would not respond to our messages or calls. She was not mad at us, per say, but she was devastated by the situation. She did not think anyone could be so evil as to scam a complete stranger who was only trying to help. DJ was so angry that I had to plead with him to not say anything he would regret. Frankly in all the years I had been with him I had never seen him so upset. "I want to drive to Golden Valley, show up on her dirty-ass front porch, grab her ugly purse from her hand and take all of Prink's money back. She is the worst, nastiest and most vulgar person on this planet.

There is no good in her at all. If she wasn't a girl I would smack her. How could she do this to Prink?" he asked.

Sandi was not ever going to give the funds back or even send us a receipt showing us if she used the money for food. She was being a completely selfish, deceitful bitch, and she had stolen from an angel. DJ and I felt so bad that we sent Prink some money to help with the funds she lost. Words cannot describe how we now felt about Sandi. She was not human. She was an evil monster who cared about nobody but herself. But we were so close to getting Amelia that we were forced for move forward and pretend things were ok. We could not yell at her or scold her because we knew she could get mad and unmatch with us. We were dancing with the devil, and she held the upper hand. We were sick with sadness, anger, hatred, and pain. We did not know how we could make it another day, let alone another three months. It was one of the darkest days of this long process for us.

Later that month, Sandi began hinting to us that her cell bill had come and that she was not sure what to do. She would not tell us how much the bill was, but she continued to ask us if we would help with it. We reiterated to her that we would only pay the $55 per month and that we had done our best to tell her before that she should never have purchased the expensive phones and plans. She tried everything in her power to get the money. She asked for advances, but we refused. She text messaged Jill every ten minutes asking for advances, but Jill also refused. She attempted to sell some of her personal goods at the Golden Valley swap meet, but unfortunately nobody bought her old typewriter, used loofahs, or rusted antique gun. She tried borrowing money from people but had no luck, nor did she manage to sell her things on a Facebook "buy, sell trade" page. Finally, she came to us and told us her phone was going to be shut off any day now for defaulting on her bill. We calmly asked her how much her bill was, and she responded by telling us it was over $400 and she had no way to pay it. Once again, we reminded her that we were more than happy to get her a cheap prepaid phone. This made her extremely angry, and she said some very mean things to DJ. We had a few hours of silence before she came up with her next brilliant idea. She said she would just go to Walmart and have them unlock her phone so she could use the prepaid service. We informed her that Walmart did not provide such a service. This infuriated her even more, and she then came back with an even crazier idea in which her friend would place her on his Sprint plan for three years if she paid him $300. We reminded her again that it was not legal for us to give her cash for such a purpose and that we would happily buy her a prepaid phone. She then had the audacity to text DJ and say, "OMG whatever. You guys make me mad." She actually had the nerve to verbalize that she was mad at us because we would not fork over $300 to her for something that a) we did not even know was valid, and b) would be considered illegal by our lawyer.

I was pretty angry by her blatant disregard for us, and I finally had the guts to send her a stern message. I told her that she owed DJ an apology for her messages and that she needed to understand that we had to follow the law. In addition, we told her that $300 was a lot of money and we were currently supporting her household, our own household, legal fees, adoption fees, her legal fees, and all of our trips to Golden Valley. She simply responded, "ok," but she never took the time to apologize to DJ. She only had a few days left until her and Doug's phones would be deactivated.

A few days before the phones were to be turned off, Sandi went into crazy mode trying to concoct any story possible to get us to pay her bill. She asked Jill for a $200 advance for the phone, but Jill refused to give her the money. Of course, Sandi sent Jill some inconsiderate and nasty text messages. She came to us with the same question, and we reminded her that all money issue had to go through Jill and the attorney. Again, she was angry with us. She now turned her attention to an attempt to sell the phones on Facebook. Doug had previously worried that they would be prosecuted for selling phones that they did not own, since the phones technically belonged to Sprint, but this did not deter Sandi. She posted the phones as new, barely used, one month old, and said that they could be unlocked by any carrier. This was not true. In reality Sprint would lock the phones so no other carrier could service them.

When no one bought the phones, Sandi began entertaining trade options, despite knowing that she needed cash to pay her bills. She discussed trades for live turtles, clothing, a corn snake, and many other crazy items. Then, we got a Facebook message that both phones had been turned off and were "gone." She would actually never tell us what she sold or traded them for, but she made it clear she had no money. She finally consented to our original offer of a prepaid phone. DJ pretty much spent a full day finding a phone for her, getting it reactivated on her previous prepaid carrier, and getting the first bill paid. She was furious that she had to go back to her old carrier and that she did not have the very best phone on the planet. You would think she would be appreciative that we got her a phone and that DJ spent hours getting it to work. Instead of any thanks, he got blistering messages about why it took him so long to get it working. She was clueless about the fact that our lives were busy with work and school and not everyone sat around all day on the couch. Our frustrations and anger toward her were peaking.

# Chapter Eight

As crazy and unstable as Sandi was making our lives, we were actually making progress. While it was still fairly far away, we could start to see a tiny flicker of light at the end of the tunnel. We had come to the conclusion, however, that if a new birth mother became available via Jill's agency that we would submit our names and profile book. We were not willing to simply unmatch with Sandi, but we were willing to do so for the right opportunity. While we were already very invested in Sandi, we could not seem to fathom the idea of spending three more months of our lives with her and her daily drama. We were truly at wit's end with her. I have never actually hated someone prior to this, but now I hated Sandi. I hated her with a passion.

Several new adoption opportunities had popped up on Jill's website, but none were the right match for us. Some wanted heterosexual couples only, a few had very serious mental health issues, and the majority were IV drug users and/or methamphetamine users. DJ and I did not want to rush into something that would likely bring more problems for our baby and us. While Sandi was a complete nut, we at least knew we would likely get a healthy baby girl. One night we were relaxing at the end of the night when one of Jill's bulletins came through via email: "Anglo baby boy born yesterday." We read all the information about the baby boy, and his medical history and birth mother's medical history were great. We also found out that he was in California and that the adopting parents would have to be there the next day if they were matched. The baby had to be adopted or he would be taken by social services and placed into foster care. DJ crunched the numbers and found a way to make it work financially. We called Jill and informed her of our decision to submit our names to the birth mother. She did as we asked and told us that we were the only couple to apply at this point. The deadline to submit had already passed.

DJ and I were overwhelmed with joy and happiness. It was almost a sure thing that tomorrow we would be driving to Fresno to pick up our baby boy! We would be free of Sandi forever! Jill told us that she would be talking to the birth mother early the next day because she was currently sleeping. She would submit our profile and see if we matched. Jill kept an updated grid on her adoption website that listed all opportunities and who had applied. We were the only name listed, and we were too excited to sleep. We began packing our bags for an extended stay in Fresno. DJ was so sure that it was going to happen that he messaged all of his teachers at school and said he would not be in class for the reminder of the week. As usual he saw the glass half-full and he could not think of any scenario where this adoption opportunity would not work. His driving desire to escape Sandi was leaving him vulnerable to a big disappointment.

The next morning came, but there was still no word. DJ was extremely excited and impatient; he kept calling and emailing Jill asking for an update, but she did not reply. I was very anxious at work because I would need to push through a lot of red tape to get my paternity leave arranged at the very last minute. I would have to explain to Human Resources what had transpired and that we would be getting the baby on this very day. I too tried to reach Jill but did not have any luck. She was oddly ignoring our messages. DJ thought he should probably check the adoption grid on her site to see if anything has changed. To his shock, there were now four couples that had applied, all of whom had missed the deadline. We were very disappointed in Jill that she would ignore the deadline and allow more people to apply. Our hope was fading quickly. As the workday came to a close, we had still not received any news back from Jill. Finally, very late in the day, we received just a very cold email stating that the birth mother had selected another family and they were on their way to get the baby. She did not even bother to call us! We wondered if she had pushed to get more applicants so she could make an additional profit off new clients. We reached her late that night via phone, and she denied our accusations. She also told us deadlines were "not really hard deadlines" and that the four other couples had applied late that night. We were not happy with Jill, and our hearts were broken. For a short time we had believed we were a lock to adopt this healthy baby boy. We had forgotten about the drama around Sandi's life and felt a complete sense of calmness and happiness. We were shocked and deeply saddened.

Amazingly, the very next day another baby girl was born and the bulletin came through from Jill. This rarely happened, and for two to happen back-to-back was rare, and had to be a sign from above. The background information on the parents was fine, and the baby was in great health. Again we were the first to apply and submit our books. For this particular adoption opportunity there was only one other couple that had applied. Again our sadness went away temporarily and we had a great sense of hope. This child *had* to be meant for us... Jill had not yet released the location of the baby, and we were once again in waiting mode. Our nerves were rattled, and we anxiously prayed to God for the right thing to happen, whatever that might be. As perplexing as it was, the very same thing happened again. Jill went silent and was MIA, not responding to emails or phone calls. Our hope was beginning to fade, and the last disappointment was still very fresh in our minds. At the end of the day we received an email from Jill. First, the baby girl's grandmother had shown up at the last minute at the hospital and talked the birth mother into allowing her to care for the child. The adoption opportunity was thus closed. Next came an even more shocking email; the baby boy that we had so desperately wanted the day before had been taken by his father at the very last hour. He came out of nowhere and snatched the baby right out of the arms of the couple who had been matched with the birth mother. The matched couple had spent nearly 48 hours with the baby, caring for him, bonding, and becoming emotionally attached. All of that was taken away from them instantaneously, probably leaving them heartbroken and permanently scarred. Jill had to correct the adoption website to make both adoptions read "CASE CLOSED." It was the first time that two adoptions had ever been disrupted to this degree so close together. Our hearts went out to that matched couple.

While we were not extremely religious people, we did believe in a higher power, and we viewed the past three days as a sign that we were meant to be matched with Sandi. For reasons unknown to us, we were supposed to get to know her and her family, deal with her antics and drama, and hopefully end up with Amelia in our arms. Maybe we were being tested. It was possible that maybe we were going to help Sandi become a better person or turn her life around. Or maybe we were matched with her to save Amelia. Maybe there was something we were to learn from all of this and we would become better people as a result. It was possible that we would never know why we were put through these trials and tribulations. As a result of all that had happened, we decided that no matter what we would ride this out with Sandi and her family. We knew in our hearts that we could weather the storm and make it until November 12th. This gave us a new sense of urgency, drive, and determination to make this work at all costs.

We immediately turned our energy to making the best nursery possible for Amelia. We wanted her to have a bright, happy, upbeat, and fun room. We had already purchased much of the furniture and had assembled the crib, changing table, and a rocking chair. Really all we had to do was decorate the room and get accessories for the bedroom and her connected bathroom. Having absolutely nothing to do with the fact that we are gay, rainbows quickly became the theme. Everyone who ever gives advice about babies always will tell you to stimulate them with colors and bright objects. We ordered a massive arching rainbow wall decal and centered it above her crib. We then stenciled on her name in a bold red color underneath the rainbow. We also purchased some *Winnie the Pooh* and *Sesame Street* decals and really made the room fun and lovable. For her bathroom, we maintained the rainbow theme by getting a rainbow shower curtain and cute rainbow towel sets from Target. DJ and I share a love for the silly adult-oriented cartoon *Adventure Time,* and we had purchased some decals from it when we thought Amelia would be Silas. One way or another we would still find a way to work the *Adventure Time* theme into the bathroom. It actually worked out perfectly, as over half of the stickers were bright colors of princesses, rainbow unicorns, and other very feminine items. When we were done with the nursery we were really in love with our work. We proudly took pictures and posted them all over Facebook and Twitter. If nothing else Amelia was going to have the cutest nursery and bathroom in town.

We had to continue to try and bond with Sandi despite our feelings toward her. We hoped that somehow, some day, our hatred would possibly turn to love. It was most certainly time for another visit to Golden Valley, but we could not bear the idea of returning again so soon. A thought occurred to me that I should call Kim and John to check in with them. They were excited to hear from us, and during the conversation I brought up the idea of having Sandi come up to Livermore to visit so we could all meet up in San Francisco. It would give us a chance to all meet, give Sandi the opportunity for a quick visit with her daughter, and would prevent us from having to make another trip to Golden Valley. To our surprise, John and Kim agreed. The plan was to meet at Golden Gate Park's massive playground, have a quick lunch, and then be on our way.

We could not afford to fly the entire family down to Livermore, so we offered Sandi the opportunity to come to visit us and the biological child whom she had placed for adoption. She pushed back saying, she did not want to leave Doug alone and wanted the whole family to come. We explained the cost prohibited us from doing that and we could only bring her. She convinced us to allow Camille to come with her, and we eventually agreed. After booking the flights, Sandi informed us that she had no way to get to the Las Vegas airport. Her car would not make it, and there were no busses that went to Las Vegas. I think she thought this was her excuse not to come in order to avoid flying, which she had told us frightened her. The tickets were already booked and we were not wasting that kind of money, so we arranged for a family member to take her to the airport as long as she gave them gas money.

For the entire week prior to coming, Sandi texted me multiple times daily explaining that she was too scared to fly and could not do it. I told her that she was flying on a big jet, the weather was supposed to be perfect, and she would not even feel the flight. She was terrified of flying after a rough flight on a very small plane out of Golden Valley airport. I assured her this would be much different and continued to talk her into coming. Honestly, I felt she would eventually back out at the last minute. I was actually very surprised when she told us the day before that she would be there.

The day did not start without the usual drama. Her ride did not show up at 8am like they were supposed to, and they were not answering the phone. I thought this was Sandi's last minute attempt to not come, but I guess the desire to see her daughter overpowered her desire not to come, because she somehow made it to the airport with about fifteen minutes to spare. She was in the air and on her way to Oakland airport.

DJ had class, so I left work early to go to pick Sandi and Camille up by myself. The flight was on time, and I had pretty much timed it out perfectly. As I was pulling up Sandi and Camille were walking out with their bags. I warmly waved at them and pulled the car to the curb. I got out, loaded their bags, and gave them both hugs. Now, I have smelled some raunchy things in my life; I dug through spoiled yogurt as a part of my first job with Pillsbury, I was vomited on during a rough flight, and I have cleaned up some nasty cat poop after an intestinal infection... but what I smelled when I hugged Sandi was off the charts. I had no idea what had happened, but she smelled like she had not showered in weeks. It was beyond body odor and into a new class of its own. When she and Camille got in my car the smell just engulfed my entire vehicle. I could not breathe. I had all the windows rolled down and she was yelling at me to roll them back up. How would I ever get this smell out? How would I be around her for the entire weekend? On a bright note, it was very nice to see Camille, and her happy smile made me excited that she had come.

I had found an amazing deal on Hotwire and got a very nice Marriott hotel for the same price I would have paid for a Motel 6. It was actually a very fancy hotel with doormen, bellmen, and a fancy swimming pool, hot tub, and fire pit area. However, before we could make it to the hotel Sandi said she was starving and needed to eat. I knew she had already had lunch because she had texted that she and Camille were eating at Las Vegas airport. She asked me to stop at Burger King, where she ordered two bacon double cheeseburgers, large fries, and the largest soda I had ever seen. She wolfed it all down before we got to the hotel, which was only a few miles away.

I dropped her off at the hotel and told her I would pick her back up shortly after DJ was done with class. Secretly I was hoping she would either shower or go swimming in the pool, as either would hopefully reduce or eliminate the odor. I helped her check in, and she seemed to feel both happy about the fancy hotel and also a bit out of place. She kept making comments about how fancy it was and showing things to Camille. I was actually happy that she was so impressed with the hotel, and I hoped she would enjoy it.

She did not like the fact that Doug was home alone, and from the moment she landed she did not stop texting and calling him. If he did not answer she would curse out loud and put on the scowl. I felt the time alone in the hotel would do her good, so I took off and headed for home.

The plan was to have Camille swim at our place, go to dinner, and then end the first night nice and early. We picked them up at the hotel and were pleased to quickly notice that she had indeed taken a shower. We could smell the soap and shampoo, but the odor from before had not quite left the car yet. We proceeded to take them back to our pool, where Camille played in the pool and hot tub and had a blast for about an hour. It gave us the opportunity to talk to Sandi casually for the first time in a long time. We did not talk about anything important, but it was just nice to not have a conversation over text or about money. She was clearly bored and did not care that Camille was having fun. She just kept saying she wanted to go and that she was starving. I guess the four burger patties, bacon, pound of fries, and liter of soda did not appease her appetite. So we struggled to get Camille out of the pool, as she was not ready to get out just yet. We were able to lure her out of the pool and then got her dressed and ready for dinner.

This was a budget trip, so we were not doing any fine dining. We ate at a local diner and all enjoyed breakfast for dinner. Dinner was pretty uneventful, and Sandi spent most of the time checking in on Doug while we played with Camille. By the end of dinner, Sandi was exhausted and ready to head back to the hotel. We took her back to the hotel and they wanted to see the pool area at night so we went in with them. It was a pretty setting, and Camille actually took the opportunity to jump into the hot tub (much to Sandi's dismay). We parted ways for the night and agreed to meet back up at 9am for our trip into the city to meet John, Kim, and Emma.

John and Kim were very amazing parents but had Emma on an extremely tight and rigid schedule. We could not meet in the afternoon because it would interrupt her nap. We could not meet at night because she had to be in bed at 7:30 regardless of anything else. Because they lived an hour away, they would have to leave at 6:00pm at the latest. Emma napped until 3pm, so that made the visit almost impossible. Thus we were forced to meet in the morning before her nap, as long as she got to eat lunch at exactly 12pm. The plan was to meet them in Golden Gate Park near the carousel at 10am. We made the short drive to the city and arrived with plenty of time to spare. As usual, Sandi complained the entire drive into town and also continuously commented on the fact that she was starving.

10:30 came and there was still no sign of John and Kim. I could see in Sandi's eyes that she was thinking they would not show up, and we were thinking the same thing. I text messaged them, and they said they had gotten a late start and would be there shortly. In the meantime, Camille had a blast playing in one of the largest playgrounds that I had ever seen. At about 10:45am Sandi noticed them walking down the path and got up to meet them. John was thin, good looking, had a 3- or 4-day-old beard, and was dressed in clothes that were too warm for the nice day. Kim was tall, thin, very attractive and had a sunhat on and what appeared to be sunscreen all around her eyes. They were kind people and easy to talk with, and we all introduced ourselves, chitchatted, and made quick small talk. Emma was seriously one of the most beautiful babies I had ever seen. She was extremely pretty, had bright blue eyes, and long, flowing blonde hair. She too was overdressed for the weather, wearing a dress, sweater, coat, and winter hat. It was also very evident that Emma was extremely bright, well behaved, polite, and adorable. This made us feel so much better knowing that these parents were able to take a baby from Sandi and raise her to be a normal, healthy, and smart child.

We loved watching Emma as she played on the playground. She was adventurous, outgoing, and interacted well with Camille. Sandi and Kim were in deep conversation about Sandi's dried-out hair (remember, Kim was a cosmetologist), and Kim was suggesting things she could mail Sandi to help with her issues. DJ and I played with Emma and Camille and also had nice talks with John. We were thrilled that Amelia would have a big sister who lived so close to us. We hoped that we would be able to establish a good relationship with the family and meet on a regular basis. We took the kids over to the carousel, where they enjoyed a ride on the antique landmark. It was very odd that Sandi showed absolutely no interest in her daughter, Emma. In fact, the entire time we spent in the park Sandi did not even look at her or acknowledge her existence. I can certainly understand that the situation is very complex, given that Sandi had placed Emma for adoption. It was simply perplexing that, after all the begging she had done to get this visit, she was completely disengaged with Emma. Instead, she sat on a green park bench with her arms crossed and a scowl on her face. I tried to bring Emma over to her to take some pictures, but she refused. I forced Emma onto the bench and tried to take a few pictures regardless, since I knew Sandi would forever regret missing this opportunity. She scowled in every picture, and Emma did not want to be near her. I was puzzled as to why she had so badly begged me to help her see Emma only to come all the way here and be completely disinterested. The fact was that Sandi was furious and pissed off because the attention was on the kids and not directed at her. We also knew that she probably felt immense pain as she watched another family raise her child. Maybe this was the reason for her behavior. We would never really know but we tried to believe that she loved Emma and was just sad that she could not care for her. We wanted to give her the benefit of the doubt and rather than feeling angry toward her; we felt sorrow and empathy.

John and Kim's time was limited due to the fact that Emma had to be back in time to nap. Thus we needed to head out to lunch so Emma could eat on time and they would have enough time to get back to their home. As a group we walked up the hill and headed to have a nice lunch at an organic crepe place. It was very busy, but we were able to get a table fairly quickly and had a very nice lunch together. Everyone loved their meal except Sandi, who complained about her food. As we were walking back to the park and our cars, Kim wanted to stop at a children's clothing store. She was in there for a long time and came out with two large bags of clothing for Emma. On the walk home DJ and I walked with John, who inquired on how things were going. We told him the truth. He did not seem surprised one bit and remarked, "That is why we only see her once per year. This was an exception to meet you guys."

As we parted ways, Sandi showed absolutely no emotion toward Emma and simply said "goodbye" emotionlessly. It was as if she were saying goodbye to a salesman at a car dealer. Kim, John, and Emma went their separate way toward their car, and we headed to ours. Sandi did really not say much, but she was glued to her phone, arguing with Doug via text. While arguing with him she was also yelling at Camille for no reason, but she clearly felt no sadness about saying goodbye to the daughter that she only saw once per year.

We took them on another quick tour of the city and showed them the Castro, the Mission, and a few other interesting parts of town. Sandi's fight had escalated from text to actual phone conversation now, which involved her screaming at Doug and some other unknown people. She was dropping the f-bomb left and right and did not seem to even notice that we or a five-year-old girl were in the car. Knowing that Sandi could not care less about the tour, we headed back over the Bay Bridge toward the East Bay. Sandi insisted on a nap for both herself and Camille, so we dropped them off at the hotel. She said she would text us in about an hour and we could leave for dinner. As she was walking into the hotel her fight had escalated yet again from a screaming match to Doug constantly hanging up on her and her immediately calling him back. The cycle continued repeatedly.

We went back home expecting to only be there for an hour. We both took short naps as well. An hour went by, then two, then three, and we still had not heard from Sandi. Then the first crazy text came: "How much is it to fly to Golden Valley tonight?" We replied that it was not possible as there were no flights to Golden Valley from San Francisco and the only flight that went there via LAX was gone for the day. We also said that her flight was not changeable and we could not buy her another ticket. We asked her why she was asking and she said that she just needed to get home now. She asked how much a bus would cost, and we explained a bus would take 24 hours to drive there. Finally we just asked her what was wrong, and she told us that Doug was having a party at the house and was drunk when he was supposed to be watching the kids.

Somehow we convinced her that there was absolutely nothing she could do at the present time and asked her what she would like to do. We suggested that she call a family member to go check on the kids. She seemed to like this idea; however, she never bothered to actually do it. She stated that she had always wanted to eat dinner at the Cheesecake Factory and that it would make her really happy if we could go. It was quite a bit out of the way, but we decided to take her to the restaurant in Palo Alto because it was a very fun little city with a great downtown. We picked them up at the hotel, and we could tell she was not in a good mood. She was yelling at Camille while also fighting with Doug on the phone. We started our drive to Palo Alto, and she spent the entire drive talking and texting Doug. Her language was beyond reprehensible to use around Camille, saying things like, "You motherfucker, if your ass hangs up on me again I will fuck you up when I get home. Who the fuck is over there right now? I hear a girl's voice. Let me talk to someone now, you fucking deadbeat drunk." Doug hung up on her and did not answer when she kept calling back. She probably called him 30 to 40 times in the car. Somehow she figured out that one of his friends was there and called him. The guy answered and basically taunted her, telling her that Doug was "free" and that she was a controlling lunatic. She cussed him out until he hung up on her and also wouldn't answer again. She then gave up on the phone for the time being and decided to badmouth Doug right in front of Camille, telling her, "Your father is a piece of shit. I am so done with him. This is it—for real this time. He is out on his ass when I get home, and we'll never see his fucking ass again. He is fucking douchebag." What a fun start to the night.

We arrived in Palo Alto, which was the home of Stanford University and a very lush and beautiful downtown. Being the home of Silicon Valley, there was a lot of wealth in the town, which was obvious by the many mansions along University Ave. It was also unique in that the entire city was filled with large trees and redwoods, making it very aesthetically appealing. When we found the restaurant there was a very long wait, so we got on the waiting list and then decided to walk around the downtown area for a while. We stopped in many of the fun shops, browsed the unique stores, and then stopped at the famous candy store, Rocketfizz. This was the king of all retail candy stores, and they sold every kind and brand of candy you could imagine. They also specialized in having the largest collection of unique sodas. You could buy anything from peanut butter and jelly soda to banana cream pie soda. Camille was loving it and looked around with her eyes wide. We told her that she could pick out one thing for herself and one thing for her brother and sister. She concentrated hard on this task and tried to find the candy that best suited her sister and brother. This showed that she was less concerned with herself and more concerned about her family. We wondered how she could still have that love and innocence within her soul given how she was being raised. Meanwhile, Sandi was outside texting and repeatedly calling an unresponsive Doug.

The buzzer let us know our restaurant table was ready, so we walked back over to the restaurant and were seated. Sandi was still texting Doug with threats and still trying to call him. Every time the waitress would come to take our order someone would pick up the phone to taunt Sandi. She would start yelling, cussing and embarrassing all of us in a public place. The waitress had to come back five times to actually take our order. Sandi complained about the meal while DJ, Camille, and I enjoyed our food. At this point, Sandi just wanted to go home, so we ordered some cheesecake to go and left.

Sandi's behavior continued in the car. A very drunk Doug finally picked the phone and said he'd had enough, was drunk, and was just going to go to bed. Sandi asked if the kids were in bed and he said that they were just running around. We could actually feel some sympathy for Sandi at this point, given that she was 700 miles away with no way home and her boyfriend, who was supposed to be babysitting, was going to pass out while the kids were still awake. She demanded to talk to Duncan and asked him if he had had dinner. Duncan replied, "No, Mommy, Daddy give-a' us no food all day." That was the straw the broke the camel's back for Sandi, and she rightfully went ballistic. She called one of her family members and asked them to go check on the kids and stay there for the night. The family member arrived to find Doug completely passed out on the floor, the kids running amok, and empty liquor bottles everywhere. The family had moved from completely dysfunctional to an absolute train wreck.

We tried to provide Sandi with as much support as we could muster and told her she should give Doug an ultimatum regarding his drinking. She was crying uncontrollably and saying that she couldn't even trust Doug for two nights so that she could go visit Emma, whom she really seemed to have little interest in. She was crying because she felt she was stuck in a relationship with a man who would never change. She was crying because he did this to her on her one opportunity to be away for a weekend. I also believe she realized what a mess her whole life and situation was and she was also very upset over that. It was one of the very few times that we felt empathy toward her and could feel her pain. It was a rare occasion where we saw Sandi raw, broken, and honest. We talked to her, tried to reassure her that things would get better, and gave her honest hugs when we got back to the hotel. This was also a confusing time as it related to Doug. On the whole, we trusted and liked him. During this trip, however, he became a different person and behaved like something we had never witnessed. We lost some faith and trust in Doug that night and began to question his character altogether. As it related to the adoption, we knew we were pretty much on our own. The dysfunction in this family was far too frequent and deep for us to put any trust in Sandi or Doug.

We got out of the car with them and went and sat at the pool for a while, trying to calm Sandi down. It seemed to work, and she actually said, "I don't know what I would do without you guys." We did not know if she just meant financially or if she meant emotionally, but we tried to think that maybe this was one instance that was not about money. Her pain was genuine this night and we did all in our power to make Sandi feel good.

The next morning, we took Sandi and Camille for a quick breakfast and had to head to the airport. Her demeanor had not changed since last night, and she was still fighting with Doug via both text and calls. She looked exhausted and she said that both she and Camille were up until 4am fighting with Doug. What a terrible situation to put your five-year-old daughter in. She kept Camille up all night long fighting with her father. We could only imagine the language and insults that were used through the night. We drove her to the airport, helped her with her bags, and hugged her and Camille goodbye. The ride to the airport was in complete silence and we felt that we had not achieved much on this trip. We had hoped to bond but instead found ourselves in the middle of a broken family's drama and trouble.

We did not feel good emotionally going home. We were tired, concerned, and could not imagine how we could last much longer neck deep in this mountain of drama. We could not fix their problems, we could not buy them happiness, and we could not magically make all their troubles go away. As a result of not bonding this weekend, we also felt like we still needed more time to try and really connect with them. We were close to their kids, but we were only ATMs to Doug and Sandi.

Sandi said that as soon as she arrived home she would kick Doug out and move on. Of course that did not happen. As soon as she got home all was forgiven, and they went on with their treacherous life in Golden Valley. DJ and I went on with our lives as best as we could; given the stress that we were under. It made us ponder what could possibly make us so much different than Sandi's family. We would later learn more about her history and specifically her mother.

For me, it made me think back to my childhood growing up in Lorain, Ohio. While we were not rich by any means, my parents always provided a loving and supportive environment. My sister and I were always nurtured with love and sheltered from all of the drama that seemed to define Sandi's life. I cannot recall ever seeing my parents fight, and I always remembered them having a warm relationship toward each other. Foul language was never used around me, and if I ever used bad language I was disciplined harshly. Unlike Sandi, my family was always very close, and we would see extended family very often by taking trips to West Virginia, where my most of my relatives lived. There was no alcoholism, no drug use, no wild parties, and we always had a clean home with food on the table. During my younger years, my dad was the sole provider as a teacher and basketball coach who spent his summers painting houses and bartending to keep food on the table. He worked very hard and eventually made his way up the ranks to ultimately become a superintendent. Despite our lack of a large income, my parents managed to save money for our college, took us on awesome family vacations every year, and had even managed to save up for a small boat that we would take on Lake Erie on most weekends. My childhood memories were excellent, and I honestly did not have any of the turmoil that Sandi caused on a daily basis. It made me sad to think about the situation for Camille, Duncan, and Carrie, and I often wondered if they would ever have a chance of a successful future with Sandi and Doug as their parents. For both DJ and I, it was a harsh reality that we had to face each and every day that weighed on our hearts. We really did care about the kids, and the more we learned about their upbringing the more we feared for their future. The hard part was that there was not much we could do to help them. Yes, our money gave them food, shelter, and other miscellaneous things, but it did not buy them love. It was also dependent on Sandi using her funds toward the kids, which was extremely rare. She would usually use the money to buy things for herself. In fact, she had become addicted to a Facebook page that allowed people to buy, sell, or trade items. We were able to see all of Sandi's posts, and she was buying things every day despite not having money. She would complain about not having any food for the family while she was buying puppies, clothing, furniture, reptiles, and even a 50-gallon turtle habitat. As hard as we tried, we could not understand her behavior and probably never would.

# Chapter Nine

I was raised as a Roman Catholic, but I learned the most from the way my family lived their lives. I was taught right from wrong, and my parents showed me daily love and affection, provided discipline, and taught me how to think less about myself and more about others. As a child and pre-teen, I was known as the kid who would befriend the elderly in our neighborhood and visit them daily. I do not know how, but I would never pay attention to their living conditions, the depressing nature of their illnesses, or even the sometimes bad smells in their homes. I was driven to them because even at that young age I felt sorry for them and knew they needed friends. I would often do chores for them or bring them leftovers from our family's dinner. On holidays I would always make them a plate and bring it over to their house on a day that was usually very lonely for them. On Haddam Drive, the street I grew up on, we had a mentally ill lady who would wake up in the middle of every night and scream and rant outside for hours until someone usually called the police. This went on for my entire childhood, and everyone in the neighborhood was scared to death of her. One day I was feeling sorry for her, and without any thought I just went over there and knocked on her door. She ended up being a very sweet lady, who invited me in for some pastries and fresh homemade grape juice, after which we talked for about an hour. My parents and neighbors were stunned when they noticed me walking out of her house. They wanted to be angry at me for being careless, but when I told them the story they could not find a reason to get angry with me.

As with all neighborhoods, we also had an older lady who lived alone in a rickety old house, and the rumor was that she was a witch. Her name was The Monkey Lady because apparently she had a pet monkey. There were urban legends that if you rang her doorbell, a trapdoor opened and you got dropped into a dungeon where you would spend the remainder of your life. Kids would not go anywhere near her home. Again, for reasons I cannot explain, it did not faze me at all, and I often knocked on her door. She never answered, but I would always pick flowers around the neighborhood and leave them for her. I never once saw her grab them, but they were always gone hours later. There was another older man, Mr. Neubower, who always just sat in his front yard in a lawn chair. I would spend hours with him, listening to his stories from years past and looking at all the memorabilia he had from his past. He was the most interesting man I knew.

The closest elderly friend whom I ever had was an old crippled man, Mike, who had severe multiple sclerosis and was confined to a wheelchair. He had a long ramp with that fake grass carpet leading to his door. He too would sit on his front porch. One day I approached him and spent the afternoon speaking to him. He was a wonderful man, kind and full of interesting stories. His sister lived with him, and she was confined to a hospital bed in the living room as she lived out her last days in agony. She would scream and moan, but I would just go inside and talk to her or hold her hand. Mike and I became close, and our relationship lasted well past my teenage years and even into my college years. I would visit him after school when I was home for college breaks, and I would always make him plates of food and visit him on holidays when he was alone. He passed away peacefully one day. I missed him dearly and still think of him often.

As I look back on it today, I wonder why I was like that. I was not a saint by any means. I was wild, probably ADD, and I got into tons of mischief and trouble. That being said, somehow I was raised to care about others before thinking about myself. Now, as an adult looking back, it was very clear to me how this came to be. My parents raised me this way and really taught me to live by the golden rule. We did not go to church every Sunday, but I was taught a different religion by my parents on a daily basis. It was to live each day to the fullest, do unto others, and to be a kind soul. My father was the poster child for this lifestyle, and anyone who knew him thought this of him. I have met very few people who did not like him, and he was known in our community as a model citizen. He lived his life to the fullest, and he was the first to help a person in need. I remember driving through the Lorain ghetto one time on our way to the store when somehow he noticed an old African American lady collapse. He slammed on his brakes, turned around, and pulled up to her house. He got out, held her head up, took her hand, and waited until the paramedics arrived. That day has always lived in my head and continues to inspire me. He was so kind-hearted to everyone he crossed paths with and never seemed to get too flustered. Even when both of his brothers battled serious alcoholism he was always there to support them rather than scold them. Both of my parents were just amazing; I could not have been luckier to have been raised in such a great environment.

Sometimes, to DJ's dismay, I would try and find reasons to be sympathetic towards Sandi. He had every right to detest her, and I fought that internal battle on a daily basis. In my heart, however, I wanted to try and help her and her family. We had been through so much that we would go back and forth on whether or not we would continue to have contact with her after the baby was born. Our lawyer had advised us that she had committed enough fraud and manipulation that we could easily terminate our visitation agreement. At the very least we could just say, "Sure, Sandi, you can come out and visit. Just save your money and you can fly here anytime." That too would work because we knew she would never have the money to do that.

Often after a bad week with her I would agree with DJ and say we needed to cut all ties after Amelia was born. I would have rage like I had never felt before in my life. Then something would happen or I would see a flicker of kindness in her and I would change my mind again. I would think about the hard life that she lived and wonder how I could justify adding more sadness by taking away her visitation rights despite the fact that she did not deserve them. I would put myself in her shoes and think how badly it would hurt to have an adoptive family whom you trusted walk away forever. For families who might be reading this and did walk away: we understand 100% why you would choose that. She was toxic, manipulative, evil in many ways, and a terrible mother. She used all of us for money and was the clear definition of a scam artist. We understand, and we do not judge you. Frankly, we respect your decision. As for me, my decision had yet to be made. The next two months would drive that decision. I hoped in my heart that I would find a way to love this woman, but it was extremely difficult.

We had already made more visits with Sandi and family than any other adoptive couple had in the past. Jill would often remark that we were doing more to help our relationship with Sandi than anyone she had ever worked with. We had made two trips to Golden Valley, had taken the family to Las Vegas, and had them come to Livermore twice. That was five expensive trips in only a few months. But that was not enough for Sandi, and she would repeatedly text us for days on end asking us to come out soon. We knew it was not about us but rather what she could get out of us. We would explain that it was extremely expensive, that we had to watch our budget, and that we had work and school. She could not comprehend this as she sat home all day on the couch with Doug watching TV. To our surprise, Doug had texted us to tell us how excited he was that he had gotten a part-time job at Arby's. We were proud of him, congratulated him, and hoped that Sandi would not sabotage the job as she had done to all of his jobs in the past. We knew she would not like him being away from her several days per week. What we did not know was that the loneliness that Doug's job would cause would send her to a new level of drama and attention-seeking behaviors.

It did not take long for her to let her loneliness spin out of control and turn her attention to us. She begged us to come out relentlessly. We told her we would be coming soon, but at the moment DJ had college exams and I was in a very busy period at my office. She did not like this response at all, and she would actually get mad at us and completely stop talking to us. She went in cold shoulder mode in an attempt to manipulate us into coming. When it did not work she went to plan B, which was—simply put—reprehensible.

Sandi knew she held the upper hand with the adoption, and she knew that DJ and I were dependent on her to fulfill our dream of being parents. She also knew that anything that involved health matters would scare the living hell out of us. Her new tactic of manipulation started by her sending us texts telling us she was having an emergency. One day she texted us, "Something ain't right. I've had six kids and something ain't right with this one. I feel like she is coming any moment." We got extremely worried and asked her what was wrong. She said her back hurt badly, she was swollen, and she was having contractions and spotting. DJ and I were terrified. It was too early for the baby to be born healthy. We did some research and learned about Braxton Hicks contractions, which were normal. We told her about it, and she said what she was feeling was not that condition. The thought never crossed our minds that she would lie about something this serious. We called her and told her to go to the hospital. She refused and used the excuse that Doug was at work and she had no ride. We messaged her relatives asking them to take her, but when they offered she refused. The next day she was apparently fine and was back at her usual game of trying to squeeze money from us. We begged her to go to the doctor, but every time an appointment came up she did not show up. We called the doctor and asked if she had gone, but the doctors would tell us she had not shown up again and had not bothered to call and let them know or even reschedule.

One night, she posted the following message on Facebook: "Gotta go to the ER… I am in labor." DJ and I saw the message and immediately starting calling and texting Sandi. She did not respond. We tried calling Doug, but he was working so he could not answer his phone. We called the hospital, but she was not there. We were seriously panicking and had no idea what to do. We called Jill and asked if we should get in the car and drive to the hospital. She told us not to do that until we confirmed that Sandi had actually been admitted and was actually in labor. Sandi continued to ignore us, so we called her sister and explained the situation. Soon thereafter, Sandi deleted her post on Facebook and responded to us. "It was a false alarm, but something still ain't right," she said. Again we asked her to go to the doctor, and she said she would the next day.

The next day she text messaged us and told us that she had preeclampsia. When we asked her questions about it she did not respond. We did our own research on the illness and got very scared. We called both of her doctors, and both indicated that she had not been diagnosed. When we called her out on it, she got angry and replied that she had given birth to six babies so we should not question her judgment. She said she was more aware of her body than anyone else.

Somehow we convinced Doug to take her to the doctor and she went, albeit with a lot of complaining. We did not know this at the time, but the doctor had told her to fast for a blood test but on the way she drank the largest fountain soda that the gas station had. It was 60+ ounces of full-sugar Mountain Dew. She went to the doctor, and she immediately texted us that she had gestational diabetes and would most likely be having Amelia early as a result. The baby could come any day, she told us.

Of course we called the doctor, who confirmed that Sandi's sugar levels were in the 200s and required further testing. However, the doctor denied telling Sandi that she had gestational diabetes and said it would require a three-hour glucose test to confirm. They had the test scheduled for the next morning. We were worried, but at least we would know the truth.

The next day came, and Sandi would not respond to us at the time of the appointment. Later she texted to tell us she felt too sick to go and had canceled. The test was rescheduled for the next day. The next day came, and she told us that she had gone to the appointment, but the doctor said she had never shown up. We called her out on her lie, and she said that she had accidently miscommunicated and what she meant was the appointment had been rescheduled for the next day. Of course the next day came and she once again skipped the appointment without calling. She had no intention of going to this appointment despite how important it was for her health and the health of Amelia. We discussed the importance with both Jill and the doctor, and they told us it was crucial that she get the test done. At this point we felt we had no choice and would have to schedule the appointment for Friday, go out there, and take Sandi to the doctor ourselves. We made the appointment and told Sandi we were coming out to visit and help her with the doctor. She happily agreed, knowing she had won the battle and we were coming to visit her.

Flying had become far too expensive to continue doing at the rate we were going. It had come to the point that we had to drive in order to make ends meet. What that entailed was a nine-hour drive from Livermore to Golden Valley through some of the most boring scenery one will ever see. I guess if you like brown dirt then you would enjoy this drive…otherwise it is pretty rough. We left late in the afternoon on Thursday so that we could make it in time for the Friday morning appointment. We made the boring drive straight through, only stopping for gas or an occasional restroom break. We made it to Golden Valley at 2am. We arrived at our usual hotel, but the teenage clerk had sold the last room to a couple who had just walked in, despite us having a pre-paid reservation. I was not in the best of moods so I was pretty hard on the kid, asking for him to call his manager, etc. We were exhausted and just wanted to get to sleep. Because there were no more rooms we made him get on the phone with other hotels and get us a room at the same rate. After flustering around for a while he found us a room and a hotel a few miles away. We arrived and crashed immediately.

At 7am we began receiving text messages that Sandi did not want to go to the appointment and begging us to reschedule it. We reminded her that we had driven nine hours for this appointment and that she needed to go. She messaged us several more times with other excuses as to why she did not want to go. She finally gave up and responded that she would do it but she was not happy and would not be fun to be around as she had not had her morning Mountain Dew due to the fasting.

We picked her and the entire family up at 8am, and she was being a complete bitch. She said that if she had to sit through this miserable test then her whole family should have to come and wait with her. What a way to treat your kids! She snapped at every word we said, complained the entire drive there, and yelled at the receptionist when we arrived regarding the fact that it would be a few minutes' wait before they could draw her first test. "What? Are you fucking kidding me? Do you realize I am starving? I need to get this fucking thing done," she yelled. As usual she won and they took her straight back. She came out and immediately went outside to use her e-cigarette. DJ went out there with her and chose some very bad timing to ask her a question. He asked if we could see the OBGYN after the glucose test because he had an opening and she had missed the last several appointments. She went ballistic on him, yelling and screaming and eventually just walking away from him. I knew when they both walked back in that there had been an altercation. She refused to agree to see the other doctor. We waited with her as the clock slowly ticked for the next blood draw. She said she was sick from not being able to have her soda and needed to get this over with. She got the next draw, and then we had about an hour until the next. We loaded up the car and drove to the nearby park so that the kids could play on the swings and Sandi could sit in the shade. It was already nearing 100 degrees, and it was not a good idea to be at the playground. The kids played, but the rest of us sat under a tree while DJ did homework.

It was time for the second to last blood draw, and Sandi was getting extremely agitated due to the lack of food and soda. She demanded to the nurses that this would be her last blood draw regardless of whether or not it would have an impact on the results. It did not matter what anyone said, she was done and they could deal with the results. She came out from the back and stormed out the door, leaving everyone behind. She got to the car and then demanded we go eat immediately. DJ and I stayed behind and asked the nurses if the test would be incomplete without the last blood draw. Luckily they said the doctors could still see the patterns of her glucose and that the last draw was only a control draw. Thus, we should be able to get a clean test result the next business day.

Sandi was ravenous and insisted on the Golden Corral all-you-can-eat buffet. DJ and I had never been there and had always avoided it due to its reputation for substandard buffet food. We were not looking forward to the meal. Sandi, on the other hand, was in her own piece of heaven and was loading her plate with everything fried, breaded, or fattening, washing it down with several sodas. DJ and I helped the kids get their plates and then we cautiously chose some safe options for ourselves. The place reminded me of the Cousin Eddie scene from *National Lampoon's Vegas Vacation*: old, reheated, and soggy food that had been sitting around for hours. Sandi was slowly getting into a better mood with each piece of fried food and each glass of soda that she downed. Within thirty or so minutes she was back to her normal scowling self, complaining about this and that.

During this time I also had to get Sandi to sign a preference sheet for the attorney that basically listed how she wanted things to be handled during the 72 hour waiting period after the baby was born. She seemed annoyed to fill it in, but the paper was for her own protection. It asked about what role she wanted DJ and I to have, what visitation would be like, and if she wanted to breastfeed. Her next few sentences were some of the most reprehensible things that either of us had ever heard from a mother. First she told us that she was tired of being pregnant and "just wanted this damn thing out of her." She referred to Amelia as a thing. An innocent, unborn baby whom we already loved so dearly was just inconvenient, moneymaking object to her. In her eyes, she truly was just a "thing." As she filled out the paperwork and the kids ate dessert, she started explaining some of the background of how her last pregnancies had happened and some details about the relationships that she had with her kids. We were astonished and stunned to hear what she had to say. She casually said that she was very close to Camille and that they had a great relationship and she loved her dearly. She then said her relationship with Duncan was just so-so because he was the middle child. She almost said it as if she were trying to say that he was just kind of an inconvenience. Her next sentence, however, left us in utter disbelief. Without any sign of remorse or empathy she told us, "It's a little bit different with Carrie. After she was born I got pissed at Doug and we broke up. I left for six months and never bonded with her. I kind of care about her, but that's about the extent of it." To say our hearts felt instant pain for Carrie was an understatement. I think we saw the last piece of good float out of Sandi, and the devil appeared right in front of us. She was making this weird smile that would have creeped out even the darkest of souls. Hearing her say that explained so much. We thought that all of Carrie's bad behavior was simply a cry for attention and love. She was the runt of the litter who had been rejected by her mother. The one human being who was always supposed to love her unconditionally did not care at all about her, and it was clear now that she knew this. Doug did give her some affection, but it wasn't even remotely enough. This poor child would probably be permanently damaged by Sandi's utter disregard for her and would need a lifetime of therapy to ever have a normal existence. I wanted to cry; I wanted to reach across the table and shake some sense into Sandi; I wanted to throw some holy water on her to see if she would melt or a demon would come lurching out of her mouth. Sandi was damaged goods from her childhood, but she had turned into the most evil woman I had ever had the displeasure of meeting. I would never look at her the same again. I would never look at Carrie the same again. I was determined to help this child by giving her extra attention or, better yet, by calling CPS as soon as my adoption was complete. Until then we would spoil her with affection.

At this point we were nothing more than "meals on wheels" to them. We came into town usually for three days, which included dinner on day one; breakfast, lunch, and dinner on day two; and breakfast on day three. In between meals we did other things that benefited Sandi. On this day we were taking them on a hike in the Hualapai Mountains. While it was 100 degrees in Golden Valley, it was 70 degrees only a short drive away. Thus we started our drive up. How far out of our way did we go to make them happy? Since we had driven our own car and did not have a van, we hired a cab to take them up the mountain. Sandi and DJ were with me, and everyone else was in the cab. During the ride up, one more revealing secret came out of Sandi. She explained to us that she had previously been a heavy IV drug user before her pregnancy, which we already knew, but also that she had spent three years in prison. None of this had been disclosed to us before, and, just like the smoking, she had lied about this on her background information. To make matters worse, her story did not hold water. We tried to remain calm and compassionate and asked her what she had done that had caused her to spend three years in jail. She said that she had run away from home so many times that she had been thrown in jail. There had to have been more to the story, we thought, but that was all she was telling.

"Why did you run away Sandi?" DJ inquired. Her response would make us better understand her very tough childhood, "well my Mom was on drugs my whole childhood and so was my stepdad. They were always drunk or high. We'd get beat every day. Eventually we were taken by CPS. We were in and out of CPS care and then my sisters just raised me. I never had food or clothes or nothin'. Finally I just took off. I couldn't take no more." It was sad that Sandi had what was likely a severely traumatic childhood. We felt empathy toward her and it motivated us to keep trying to connect with her. The rollercoaster of emotions continued for us. At times we felt hatred toward her and then we would come to empathize with her. It was very confusing for all of us. Despite her horrific childhood, why didn't she try to make life easier and better for her own children?

We found a very nice trailhead and started having some fun family time exploring the forest, monstrous boulders, and unique wildlife. The smell in the air was of fresh pine and cold mountain air. It was a refreshing change from Golden Valley. Sandi bitched and complained and Carrie peed her pants again, but we all had fun going on a small adventure. DJ and I pretended with the kids that we were on an *Adventure Time* quest and gave the kids fake swords and told them to go look in caves for the Ice King. They were really having a blast and had really bought into the idea of using their imaginations. As remote as this place was, we came upon a large doe that was standing in some low brush. I expected her to run instantly, but instead she stared at us, sniffed the air, and then started walking toward us. One would think that the kids' laughing and sudden movements would scare any wild animal away, but it did not. She stopped very close to us and looked directly at us as if she were there to tell us something. She got closer and closer to us and then stopped. She was within arm's reach, but we told the kids not to try to touch or pet her. She allowed us to observe her for about ten minutes, and then she casually turned around and slowly trotted away, looking back several times. There seemed to have been some meaning to this odd turn of events, but we could not really comprehend it. We just knew it was something good.

We had to make two trips from the trail to the restaurant because the cab was gone and we only had one car. So I made two trips taking two different groups up the mile long road to the Hualapai Mountain Resort restaurant. Again it was "meals on wheels" time. On the first trip up we had a large elk walk along the road next to us. It was a marvelous thing to see such a large and beautiful animal so close. We stopped and watched him for a short time and then dropped them off at the restaurant. We also saw a poor little squirrel that had obviously been hit by a car and was sadly flopping around in pain on the side of the road. We all felt sorry for it, but Sandi turned with a big smile on her face and said, "Ha, that is exactly what Doug's cat looked like when I killed it." I said nothing to her other than giving her a very mean look. What an evil and sick thing to say. I turned around, went back to the trail, and took everyone else up to the restaurant, sick to my stomach from Sandi's comment.

For the Golden Valley area, this was a really nice place that had an amazing atmosphere and menu. It sat atop the summit of the mountains surrounded by towering pines, boulders, and rocky terrain. They usually had live music playing on the large and rustic outdoor patio, which had warming heaters. This restaurant was a real treat for Sandi's family and also a treat for us. We hoped that, despite our growing dislike of Sandi, her family would at least enjoy it. Selfishly, it would be nice for us to have a great dinner as well, given the stress and drama that we had recently been facing. Sandi was already not enjoying herself at all and was yelling at the kids, complaining about the table, and sitting with the all-too-familiar scowl. We ordered some appetizers, including some stuffed mushrooms. It was a Sandi-sized fried platter from Heaven. I've really never seen her eyes light up like this—not for Doug, not for her kids, and definitely not for anything kind we ever did for her. She was smiling, talking politely, looking upbeat, and seemed to be actually enjoying herself. She could not stop talking about how amazing the fried mushrooms were, and she was eating them like popcorn. With absolutely no regard for price or what we had to pay Sandi ordered the most expensive rib eye on the menu, a side of fried shrimp, and steaks for the kids who never ate, while Doug ordered a king-cut prime rib with a Creole shrimp topping. They did not hold back, ordered dessert to go, and did not say one word of thanks to us. The bill? $250 and some change, but at least Sandi was happy.

There was no way to take a cab back down, so we had to all pile into my little car and carefully drive down the mountain. We dropped them off at home and again did not receive a work of thanks. To our dismay, they invited us into their home to stay for a bit longer before we went back to the hotel. The trailer home was far on the outskirts of Golden Valley and near the airport. It was an older trailer park area where every other trailer was either abandoned, overgrown, or the windows were covered in cardboard. Most of the homes had several broken-down cars in the front yard along with tons of garbage. There were a few nice trailer homes peppered throughout the neighborhood, but not many. One completely trashed home had cardboard covering the windows with a note written on it that said, "Dog Bits (sic)." I wanted badly to take a picture and post it on Facebook, but I was able to resist the temptation.

As we pulled up to Sandi's home, we were somewhat surprised that the home was far nicer than we had envisioned. It had a huge dirt yard, several fruit trees, and a big fence surrounding the entire property. There was also a large porch where they had several chairs. We stayed outside and talked for about an hour as the kids clung to DJ and me, looking for much-needed attention and affection. They had a few dogs and a few cats at this time, and all were constantly licking us or jumping on our laps. They were very dirty and smelled terrible. I had to use their bathroom, but I was really not looking forward to it. They told me to just go ahead and go inside. I entered the home and gagged immediately due to the smell. There were dog and cat feces all over the carpet, which appeared to have once been beige but now was covered in a film of black dirt. In one corner there was a pile of old towels and blankets that served as the bed for all three kids. An old mattress was on the floor, where I assumed Sandi and Doug slept. Debris littered every room. Walking back to the bathroom, there was an overfilled cat box with feces both in the box and outside of it. The bathroom was something out of a horror film. The sink and shower were covered in a brown film of dirt. There were toothbrushes on the floor and just lying in the dirty bathtub. Garbage was all over the place, and the toilet was nearly impossible to describe. The bowl looked as if it had not been cleaned in years, and there was a thick brown layer of scum covering the entire inside. There were human feces on the toilet seat and on the back of the toilet. There was no soap to wash my hands, so I walked to the kitchen to see if there was soap there. There were weeks of dirty dishes piled up, covered with rotting food that smelled like the inside of a trash bin. There were two completely overflowing garbage cans with flies inside and flying around. Three old fashioned sticky tape fly traps hung down from the ceiling. I could not take any more and had to get out or I was going to vomit. I made my way back out to the porch and mentioned to DJ that it was time to go back to the hotel.

The next morning we had to take them to breakfast, of course. Sandi decided to invite her brothers and sisters to attend and asked me if I could pay. I kindly said that I couldn't pay for her family and that I had a limit to my budget. She got mad and cussed me out but still had them come. They were actually very nice, kind, and easy to talk to. I had no idea how Sandi was related to them. They all worked two jobs, attended college, and had normal lives. We had a pleasant conversation as Sandi ate her country fried steak and side order of sausage gravy. She did not really even acknowledge her family and sat alone at the end of the table absent from any conversation. We finished eating and quickly made it known that we had to get on the road so we could get home at a decent hour. As we left, Duncan and Carrie completely broke down in tears and begged us to please not leave. Duncan always ended his words with the letter "a" and would say, "Please don't leave-a me. Take-a me with you. Come back-a." We gave them big hugs and promised we would be back soon.

Sometimes bad luck comes in cycles. On the way home, while driving in the middle of nowhere in the Mohave Desert, we had a tire blow out. It was 110 degrees and more like 140 degrees on the pavement. Within five minutes of attempting to change the tire, I was drenched in sweat. Cars were driving fast and right by me with no concern despite our emergency flashers being on. It took me a long time to change the tire given the heat. The wheel itself must have been 200 degrees or more, and we had to take our shirts off and use them like oven mitts just to get the tire in the trunk. The next problem was finding a tire store in the middle of the Mohave, given that we could not drive 400 miles on a donut. Thankfully we had a signal and our GPS took us to a small local garage. We were expecting to be ripped off and get an enormous bill. Just when you are losing faith in humanity, you meet good people. This man, who barely spoke any English, changed the tire, put a brand new one on, put the spare back in the trunk, and only charged me $80. We thanked him many times and made our way back on the road.

The road is a lonely place even when you are riding with your partner. With nothing to see but open land and desert it easily causes you to reflect upon your life, thinking of both recent and past events. We drove quietly and were both thinking about how much our lives had changed since the beginning of May. While we had both had our ups and downs in life, we had a very stable home and were financially stable;

I had a great job, DJ was finishing school, and we both had loving and nurturing families. With the car seat still in place in the rear of the car, we both dreamed of the end goal of having Amelia come home for the first time and of meeting her in the hospital in a few weeks. It was clear that a lot had happened to Sandi in her young life, but how had she turned into the mean, cold, and selfless person we had come to know? It was possible that we would never know. Maybe she was just a bad seed in general, or maybe it was a combination of her past and current living situation. Maybe she had a mental disorder. What we did know was that we would never be anything like her as a parent and that her behavior reinforced everything that we never wanted to be. The sole focus of our lives would be Amelia when she was our daughter, and nothing and nobody could ever change that for us. We would do everything in our power to ensure that she would have a bright future. If that meant keeping her away from Sandi's family, then we would do all in our legal power to ensure that happened.

# Chapter Ten

Time was now on our side, and the pregnancy was in week 32 and progressing nicely. While Sandi had refused to see her OBGYN, the last ultrasound was great, and the baby was fine despite being slightly underweight. The issue was that Sandi could easily go into labor at any time given her smoking and high-risk pregnancy. Due to these factors, we had already packed our emergency bags, put all the essentials into DJ's car, and had pet-sitting services prearranged. We were ready but still hoping it would be a few more weeks to ensure Amelia would be safe and healthy. The results of the three hour blood sugar test had come back and it confirmed that Sandi did not have gestational diabetes. The doctor had concluded that during her routine OBGYN visit her glucose test was flawed as a result of her large intake of sugary soda earlier in the day. He had mentioned that Sandi told him long after the test that she had consumed the large soda minutes before the initial test. Why did she not mention this before? She could have saved us valuable time and a trip to Golden Valley. It was obvious that she had concocted the entire story and illness for attention and another visit. We were livid and as always there was nothing we could do.

Sandi had learned that she could easily manipulate us into coming to town by either ignoring us or by causing drama that required us to drive to Golden Valley to ensure that things were ok. We would probably never know why she wanted us down there so badly except for her loneliness and desire for "meals on wheels." We walked on eggshells as her drama intensified. No matter what we said, she would get angry and turn it into a huge fight. After two big fights and her claiming that she was "done," we had to take another trip to Golden Valley to try to keep things afloat. We had made this decision at 6pm on a Saturday after we noticed that she was really losing her cool; we felt obligated to go. I had to use two precious vacation days, Monday and Tuesday, and it worried me because I knew I would need these days for the delivery. We made the long drive in record time and soon were checked into the hotel.

For reasons unknown to me, Sandi and her family had absolutely no money, no food, and no personal supplies. We wondered what she was doing with her food stamps because they did not seem to be going toward food, since her refrigerator was empty. The kids were in torn and dirty clothes, and even Doug did not have any usable clothes at this point. This pulled at our heartstrings, and despite our feelings about Sandi we took them shopping at Walmart for some essentials. We needed them to be stable for a few weeks, with food and supplies, and we wanted the kids to have some new and wearable clothing items. We spent about an hour and a half at the store and purchased them several weeks' worth of food, supplies, toiletries, and some new clothes for Doug and the kids. Doug thanked us many times, and the kids were excited about their new clothes. Sandi was upset because nothing that we purchased was specifically for her. She did not thank us, and she actually complained that we had not purchased her anything, saying, "My God, you guys do all this for the kids and Doug, but nothin' for me. I never get anything from you guys. What the fuck?"

We took the bags back to their home and helped them load everything into the house, refrigerator, and freezer. While doing so, I happened to be sitting next to their computer when instant messages started popping up on the screen. They were all for Doug, and, to our surprise, they were all about drugs: "Yo, bro, I need some of that good chronic weed. Can you meet me later?" "Hey, Doug, need some of the green; when can you meet up?" "Doug, need a QP TODAY. Call me ASAP." All the messages were from different people, and they all came in the span of a few minutes. This explained why Doug was always hesitant to work. He clearly had an illicit side business going that supported his drinking and other activities. Sandi must have known about it, since the messages were not private in any way. The strangest part was that one of the messages was a reply from Doug to a friend asking if he would smoke pot with him: "Sorry, bro. I hate the shit. Hate how it makes me feel. My girl MAKES me smoke it every day because she hates my personality." This was just another great thing to add to the daily soap opera of Sandi and Doug's lives. Why were we surprised; we should have known better. At least now we knew where our money was going.

We continued the day with our next "meals on wheels" campaign and took them to lunch and dinner. After running a few errands for them and taking the kids for ice cream, we brought the kids back to the hotel for some swimming. We had fun swimming with them and watching them jump and play, even while Sandi scowled in the corner. Carrie was running on the wet floor when she slipped and hit her head very hard. Sandi was in tears laughing and thought it was the funniest thing she had seen in a long time. "You see; that's what happens when you run. It's your own damn fault." Doug got out of the pool, checked her head to ensure she was ok and not bleeding, and held her while she cried. It was yet another example of Sandi's complete disdain for Carrie, and the laughing seemed just evil. What mother would display such hatred toward her child? DJ could not bite his lip any longer, "How do you possibly think that is funny Sandi?"

We dried them off, got them changed, and loaded up the cars to go to dinner. This time we were staying in town and eating at a Mexican restaurant that I had dined at during a past trip. The meal was uneventful and actually rather nice. There was no yelling, no fighting, and the kids were well behaved. Then suddenly, Mama came into the picture without warning.

We knew very little about Sandi's mother other than what we had been told about her childhood. We knew she was an alcoholic and meth addict who was married to an abusive fellow addict, and we knew she lived in a tent somewhere in remote Oregon. Occasionally she would make rude comments on Sandi's Facebook page, to which Sandi would immediately reply, "Do not test me, Mom. I WILL fucking block you." Beyond this, however, we had had no interaction with her, and she was almost never mentioned. During dinner, Sandi got very concerned and asked DJ and I both to block her on Facebook, as she was concerned that her mom was seconds away from sending us a message. She was clearly upset and would only say that her mom was saying terrible things. It was very obvious that she was in a very intense fight with her mother over text, and she kept saying, "I *cannot* believe she just said that."

Doug was talking to us about what a bad person Sandi's mom was and what a bad person the husband was. According to Doug, the last time the two of them had hitchhiked up to Golden Valley for a surprise visit things had almost turned physical between the two of them. They were staying with one of Sandi's siblings, everyone was drunk, and Doug ended up in their front yard challenging the husband to come out and fight. From Doug's perspective, the husband had said something so bad that he felt compelled to go end it on the street. The husband had refused to come out, and Doug had just shouted expletives at him from the sidewalk. As Doug was telling us this, his phone beeped, and it was a message from the mom and the husband. He looked stunned and got very angry, saying, "That bitch can say whatever she wants to you, Sandi, but not to me. That disgusting cunt is now talking shit about Drew and DJ, and now I am going to fuck up that bitch and her pussy man." Sandi begged him to not reply and not continue the drama, but he refused. DJ and I were completely caught off guard that we would somehow be involved since we had never met her or even spoken to her. While we knew it was going to be bad, we were dying to know what the toothless tent lady was saying about us. Sandi was adamant that we not see it. Doug was going back and forth with her and was so mad that he was pacing. He was sticking up for DJ and me, which was actually really awesome to see. He even went as far as to say, "Man, guys, you have saved my life so many times, and I am so thankful to you and always will be. I ain't gonna let this crack ho talk any shit about you. She can say whatever she wants about me, but since she brought you guys into this, it is on. Oh man, just let those two show up here." He was dead serious, and there was no doubting his anger. In an odd way, it was very refreshing and comforting to know he really cared about us.

Sandi and Mom continued to text-fight, as did Doug. Now the husband was chiming in, and according to Sandi the things that they were saying about us were too bad for them to show us. The mom was threatening to take a train or hitchhike down to Golden Valley. Sandi had no way of keeping a secret, and eventually they both showed us the messages, apologizing as they did so. I must say, in my 38 years of existence, nobody had ever talked about me like Sandi's mom and her husband did. I have never been gay-bashed or had gay slurs thrown at me, so this was a first. DJ had endured years of abuse from his conservative town and had thicker skin than I did. That being said, these messages were even hard for him to read:

The messages to Sandi read:

"You dirty nasty skanky baby selling ho. I wish you was never born. I may have had my kids all taken away from me from CPS but at least I could feed 'em. You sell 'em. You nasty ass bitch."

"How dare you sell my grandkids again? Especially to some nasty, flaming faggots. Faggots rot in hell. Sinners. You are giving my grandbabies to fucking sinning faggots and butt pirates. You don't deserve to live."

"I know you was a lesbian too but you got fixed by God. You have no right to do this with these bitch ass fags. I am coming down there. You are a no good, completely worthless piece of fucking shit."

"I shoulda never had your shit ass."

The messages to Doug said:

"Not only is you a fag and dick sucking bitch, but your sorry ass is givin' my grandkids to sick, perverted faggots? My husband is going to kick your dick suckin' ass bitch."

"Heeeey Doug. Fag. Fag. Fag. Cocksucker. Piece of shit faggot."

Next, the husband had messaged Doug:

"Man when I see yo sorry punk ass in Golden Valley I'll whip the fag out of your ass you bitch."

"You pussy ass fag, let me see your punk ass and I'll show ya a real man."

We drove back to Sandi's house, and all three of the kids were already asleep in the back of the car. We had to carry two of them in and place them on their pile of clothes and sheets to go to sleep. Camille stayed awake to watch some cartoons while both Doug and Sandi continued arguing with the ever-so-pleasant mother and husband. Sandi was telling her mother how she would never allow her to see the kids again and that she was cutting her off forever. She told her mother that if she ever came to Golden Valley Sandi and her family would leave, so she should not even bother trying to find a way down. The mother continued saying some of the nastiest things I had ever seen from a mother to a daughter until Sandi finally decided to block her. Doug continued defending us and showed us some of the messages that he sent to both the mother and husband. They were pretty brutal, but it felt nice that he cared enough to really stick his neck out for us. It was obvious that he was truly angry about the verbal assaults and gay slurs, and he kept saying that "we were family and nobody fucks with his family." As a result of Doug's messages, the husband actually backed down, apologized to him, and asked him to forgive him and not beat him up next time they saw each other.

The drama ended. We had seen a glimpse of Sandi's mother, and it was something I never wanted to see again. DJ and I were genuinely worried that this crazy, drug-addicted lunatic would show up during the delivery of Amelia and really cause a lot of complications. We discussed the strategies we would use if she showed up. We would call security, tell them that she had threatened us and was a meth addict, and then threaten to call the police. Even the mention of the word "police" would have this woman running for the hills. As a precaution, we did as Sandi had asked and blocked her from messaging us on Facebook just in case she decided to turn her anger toward us.

While Sandi was a terrible person, this mother was even worse, and we had some temporary sympathy for what her life was probably like growing up. It was no wonder that all of her children had been taken away by CPS, and it was not surprising that Sandi had tried to run away multiple times. While we felt sorry for her, you would think Sandi would want the exact opposite life for her children. Why was Sandi putting her kids through some of the same angst that she had grown up with? Are people born evil, or are they nurtured to be evil? In the case of Sandi's family it appeared that generations of mental and physical abuse had passed themselves along like a bad gene.

There was little hope for Sandi, and sadly there was little hope for her innocent children either. There was little we could do for the kids other than to continue to try to show them some love and affection and give them some semblance of a "normal" life during our visits. DJ and I had discussed what to do about their home life after the adoption, but we had yet to come to a final decision. Many people in our lives whom we trusted suggested that we call CPS and tell them everything in the hope that they could try to save the kids. Maybe it was not too late for a loving foster family to take them in and give them a good life. Maybe someday we could help them or even adopt them. It was probably not realistic, but we wanted to find any option that would help these poor little souls.

"Meals on wheels" continued the next morning as we met the family at a new breakfast destination of Sandi's choosing. We had to get on the road to make it back at a decent hour, so we made the breakfast short and sweet. We went through the usual ritual of Duncan and Carrie crying and asking us to please not "leave-a." We said goodbye and were back on the road for the long desert drive.

As we drove, we realized that Sandi had manipulated us to the point that we no longer felt we had lives of our own. Our lives revolved around Sandi in our ultimate quest to get the child whom we already loved. We no longer had our beloved weekends; we did not have time to clean our house, do our laundry, or even get a haircut. We were both very close to our families, but we were even neglecting those relationships. I spoke to my parents and sister very infrequently and had almost no interaction with the nieces I so dearly loved. I was often distracted at work by Sandi's behavior and constant texting, and it was probably showing in my work. I was lucky that the staff, boss, and owner of my company were very understanding. DJ was struggling to keep up with his school, and it was beginning to show in his work as well. He too was disconnected from his family and friends. For me, the saddest part was having to leave my dear 14-year-old cat Boomer at home almost every weekend. He was extremely needy and was always starved for attention. It may sound silly to some, but he was old and I felt like I was wasting whatever time I had left with him to accommodate Sandi's insane behavior. But as Jill kept telling us, "You're almost there. I think I can, I think I can, I think I can…"

# Chapter Eleven

We had made it a long way, and, as Jill said, we were "living miracles to endure Sandi for this long." Jill called often to encourage us and tell us how close our travails were to being over. We were only six weeks away from the planned C-section. Our hopes and dreams were hinged on making it only six more weeks with Sandi. We had to tolerate her manipulation, poor behavior, and constant need for attention for just a little while longer. DJ and I decided that we were in the home stretch and would do anything to simply avoid fights or conflicts with Sandi so that we could make it to November. We had hundreds of people praying for us and Amelia, and thousands of people were cheering us on. We were ready for the "last lap," and we could almost see the finish line.

Sandi was on a whole new level of craziness by this time, and Doug was informing us that she was impossible at home. She was crying, yelling at him and the kids constantly, trying to invent new ways to get money from us, and buying things with their small amount of money at the local swap meet and online. She had no regard for money, and as soon as she received our weekly funds she spent them on herself. She could not manage money at all, and as a result she would always squander all of their money before they could even get to a grocery store. She had also given up on trying to use the baby's health issues as a plan to get us to come out. It had stopped working once we were able to inform her that we had spoken to all of her doctors. Now she was turning to new tactics. She would purposefully start a big, dramatic fight with DJ or me. It did not matter what we said, she would jump on it and do everything in her power to start a major confrontation. We were always walking on eggshells, and she knew it. If we did not fall into her trap, she would just tell us that she was mad at us and would not talk on the phone or answer any text messages, even if they were important. She knew she had us by the balls, and we could not do anything about it. She always started this on a Wednesday, and her fake anger would peak on Thursday night. DJ and I were helpless as she would threaten to unmatch with us, never talk to us again, or various other severe threats.

We did not get much time to ourselves, but we were ok with that. We would do absolutely anything at this point to get Amelia. We did, however, have one special day that we will never forget thanks to my amazing colleagues at work. They threw us a massive baby shower on a Wednesday afternoon, with all the bells and whistles. DJ was invited, and we were warmly greeted with applause, clapping, hugging, and smiling faces. They had put an enormous amount of work into this event, and I was blown away. I was a diehard Cleveland Browns fan, and somehow, all the way out in California, my colleagues were able to make the whole theme and decorations about the Browns. They had an orange and brown diaper cake, orange punch, orange and brown streamers, and tons of orange and brown desserts. We played baby shower games like "guess the melted candy bar in the dirty diaper" and "pin the ribbon on the Cleveland Browns' mascot." They showered us with amazing gifts and presents that we would be forever grateful for. It was an amazing and happy day, and we shared every moment of it with our Facebook family.

Sandi was on our Facebook page, and she had commented on our baby shower pictures. I cannot be sure, but I think these pictures set her off in some weird and unexplainable way. We had no choice but to drive down there after she made threats regarding ending the adoption and then stopped talking to us. She repeatedly text messaged us saying that she was scared, but she would not tell us what she was scared of. One night, after going back and forth with her, she pulled out her ace in the hole: "I'm scared ur gonna cut me off like the last family." All night long, despite anything we would tell her, she would use this new weapon. "You guys are acting different. I'm scared you are gonna screw me, like everyone else. Everyone screws me. I know you guys are gonna too." We assured her that this was not the case and that we had every intention of keeping our visitation promises to her. Nevertheless, she made it completely clear to us that she was now having second thoughts about the adoption. I called Doug and asked them why they suddenly did not trust us. He told me that Sandi was completely out of control this particular week and was acting like this to everyone. He said they still trusted us and considered us family. Regardless, we were still scared about Sandi's behavior and threats. Unable to talk her down, we sadly and reluctantly agreed to come down to Golden Valley again. Sandi claimed she wanted to "talk to us about something important." We knew it was just "meals on wheels," but we were not willing to take the risk.

After the repeated long and brutal road trips, the tire blowout, and the 18 hours of lost time that driving to Golden Valley caused, we decided to fly down there this time. It was more expensive, but we just could not manage to muster up the energy and enthusiasm to drive down again. We arrived once again in Las Vegas and drove a rental car down to Golden Valley. We knew Sandi well by this point and never expected her to be appreciative, but our welcome in Golden Valley on this trip was too much even for us. We would usually meet up, talk, and then proceed to do something. Instead, on this trip she had text messaged us to meet them at the 99-cent store. We knew where it was and drove to the parking lot, where we saw their empty car; they were already inside. We walked in, and they did not even greet us; they just continued shopping. Doug was clearly as high as a kite and could barely keep his eyes open. They had an entire car full of Halloween decorations, Sandi's latest obsession, that they were expecting us to buy them. At this point, Sandi was not even asking, and we knew she would threaten to cut us off if we refused. Since we had decided to do anything for Amelia, we played along. We even went back to their house and helped them to install all of the decorations. We created a graveyard scene with skeletons, glowing hands, flying ghosts, and strings of skulls. It looked great, and the kids were very excited. We knew it would last about 24 hours before the dogs and various other animals ripped it apart, but for the time being everyone was happy.

As was usually the case on these trips, other than feeding them, we took them somewhere fun for the day. There was nothing going on in Golden Valley that day except a bounce-house and an alpaca festival. Sandi refused to go to the bounce-house because there was nothing in it for her, and she claimed there were too many germs. Our only option was the alpaca festival, which was a short drive down I-40E. I had looked it up on the Internet and it seemed like it would be fun, with games, rides, food, and playing with the alpacas. Unfortunately, to everyone's disappointment, it was a big bust. There was nothing there but a few old alpacas and an owner who was trying to sell them. Doug was still pretty loopy and was not making any effort to have fun. This idea was my mistake, and we only stayed for a short period of time before we left. Sandi complained the entire car ride home, and the kids were behaving terribly as well. Sandi cussed and screamed at them, and, to make matters worse, Doug was now coming down from his high. He was complaining about an abscessed tooth that he had now had for three weeks. Not only did it hurt and force him not to eat, but the pus also ran into his stomach all night, causing him vicious nausea.

I am not trying to be mean, but neither of them had ever visited a dentist other than to have a tooth pulled. It was also evident that neither ever brushed their teeth. While I understand that they had economical obstacles, brushing your teeth (and your kid's teeth) is pretty much a necessity at any income level. The kids had completely rotten teeth and often complained about toothaches and pain. Sandi had most of her molars pulled and Doug...let's just say I have seen better sets of chops on episodes of *The Walking Dead.* Due to the rot and decay, both of them had breath that could make a tin can melt. We had tried many times to drive them to the free dental clinic in Flagstaff for treatment but they had refused. At times, it honestly made it difficult to be physically close to them due to the odor. We felt terribly sorry for all of them and we tried our best to help them. Having these issues was completely normal to them, but we could not help but feel very sorry for the whole family.

We had a very melancholy dinner at a local Mexican establishment, and neither Sandi nor Doug were talking much. It was an odd feeling, like something just was not quite right, and it did not sit well with DJ or me. The kids were on their absolute worst behavior, and we found out at dinner that it was because they had all consumed Doug's coffee that day. They had been hyped-up on coffee all day, and now they were crashing and it was ugly. All of them were crying, Sandi was screaming, and

Doug was absent altogether. At one point Sandi smacked both Carrie and Duncan alarmingly hard on their faces. The hit left red marks on their cheeks. When Carrie escaped from her highchair Sandi kicked her in the stomach with all her might, leaving her on the floor wincing in pain. Doug yelled at Sandi for hitting the kids, which started a huge fight between them. DJ scooped up Carrie and comforted her in his arms.

It was time to go, and luckily for us we had a very early flight out of Las Vegas the next morning. We dropped them off, said our goodbyes, received no thanks, and made our way back to the hotel. We had also told them that we could not, under any circumstances, afford to come out the next weekend. We told them we would be back in two weeks and made it clear there would be no trips in between. Sandi was very unhappy about that.

Back home, DJ and I prepared for a nice weekend of doing nothing. We needed the time to simply unwind and relax. DJ had a full schedule of school ahead of him, and I was catching up on work and having a very productive week. That Thursday, unbeknownst to me, DJ and Sandi had a small argument. DJ messaged me that he was having a bad morning and that Sandi was asking him for money. He kept telling her that all money matters had to go through Jill, but she just kept texting him. She kept telling him that she wanted us to visit, and he continued to explain that it was not possible this weekend. She reverted back to being scared about us abandoning her and sent him twenty or thirty more texts. He was not doing well on a math test he was taking as a result of her pestering, and he was also sick from some antibiotics that he was on at the time. Then, without warning, he snapped at her and said some pretty rough things to her; it was nothing terrible, but it was enough to send her into a tailspin. At this point I was getting his messages forwarded from her phone to mine and she was crying. She was furious and said that no one could talk to her like that, especially not DJ. She insisted that she did not trust us and that "the truth had finally come out." Then she stopped talking to us altogether.

Knowing how far we had come, I knew I had to clean up this mess quickly. I too had had some blowout fights with her due to her insane behavior, so I was confident I could fix this situation. I asked DJ to apologize profusely, which he did, albeit reluctantly. She refused to talk to him, but thankfully she started talking to me again. I explained that DJ was having a terrible day, although that was no excuse for what he had said to her. I told her he was sorry and did not mean what he had said. As soon as she calmed down she started asking me for money to put to a new car. As per the law, I told her that I could not do that, nor could I afford it anyway. As a result, she pulled the silent treatment on me. I did not react, which made her furious. She texted me, "OMG Andrew, all I am asking for is a fucking reliable car. You CAN afford it. Why don't you never help me? I am tired of this shit."

This late in the game and with Sandi so angry at us, we had no choice but to get in the car that Friday night and drive back to Golden Valley. I will be honest: I was very angry with DJ that we had to make yet another trip. Though I had done the same thing in the past, my actions hadn't resulted in an emergency trip to the desert. Two hours into the drive I forgave DJ, and we started strategizing about how we could make Sandi happy again. DJ text messaged her and told her that we were heading to Golden Valley to apologize in person. This immediately lifted the anger and silent treatment, and she stated how excited she was that we were coming and how important it was that we were. She would not tell us why it was important, but she claimed she wanted to talk. Of course she then started planning what we could do for fun on the visit. Her anger was already gone, but we were already halfway into our drive.

We arrived in Golden Valley at 12:30am and checked into the hotel, where they knew us by name by now and said, "Back so soon?" We nodded unenthusiastically. We were exhausted, emotionally down, and just numb. It did not take me more than three minutes to fall asleep. Though we got seven hours of sleep, it felt more like it had been no more than ten minutes before the sounds of our phones filled the room. One text, two texts, three texts... We knew who it was, but we did not want to get out of bed to look. "Where do ya wanna meet for breakfast?" No hello, no good morning, and no greeting of any kind. It was becoming extremely difficult for us to put on our fake smiles, our fake kindness, and our fake generosity. It took everything in our power to crawl out of bed, shower, get ready, and head out to meet them at the restaurant of their choice.

Every once in a while you get surprised in a way that you never expected. We were expecting the same cold greeting, an angry Sandi, and a non-responsive Doug. But we were astounded when we got out of the car and they all came running up to hug us and tell us how much they had missed us. Even Sandi was smiling! We all hugged, and the excited kids jumped all over us, wanting to be picked up. Sandi was excited and said that she had a special present for us. She took a package out of her car and pulled out a new, beautiful baby blanket, saying, "This is for Amelia." We did not know what to say—we were stunned. I almost cried. Words cannot describe how much this small gesture meant to us. She had never shown any affection toward us, and she had certainly never done anything nice for us. Her gift meant that not only did she actually care, but also that she really intended to give us her baby. To really top things off, she also told us that she was crocheting us a homemade baby blanket, which would take weeks to complete. We were truly blown away by this turn of events and gave her a huge hug.

This started what would be the only somewhat pleasant trip that we ever had with Sandi and her family. There were a few snafus, but then we did not expect a perfect trip. After breakfast, Duncan and Camille insisted on riding with us to Walmart, where we intended to buy a few things we had forgotten to pack. On the way, we were talking to the kids and, as the saying goes, "kids say the darndest things." Camille and Duncan told DJ that they were getting their Halloween costumes at Walmart. We knew where this was going and decided to play along. "Oh yeah?" DJ said. "Who told you that?" Camille replied, "Mommy told us you were buying us all our Halloween costumes today." DJ was immediately furious, and I had to remind him of our new motto: "anything for Amelia." That being said, neither of us could believe Sandi's audacity in assuming we would buy all of their kids Halloween costumes without asking us about it. Had she only been nice to us so that she could further manipulate us?

We ended up at the hub of Golden Valley, Arizona, the Walmart, and began our costume-shopping adventure with the family. Having no kids of our own, we had to admit that it was fun to see how excited the kids were. Duncan pulled out rubber swords, and DJ and I had an *Adventure Time* battle with him. He was as happy as I had ever seen him. Camille was rifling through all the Disney princess dresses while Carrie was dead set on being a bumblebee. They were all extremely happy, and DJ and I knew they would look adorable in their new costumes. Seeing the kids happy made the trip worthwhile. Doug and Sandi tried hard to put other things in the cart, but we walked straight to the self-checkout stand, paid for the costumes, and headed for the exit.

Back at their house, we sat on the porch and waited for them to get ready, put their costumes away, and basically get situated. I was observing the neighborhood and looking at the home across the street, which had burned down a few visits ago. Every house must have had a minimum of five dogs and five cats plus one wheel-less car. Every person outside was smoking cigarettes, and they all had beers in their hands. I was pretty sure that it was the start of a new Stephen King horror story as about 5,000 biting flies descended on the house and us. The pitbull was tied to her chain, two cats were pissing in the flower box Carrie was playing in, and Duncan was playing in a puddle of water, dirt, and dog poop while flinging the water in every direction. The dog vomited, ate a few bites of it, and then had a follow-up bout of diarrhea. Ranger, the little puppy, then proceeded to eat the vomit and lick up the diarrhea. It bolted for DJ, who screamed and lifted his legs in terror. The puppy had run through a puddle and was frantically jumping up and trying to lick DJ, who was scared as hell. DJ pointed the dog in my direction, and now both hounds came running up to me trying to lick me and jump on me. I too was horrified, and I pushed the dogs away. Now the flies had gone from 5,000 to 10,000 and had overtaken the porch. The kids were still playing in the poop-mud, and at this point their shoes were off and they were running in it in their bare feet. We somehow avoided getting muddy or licked, but the kids were disgustingly dirty, and then a stinking and dirty stray cat jumped on me and curled up in my lap. I could see the fleas jumping on its fur like popcorn on a campfire. My shorts were covered in muddy cat prints and flies swirled around the poop, mud, water, and vomit combination. Doug and Sandi were now out of the house and noticed their dirty kids. Sandi began screaming and cussing at Doug to clean up the poop and vomit, shouting, "God damn it, Doug, clean up this fucking mess now! I hate these fucking mutts. Camille, get the fuck over here and get your God damn dog." Sandi smacked Camille on the back of her head and then kicked her hard on the butt. Doug brought out a disgusting shovel and started getting the mess up, but every time he tried Ranger would run up and get in the way. Then out came the hose, which seemed to get rid of most of the mess but attracted more flies. Doug hosed the mess right into the area where the kids played without any regard for them. Doug looked at the dogs, laughed, "Oh, you dirty dogs," and proceeded to kiss the pitbull on the mouth. DJ and I immediately made eye contact, stood up, and said in unison, "Ok, are you guys ready to go?" We got into the car and used nearly half the bottle of the hand sanitizer that was strategically placed in our cup holder.

Away we went, heading to the only fun family place that we had not yet taken the family to. It was Keepers of the Wild, a well-known wildlife refuge and zoo about 25 miles outside of Golden Valley. It was expensive, but, once again, we footed the bill in order to give the kids a day to remember. It was hot, Sandi was 33 weeks pregnant, and the zoo was a dirt trail with lots of hills and rough paths. Despite these factors, Sandi was more excited about the animals than anyone, even the kids. The kids were enjoying themselves and following the park rules, but Sandi was not having any of the lazy animal routine that was normal for a hot day at the zoo. She yelled at the parrots, "Talk, God damn it! Say something!" Next were the lions and tigers, which were sleeping in the small patches of shade. "Wake up, dumb tiger! Fucking move or something!" she screamed. "Doug, throw a rock at it or something. Wake them up. Fuck, we didn't come out here to watch them sleep." Thankfully Doug did not react and kept walking down the path to show the kids the other animals. Despite the intense heat, DJ was doing his usual 'make-believe' with the kids, "Let's pretend we're in the jungle and we are trying to safely return to our cave!"

For a zoo in Golden Valley, this place was quite remarkable, with many exotic animals in very nice habitats. The whole group had fun walking around the park and having a laugh at the various cute and cuddly animals. Given the intense desert heat, we found a shaded bench near the monkey village. There was a large male baboon in a large cage, and he was observing us while poking around the ground with a stick. For reasons unknown to us, he was completely fixated on Sandi. Sandi must have picked up on this, and she went right up to the cage and started to annoy the baboon by yelling at it, taunting it, and making annoying noises. In a sudden fit of rage, the baboon went completely crazy, jumped up on the side of the cage, roared at Sandi, and started shaking the cage. It scared the living hell out of her, and she screamed. For most, that would have been the end of it, but now Sandi thought teasing the animal would be entertaining. She kept at it and was now yelling at the baboon and making faces at it, assured of protection given the cage and fence. The baboon did not agree that the fight was over and put on a show of domination by running around the cage, kicking balls, and pounding its chest while roaring. Sandi continued while everyone told her to cut it out. Finally, when she turned her head away, the baboon picked up a pile of small rocks and threw them at Sandi, hitting her on the side of the head. It would have gotten ugly, as she was very mad about the rocks and was getting ready to retaliate when a park worker came out yelling, "You are upsetting him! Please do not taunt or tease any animals here." Like a preteen kid on a field trip would say, Sandi replied, "He started it!" DJ and I looked at her as if she was completely crazy.

The heat of the day was too much for a third trimester birth mom, so we headed back to the gift shops, got some drinks, and started back toward town. The plan was to go to the town's annual Oktoberfest and enjoy some fun, games, and street food. We arrived to find only a few booths selling some tacky crafts and a large beer garden with live country music. A pretty girl walked by, and apparently Doug took a look at her large breasts, which Sandi noticed immediately. Thus started an intense public fight between the two of them. Sandi was relentless and threw every curse word known to man at Doug. He just stood there and took the verbal assault like it was just a fact of life. As the fight toned down the kids headed over to the massive, original Santa Fe steam train that had once brought prosperity to Golden Valley in the 1800s. It was quite the sight to see and was still in remarkable condition. It had steps leading up to it so the kids could play in and explore it. Sandi screamed at Doug because Duncan had run over to the opposite side of the train and was by himself. "Go get your fucking son!" she screamed. As Doug was running to get him, out of the corner of my eye I noticed Carrie climbing up a large staircase leading to the train's engine. Right as she got to the top step, which was about ten feet from the ground, she slipped and fell off the stairs, landing directly on her head. I sprinted to her, rolled her over, and checked her entire head for any signs of injury. Thankfully, DJ and I had both been fully trained in adult and child first aid for the home study. She started to cry, and I knew that she did not have any major injuries outside of a possible concussion. I picked her up, and she clung to me as she shook and cried hysterically. DJ was with me, and we both tried to comfort Carrie. Camille was laughing, and Sandi and Doug were in a heated argument over whose fault it was that Carrie had fallen. I brought Carrie over to Sandi and handed her to her, at which point Sandi started crying. I do not know why she had not shown concern before, but now she was crying, yelling at Doug, and saying we needed to go to the hospital. We tested Carrie's eyes, which didn't show any sign of concussion, and she was now calm and walking on her own. Sandi yelled at Doug for about thirty minutes as we all stood there shaken up by the accident. She put 100% of the blame on Doug, who had done nothing other than listen to her by going to get Duncan. Sandi showed more interest in yelling at Doug than she did about her youngest daughter.

We ended the long day by having a very casual dinner at a local pizza place. Sandi was in a horrible mood, claiming that she was extremely tired from the long day. During dinner, she and Doug got into no less than five fights that involved swearing and yelling. The kids were basically falling asleep at the table, and we knew it was time to put an end to the day. Within a few minutes of dropping them off, ungrateful Sandi sent us a text that read, "That fucking food made me sick."

As usual, DJ and I had a long ride back to California, so we needed to hit the road early. As was the norm with Sandi, she was thirty minutes late to breakfast and had also texted on her way that she needed gas. So DJ filled her car up with gas, and we ended our trip having another "meals on wheels" breakfast at Cracker Barrel. Saying goodbye this time seemed slightly more meaningful than times in the past, and Sandi showed some genuine sadness that we were leaving. She promised us that it would be a quiet and drama-free week and that she would be working on the crocheted blanket to keep her busy. We played with the kids for a little bit longer on the large rocking chairs that are outside of every Cracker Barrel and then gave them our usual goodbye hugs. It actually felt like they were making an attempt to show some appreciation toward DJ and me. Like complete fools, we bought into it 100% and expected the coming week to be quiet.

*Chapter Twelve*

The rollercoaster of emotions continued when we returned back to Livermore. We spoke at length during the car ride home about how much better Sandi had been on this trip, albeit not perfect. We were happy that we had made some progress and that things were looking up regarding our relationship with Sandi. This somewhat warm and fuzzy feeling did not last long. Like a 4th of July fireworks show, it was bound to quickly fizzle out.

It did not just fizzle; it came to an abrupt and nuclear ending. To be honest, this next sequence of events brought DJ and I within minutes of completely walking away from this adoption despite all of our time, effort, and financial investment. If it were not for our attorney and Jill, I am fairly certain that both of us would have told Sandi what we really thought of her. Thankfully, the attorney and Jill talked us down from the ledge and brought things back into perspective. Both of our families also provided words of encouragement and support. We were now only days, rather than months, away from our daughter, and we had to keep ourselves composed. I wondered if Amelia would ever know how hard we had to fight for her, or if she would ever know the life that she could have been sentenced to with Sandi and Doug.

To begin the week, Sandi started my Monday off with text messages about how she could not stand being pregnant for another day. While she had missed the last five appointments with her OBGYN, suddenly she was texting DJ and asking him to make her an appointment. She wanted both her OBGYN appointment and ultrasound appointment moved up to the beginning of the week. When I asked her why, she stated that she could not be pregnant one day longer and that she "needed this thing out of her." She had been fine the day before, but suddenly she was dead set on having the baby early despite Amelia's low birth weight. At the last ultrasound, the doctor had told us that Amelia was under the average birth weight by about two weeks and needed more time to grow. Sandi did not give a damn about this factor and was now planning on asking the doctors to take the baby out early. While we were furious at her for having so little concern for Amelia, our nerves were calmed when Jill and the attorney told us that no respectable doctor would perform an early C-section for the simple reason of convenience for the birth mom. Try as she might, the baby was only going to come when she was ready. This did not sit well with Sandi, who bemoaned having to be pregnant for four more weeks.

While Sandi was predictable in her manipulation, tardiness, canceling appointments, and always being in a bad mood, we could never predict the next thing that would set her off. She was as volatile as a combustible gas or a geyser. In this case it was something extremely simple and it was something she had done several times in the past for her previous adoptions. Adoption law requires that a social worker visit the birth mother and father at least 10 days prior to birth. The adoption cannot proceed without these visitations, which are designed to protect the birth mother from being forced into a decision regarding the adoption. The same social worker then goes and visits with the birth family for a second time right before signing the consent to adopt paperwork. This is not only common but also a part of every adoption that involves California and most other states. Sandi had already had two past adoptions and was well aware of this process.

I spent hours trying to find a social worker in the Golden Valley area, but there were none to be found who did adoption services. We confirmed that none existed with a local adoption attorney. Thus the only other option that we had was to use an adoption lawyer who would represent Sandi and Doug, paid by me of course. I found a lawyer in town who was willing to do the visits for $750, which was a very fair price. I informed Sandi to expect a call from her in the next few days. Sandi immediately replied, "Why do I need to do that? I'm too busy. I know the laws; I have done this twice." I explained that it did not matter if she knew the laws, as these were required visits for the adoption to proceed. She was extremely annoyed, but she reluctantly agreed to do the visit with the lawyer.

In preparation for the meeting, the lawyer explained to Sandi that she would be doing one visit with both Sandi and Doug together and then would have a separate fifteen-minute interview with each of them. For reasons still unknown to me, this fact completely set Sandi off. This brief exchange set in motion the craziest tirade that I have ever seen from an adult. Sandi was livid that someone would dare try to talk to her boyfriend without her being present. We again very kindly explained to her that it was the law and had to be done.

"How could you do this to me, Andrew? How fucking dare you?! How DARE you?! We are not comfortable with this and we refuse to do it!" she hollered. "You can't do this to me. It isn't right. This is way too much stress to put on a birth mother. Why are you doing this to me?"

We were flabbergasted and had no idea what to say. She went on like this for hours, texting DJ, Jill, and me non-stop. We did everything we could and talked to several attorneys. The truth was clear: she had to do the visit or the adoption could not proceed. The fact of the matter was that Sandi did not want anyone to talk to Doug alone because she was afraid of what he might say. Due to the fact that Doug had a tendency to be bluntly honest, Sandi feared that he would say something that she did not like. She feared that if asked, Doug would cave-in and tell the attorney that Sandi had been manipulating us for money. She feared he would disclose details about the fabricated relocation, the fake illnesses to get us to come, and the lies regarding her need for money. As a result, she would not let Doug out of her sight. What she did not realize was none of this would have mattered to the attorney. She was only there to explain the law and to ensure that we were not coercing her into the adoption.

Sandi then demanded a new lawyer of her choosing, but she insisted that I provide her with a list of names and phone numbers. I called about 50 places that afternoon, but each one gave me the same frustrating response. They would answer the phone, I would tell them Sandi's name, and they would immediately say, "I'm sorry, but we refuse to work with Sandi. We know her well." Finally I spoke to a very well-known attorney who had represented the family of one of Sandi's previous adoptions. He told me sternly, "Andrew, I have worked in this business for 35 years. I have seen thousands of birth mothers all over this country. But I have never met anyone as evil as Sandi, and I would never under any circumstances work with her again. I am sorry, and I wish you the best of luck. Goodbye."

I was quickly running out of options, all because Sandi refused to allow Doug to be alone with someone for fifteen minutes. I was starting to feel angry and frustrated. Through a miraculous referral, I was able to find the attorney who did the visits to Sandi for the last adoption. When she answered the phone I was nearly in tears, and I think she could hear the desperation in my voice when I explained the situation to her. "Oh, my poor dears," she said. "Sandi is the absolute worst individual on this planet. My thoughts and prayers are with you. I told myself I would never involve myself with that girl again, but I can tell you really need help." She was based out of Phoenix, and it was a three-hour drive to Golden Valley, so 6 hours at $200 per hour would cost me $1200 before she even did any work. Out of the kindness of her heart, she agreed to do the work and reduced the travel fees to $500 per trip. She warned me that she also had to charge me for any texts or calls that Sandi made to her. The last time, she said, this had cost the family thousands of dollars. Barring any complications, she estimated the cost would be about $3500. $3500 versus $750 for the attorney in Golden Valley for the exact same services. She also warned me that the when she had worked with Sandi in the past, Sandi would change her mind about signing the consent papers when the lawyer arrived. She would then have to drive back to Phoenix and charge the family for the trip. This had happened three times before Sandi had signed the last agreement. Thus I was looking at a potential bill of $5000 to $7000.

I was sure that when I explained this to Sandi she would understand and just use the Golden Valley lawyer, but I was wrong again. I told her the difference in costs, and she went off on me. This time, however, she had crossed the line, and it was almost too much for me to tolerate. I couldn't believe what she said to me:

"How dare you, Andrew? I don't give a fuck how much it costs. I want the lawyer in Phoenix. I refuse to work with the lawyer in Golden Valley. I refuse, and so does Doug. How dare you not care about how I feel and how this affects me? You guys are selfish and always have to get your way. You do nothing for me or my family. Ever! Everything is always about you. For once do something for fucking me."

I could not believe what I was hearing. The truth was the exact opposite. We had done everything for Sandi and her family and had gone above and beyond what anyone would do for a birth family. In the words of Jill, "Frankly, I can't remember a time when you guys got your way. You have done everything for her. She has trampled all over you guys. Actually, she has abused you. You have never once gotten your way, and you have dedicated your lives to that family."

At this point I was so stressed and furious that I left work and went home. I needed to vent by doing my usual stress reduction exercise of running and running hard. I walked into the house, and DJ knew by the look on my face not to talk to me. I was angrier than I had ever been. It was like everything that had happened over the past six months had been buried and suppressed by my mind, and now it was all coming out. I was close to snapping. I kicked the wall, threw my keys, kicked an air freshener out of the wall, and scared the hell out of DJ, who was just sitting at his desk. I made a beeline for the gym and jumped on the elliptical, cranking faster than I had ever done in my life. Thoughts swirled around my head. Then I got several texts in a row from Sandi, all still bitching about the lawyer. "How dare you put me through all this stress, Andrew? You are just like the last couple, who abandoned me and don't talk to me. I don't trust you guys anymore. You never do shit for me! Now I am thinking twice about all this." I was now running at about 11 mph, and my blood pressure must have been off the charts. I was thinking about everything we had done for them: advances, gift cards, clothing, medications, dentist bills, grocery shopping, Halloween decorations, costumes, trips to Las Vegas, trips to the zoo, and thousands of dollars in restaurants and hotels…

I was just about to snap when I text messaged DJ and told him to please run to the gym to take my phone before I messaged Sandi how I really felt. He knew I was not kidding and was there in about 15 seconds. He took my phone, and I pressed on. It was the most vigorous workout I have ever done in my life. I burned 1010 calories in 40 minutes. I was drenched in sweat, but I was now even angrier than I was before the workout.

When I came home DJ was on the phone with Jill. When I came in he handed me the phone, and I screamed some terrible words at both of them before storming upstairs. DJ told Jill he would have to call her back and came upstairs to see if he could calm me down. The entire time Sandi had been texting DJ the same horrible messages she had been sending me. She was insinuating that she was going to pull out of the adoption if we did not use the other attorney. As opposed to fighting with her and allowing her to win, we both simply said that if she wanted to talk she would need to call us; there would be no more text messaging. This infuriated her even more, and she said more terrible and hurtful things to us. We held our ground and told her, "Sandi, we are not playing this game. If you force us to use this expensive attorney because you refuse to work with the one in Golden Valley then we cannot proceed with the adoption. Plain and simple!" She continued to text us and Jill horrible messages and even made a post on Facebook that she knew we would see. Surprisingly, we held our ground. My father and I had been on the phone during the course of the events, and he told me we would just have to call her bluff and take a chance. So we put our phones down and did not read any of her messages despite the nonstop beeping from our cell phones.

Around 9pm there came a silence that was as peaceful as Christmas Eve. DJ and I were both sick to our stomachs and did not even know if we were still matched with her. We were so nervous we could hardly eat. Jill called, we explained the situation, and she suggested that Sandi would more than likely forget about everything by tomorrow and act like nothing had ever happened. We did not know what to think. Then, at about 10pm I got a text message and decided to look at it. It was Sandi, and what she said illustrated just how cold and heartless she was.

"Hey guys, I need a $50 advance tomorrow ok?"

I replied back, "Are we still matched?"

She quickly responded, "Of course, y wouldn't we be?"

Just like that it was as if nothing had happened. About the same time Jill called and said Sandi and Doug had agreed to use the local attorney. We felt like we were on a different planet, like the day had just been a bad dream. Was I a character in *One Flew Over the Cuckoo's Nest* or was this actually reality? Was this woman so selfish and narcissistic that her behavior had actually been real?

I will tell you that I have experienced anger many times in my life, as we all have. Normal anger for me was the Cleveland Browns getting blown out by the Steelers or losing by a last minute field goal. Anger was that stupid fight we all have with our spouses. Anger was how we feel toward God when we lose a very special person in our lives. Anger was not getting a job you interviewed for. Anger was watching our crooked politicians during an election. What I experienced on this day was not anger, it was complete rage and hate. It was not something I was proud of, but I had to be honest with myself. It was 6 months of taking Sandi's abuse and manipulation, all of which bubbled up on October 7th, 2014. It was not fair to DJ, Boomer (whom I also scared), or to my own health. I had allowed Sandi to flip a switch in my mind, turning me into someone I was not.

Ultimately, things ended up being ok. The small feelings of sympathy that I had for Sandi were now gone, and the small amount of love I had for her was washed away in tears. From that day on I would never think of her in the same way, nor would DJ. While we prided ourselves on being honest people, DJ and I knew the remainder of our time with Sandi would be an act. We would pretend to be kind and patient with Sandi regardless of how we felt, all for the sake of Amelia.

# Chapter Thirteen

It was now mid-October, and the fall fog was beginning to creep into the Livermore valley from the Pacific each morning. The extreme heat was beginning to give way to cold mornings and cold nights, and all around us the wineries were harvesting the last of their grapes. The smell of wood burning and the grape harvest was in the air. We were getting close to our dream. Fall was symbolic of not only Amelia's birth but also the start of a new chapter in our lives, one that we were very excited to experience. In less than thirty days we would be holding Amelia in our arms and playing with her at the hotel while we waited for the adoption to clear in Arizona. Often I would find myself daydreaming at work about Amelia's first Christmas at my parents' home in Avon, Ohio. I had dreams of playing in the snow with her, sledding, building a snow fort, building a snowman, and introducing her to everyone in my extended family at holiday gatherings. I dreamed of reading her books before bed and rocking her to sleep. I envisioned DJ and me taking her on long fall walks in Livermore. I thought about holding her when she needed me and taking care of her when she was sick.

Despite these dreams, and given Sandi's increasingly odd behavior, I would often have terrible and vivid nightmares of losing Amelia as well. I would wake up in a pool of sweat, having dreamed of having to send back all the gifts our family and friends had sent because Sandi had interrupted the adoption. What would I tell my Facebook family? What would happen to Amelia? Would her future be written for her, given the environment she would grow up in? I had reoccurring nightmares of Amelia being the fourth child to curl up on the dirty pile of blankets to sleep with Sandi laughing and looking at me in the eye. In these dreams Sandi's eyes were pulsing red, and I would smell smoke and this odd frankincense odor. I imagined the grave disappointment of both of our families. Would we ever be able to afford to attempt adoption again? Would we be too heartbroken to even try? Would my relationship with DJ be ok given such a massive loss?

DJ's stress level was immense. He was unfocused in class, had a difficult time concentrating on homework, which often led to stress eating. On most days, he was so exhausted by the time he was done with his day that we would just come home and crash on the couch. Having any type of normal social life was now out of the question. He and I both were simply puppets in Sandi's show.

As October progressed, Sandi was getting more and more unpredictable, and her volume of texts increased to unmanageable levels. She was sending threatening text messages to us saying she was having second thoughts and that she assumed we would abandon her like the other two families had. At the very same time my health screening for work was required, and I was having probably the worst and most stressful day ever when I had to go. My blood pressure was sky-high, and thus I failed the test, which cost me the chance for a 25% decrease in my premium. Not only was Sandi draining my accounts directly, but she was now indirectly affecting my financials. Sandi also mentioned that a child she had placed with an adoptive family in Arizona was celebrating her first birthday. The family had cut all ties with Sandi and Doug after the consent was signed. Sandi said she was devastated and was feeling extremely depressed as a result of the birthday. While my initial instinct was empathy, I knew there was more to this story.

With some miraculous sales skills from my days in the business world, I was able to get Sandi to give me the adoptive parents' contact information. I immediately text messaged them, explained who I was, and asked them if they would be willing to talk. Their immediate response was chilling:

"Dear Andrew,

Thank you for reaching out. We were not expecting to hear from you until after the adoption was finalized and therefore we need to ask you, how you got our number. We do not know you, but you should know that we pray for you every day. We were also surprised by your message because all along we had been told your child was a boy. We are thrilled that our daughter will have a sister, but we were just caught off guard. Please know that we are with you in spirit each and every day, and we pray for you constantly. We know what you are going through. That being said, we cannot do any more than pray for you at this time. The trauma and pain that Sandi put us through still lives with us every hour of our lives. The things that she did to us and the terror she caused in our lives is something we cannot relive right now. We struggle every day with our own pain caused by Sandi. We are blessed with an amazing baby daughter, and we could not be happier. She is the pride of our lives. But what Sandi did to us cannot be explained here, and we simply cannot relive it at this moment. We want you to be a part of our lives, and we are so happy our daughter will have a sister, but for now we need to remove ourselves. We cannot wait to meet you and your daughter. We will continue to pray for you, and please know you have two people cheering you on. Keep going; you are almost there!

"PS – Antacids and hard liquor really help. Good luck and stay in touch after the adoption."

She ended by sending me pictures of their beautiful and happy one year old.

We had already been scared, but after receiving this message we were petrified. What could Sandi have possibly done to this poor family to drive them to this point? We had heard rumors that Sandi and Doug had left the hotel in the middle of the night and had changed their minds many times, but what was the real story? We knew that over time we would learn the truth, so we granted this family their space. Over time they would slowly warm up to us and check in on us. We were certain that someday we would all be together. In fact, one of the last messages that we got from them read, "There is a slight chance we will be in the Bay area in December. Wouldn't it be amazing if all three families and all three sisters could get together?"

To go along with her constant threats and the new information from the other adoptive family, now Sandi was telling us she was not going to her next ultrasound, which was extremely critical. This ultrasound would determine if Amelia was growing or if her growth had plateaued. In the case of the latter, they would be forced to take her out early via an emergency C-section, as the lack of growth would indicate a failing placenta. Sandi had missed every OBGYN appointment for the last two months. We were driven to tears when she started the messages about not going to the last appointment, followed by threatening emails. I very rarely wear my emotions on my sleeve, but her games, mental anguish, lack of concern for her kids and Amelia, and her lack of any empathy at all brought us to our lowest state of morale. DJ and I didn't know how we would make it.

On Thursday of every week, my job requires that I go to the small farming town of Livingston, CA. It also happens to be an hour and a half closer to Golden Valley than Livermore. On this particular Thursday DJ, Jill, and I had all been immersed in text messages from Sandi, none of which were pleasant. She told us she would be canceling her ultrasound appointment. It did not take us long to realize that we would be embarking on yet another trip to Golden Valley. DJ got the house ready, called the cat-sitter, packed both of our bags, and started over the Altamont Pass to come and meet me at work. The usual one and a half hour drive turned out to be almost double that, as DJ got stuck in horrific traffic. When he finally made it to Livingston, I took over the driving, and we were on our way. We let Sandi know that "meals on wheels," was coming, and she got extremely excited. All of her threats and insane text messages stopped.

The universe was not aligned the right way for DJ and me that night. We hit another horrific traffic jam both before and after Bakersfield. We did our usual three-hour shifts, and DJ took the wheel near Mohave. Our wonderful night continued with the sight of blue and red flashers in the rearview mirror as we missed the sign going down the mountain that changed the speed limit from 75 to 65 mph. The officer left us with a very sizable speeding ticket. We made the best of the drive, but due to all the traffic jams, stops, and the speeding ticket, the drive was almost three hours longer than usual, and we did not get to the hotel until 1:30am, with hardly enough time to sleep before Sandi's ultrasound appointment at 9am.

In what felt like a minute, my short night of sleep was over as my alarm sounded at 7:30am. Only a few minutes later Sandi was text messaging us asking us where we would meet them for breakfast before the appointment. We calmly explained that we were exhausted and would meet them at the doctor at 9am and could go to breakfast after. We got into the car and made the short drive to the place that would do the ultrasound. Just as I pulled in, Sandi called my phone.

"Oh my God, Andrew, I can't make the fucking appointment!' she sobbed. "Doug took off running down the street to go drink. I can't go without him."

"Sandi," DJ said, trying to hide the anger in his voice, "we drove 11 hours last night for this appointment. We are coming to your house to get you."

We quickly stopped in the doctor's office, and they told us that they were full the remainder of the day. We literally begged them, explaining that we had come all the way from Livermore for this appointment. Well, our tearing eyes and pleas got to them, and they said to just get Sandi there.

We drove to Sandi's house to find her pacing in the front yard and screaming at her kids. "Fucking stop that, Duncan! God damn it, Camille! If you fucking do that one more time…" She smacked all three kids in her rant and also pulled them by their arms so harshly that I could feel the pain myself. All three kids were on the ground crying. DJ and I managed to pick them up to comfort them. Sandi insisted we drive from trailer park to trailer park looking for Doug, and I was pretty sure she would kill him if she found him. After circling the lovely neighborhood for thirty minutes, she finally caved in and allowed us to take her to see the doctor. As a result of missing her appointment, we were forced to wait until the doctor had free time to see her. "Why the fuck are we here?" she complained. "Someone go get me a Starbucks!" Call me an idiot, but I wanted out of her presence so badly that I happily left the office and, along with Camille, went to get coffee. It was nice to spend a few private moments with Camille despite the fact that she smelled as if she had not bathed in weeks. I felt so sorry for her. I bought her a few cake pops to eat while the coffee was being made.

"So, how is school going, Camille?" I asked.

"School?" she replied. "Mommy never does school. She's always on my computer."

This answer broke my heart. I knew she would never get a real education. How could Sandi home-school her kids when she herself had no self-discipline or education?

I arrived back at the office just in time to be called into the back. Sandi brought all the kids into the examination room, along with DJ and me. The very kind doctor came in, explained everything, and started the ultrasound. It was amazing to see Amelia this close to us and to watch her move and wiggle around. He took all of her measurements and did the usual examination of her vital organs. "Well, so far everything looks good, and your baby is still a girl," he chuckled. It was now time for the important examination of the placenta and to see if Amelia had gained any weight. He noted that the placenta still had some non-functioning areas, but the main veins were still functioning very well, so he considered it normal. He got to the screen where all the measurements automatically calculated, and I saw the good news before he could even say it. "Well, Amelia has made a lot of progress this week. She is 4 pounds and 10oz, and she is now close to the normal range. Which means she will probably be about six pounds, and we will keep the original due date of November 17th. We will plan for the C-section on November 12th."

DJ and I were tremendously relieved, and a lot of our worry about Amelia instantly left our minds. Our celebration ended quickly when Sandi remarked, "Oh my God, I can't take this any longer. Can't you take it out of me now? I had all my kids at week 36. Take it out."

The doctor gave her a perplexed look and said, "Sandi, we cannot take the baby out early just for your convenience. No credible doctor or hospital would do that. It is best for the baby to go as long as possible. You are just going to have to wait."

The doctor concluded by telling her the warning signs of early labor and asking her to be sure to attend all of her upcoming appointments. She indicated that she would, but we were smart enough to know otherwise. On the good side, Amelia was healthy and growing, but on the bad side we would have to deal with Sandi for at least three to four more weeks.

We left the office with a crabby Sandi and agreed to meet at a famous Route 66 diner for lunch. DJ, Camille, and I went right there while Sandi insisted on going home to try to find Doug. The three of us waited for nearly an hour with no sign of Sandi. We messaged Sandi and asked what was going on. In another astounding message she casually said, "Oh, we'll just get take out. Get us three bacon double cheeseburgers, 3 fries, one kid's meal, and I need a root beer float." We sat there bewildered as we reread her message and thought how little respect she had for us. It actually hurt. The three of us sat at the nostalgic diner and enjoyed our fattening lunch while the conversation came to a complete halt. I am not sure what Camille was thinking, but she seemed sad. DJ and I were pondering how we ever wound up in this ugly situation. We talked to Camille quite a bit and learned how neglectful Sandi and Doug really were. When we asked her if she took a bath every night she said, "No, Mommy and Daddy don't even take showers." DJ asked her when she took baths, and she looked puzzled and said, "Not very much."

"Meals on wheels" was now truly on wheels as we delivered the bags of greasy food to Sandi's house. She and the kids grabbed the bags of food and quickly started eating without even thanking us. DJ and I were both livid and said we had to go back to the hotel to take a nap and so DJ could do homework. They all looked taken aback but did not say anything as they finally figured out that we were both hurt and irritated. DJ was especially upset and could not believe they had treated us so poorly. They had such little respect for us that they didn't show up for lunch and then asked us to bring them take-out. Sandi's brother, who was a very polite and kind young man, actually walked us to the car and apologized on behalf of his entire family. While this was nice of him, it still did not make us feel any better. At this point there was very little that should have surprised us.

Not much was said on the car ride to the hotel, but we were both thinking that things with this family were quickly deteriorating and we were being used more than ever. We stayed with our motto of "anything for Amelia." DJ took a few hours to get some schoolwork done, and I took a long and much-needed nap. As I drifted to sleep, haunting images took over my mind. In my nightmare, loud music was playing, and I could hear Doug and Sandi on the porch laughing, drinking, and making jokes about the money they had taken from us. The aroma of marijuana came in through the tattered screen door, and the dogs were barking. I looked over to a dark and dingy corner where the carpet was black with dirt and piles of dog excrement. The kids were cuddled together, shivering, on the dirty, damp pile of towels that was their makeshift bedroom. There was a black widow spider right above them, seemingly looking down on them. All of the kids were covered in dirt and grime, and they begged in unison, "Please help us, Andrew." Duncan looked at me with his big eyes and said, "Please help-a me, Andrew. Please help-a, me…" I woke up in a pool of sweat, and tears filled my eyes. Once again it made me ponder how I could help these kids someday. I knew that I could indirectly help by giving them essentials like clothing, hygiene products, and toys to make their life somewhat more bearable. But I knew I needed to do something now.

DJ and I went to Walmart before going back to the house, where we purchased several household items, toiletries, and things that would help the family. Then DJ made the decision to do something that would make the entire family feel more normal, especially the kids. He did it out of the goodness of his heart and from his own separate bank account, even though money was tight because he was paying for school. The family did not have cable at the time and only owned an extremely old box TV that did not work. DJ found a cheap "smart TV" and purchased it, thinking that even if they were terrible to us, he would still show their kids some love and excitement.

We text messaged Sandi and told her that when we arrived that everyone should be on the porch with their eyes closed and their backs turned. As always Sandi pushed back, but she finally agreed when DJ said we would turn around and go back to the hotel if they did not comply. Together we carried the TV onto the porch and told them to open their eyes. The kids knew immediately what it was and started dancing, running around, and screaming with joy. Doug turned to us, gave us a genuine hug, and his eyes welled with tears. "Man, guys, we've never had a real TV," he said. "This is the nicest thing anyone has ever done for us." Sandi was excited too, but she was screaming and cussing at the poor kids not to touch it. Doug and I hoisted the very heavy old TV and carried it to the garage. Together we all worked to set up the new TV, get the stand together, and walk through the setup. I also gave them access to my Netflix account, which would instantly stream movies to the new TV. DJ and I set everything up as the family sat in a circle around the TV in amazement. We pulled up the kids' section of the movies, and the kids sat with their mouths open as they sorted through the hundreds of movies for children. They could not believe their eyes. As soon as Doug was about to turn on a kids' film, Sandi stood up and screamed, "This ain't for kids right now, damn it. This is for adults." Camille then whispered into my ear, "Mommy thought the surprise was going to be a new car." Once again I was astounded—the nerve of this woman to think that someone would just buy her a new car! Not only could we not afford a car for them, but it would have also been considered illegal under adoption law. I was sick to my stomach and did not tell DJ about this until much later in the day.

A different kind of family would have shared the fun, played some kids' games, or watched a family show. Instead, Sandi insisted on turning on her new favorite show, *The Following* with Kevin Bacon. This was a violent and graphic show about a murderous cult and a serial killer. Sandi turned the show on, told everyone to "shut up and be fucking quiet," and started watching episode after episode. During one scene, as throats were being slashed and another victim was being repeatedly stabbed, I noticed Camille cover her eyes and ears. Duncan and Carrie were watching with no reaction. I could not believe that Sandi would allow her kids to see this violence. DJ and I felt sad that our kindness had resulted in more of Sandi's selfishness.

We decided to take the kids outside to play until Doug and Sandi finished their marathon of shows. We wanted the children away from the violence that was being depicted. When Sandi came out, she was irritated and said, "There is nothing to do in this town. Where are you guys going to take us for fun?" We politely reminded her that we did not live in Golden Valley and therefore did not know what there was to do for fun. She used her phone to Google ideas and wanted us to pay for a $160 round-trip cab to a nearby city to eat at Bubba Gump Shrimp. We quickly shot down that idea, which really aggravated her.

We settled on a local barbeque restaurant that was good enough for Sandi but cheap enough for DJ and me to not break the bank. It was an uneventful dinner, and we made sure to spend a lot of time with the kids. Sandi was exhausted, so we drove them home immediately after dinner, and she said she was going to watch the remainder of season one of *The Following*. The kids begged to watch some cartoons, but she refused.

The next morning we met them for breakfast at another local diner and actually had a nice conversation about the adoption. We wanted to leave at a decent hour so we did not get home in the middle of the night again, but we had also promised to do something with them before we left. Nothing anyone said was a good answer for Sandi, so we overruled her and decided we would go to the park and play a game of kickball. The idea to play kickball was her younger brother's idea, and he suggested we go to the dollar store to get the kickball and some drinks. He offered to pay, but when we pulled up to the store he sat in the back of the car and did not get out. All of their eyes turned to me. DJ was visibly upset, but I had to continue on with my fake smile and purchase the items. It was the dollar store, so it was not much of a financial setback, but it was, once again, the sheer audacity of Sandi and Doug that made us perturbed.

The park was actually quite nice, with green grass (rare for Arizona) and surrounded by large pecan trees. Some of the leaves had started to fall, so the smell of autumn was in the air and the crunch of dry leaves was beneath our feet. We all had a blast playing with the kickball, throwing a football, and we even tried to teach the kids how to catch a ball. No one had ever shown them how to do that. Doug, Mike (Sandi's brother), and I all had fun running routes and throwing the football. We played hide and seek with the kids while Sandi sat pouting in the car and cussing at everyone. Finally Mike insisted that Sandi get out, and with much hesitation she agreed. She told us she had played volleyball in her youth and we should try and play that instead of kickball. Sandi ruled the roost, so she immediately got her way. To everyone's surprise, she actually went from very crabby and pissed off to having a great time. We all got in a circle and tried to make it around without the ball hitting the ground. Everyone was laughing and having a great time while the kids played on their own with the football. It was very odd to see Sandi laughing and being normal. It made me wonder if her haunting past, her horrible childhood, and jail had hardened her and made her cold. Regardless, for about sixty minutes I saw her laugh, play, and have some fun. It was heartwarming to see her this way and it made all of us happy. For that one hour, she somehow put aside her past, her trauma, her abuse, and her anger to just have fun.

Sweaty, tired, and hot, it was time for DJ and me to get started on our long trip back to California. Although things were not perfect, we were certain that we had finally made progress with Sandi and would have a quiet and restful week and weekend. We made it clear that we could not come back the next weekend because we had to catch up for being gone so many weekends in a row. Sandi said she understood. We were prepared for our first quiet weekend with time to ourselves. But we were as naïve as a Cleveland Browns' fan who holds out hope every year for a winning season. The last thing she said to us was, "Hey, don't forget to fill my gas tank!" We also took the opportunity to remind her of the crucial Monday appointment with the lawyer to explain her consent rights. She promised to go and said there would be absolutely no issue with the meeting.

On the drive home the moon was full, vibrantly bright, and low in the sky. We were riding the pink cloud of pretend enthusiasm, and the drive seemed to fly by. Sadly for DJ, just when things were finally going smoothly, he was pulled over again for speeding. This would be the prequel to the roughest week of our adoption process. We would soon be meeting Dr. Jekyll and Mr. Hyde, in a week that I will never forget as long as I live.

# Chapter Fourteen

S unday was a glorious day for me: I was finally at my home, on my couch, and had nothing to do all day. My Cleveland Browns had miraculously blown out the Pittsburgh Steelers, which had not happened since 1989. So I was having a great day and even got to enjoy a long and stress-relieving 4-mile run. We were very confident that our fairly successful visit with Sandi over the weekend would translate into a quiet and drama-free week.

Like a sudden cold breeze blowing in right before a severe thunderstorm, late on Sunday trouble started brewing. First there were messages about how the baby's head had suddenly become much lower and that Sandi was scared the baby was coming. We responded, as always, that she should go to the hospital. Eventually she messaged us again and said that she was feeling very fatigued and could hardly even move. She then said she was bored and needed to get out of the house, which completely contradicted her previous story. Next came the messages about wanting us to come down to Golden Valley that coming weekend and we reminded her that this would be one weekend that we could not make it. "Y?" she asked. "It is important you are here." This was nothing new to us, so we just ignored her question and went into our TV room to relax and watch one of our shows.

We got about one hour of relaxation before both of our phones started to volcanically erupt in a spew of text messages. "I am so sick." "My back hurts and I am puking." These went on for a while, and we were both wondering if she was prepping us for a Monday appointment cancelation. Our worries were validated by the next text from her: "Hey, can you change my appointment tomorrow? I can't get up that early." We were beside ourselves and did not even know how to respond. For one thing, we were angry that she was doing this for such an important appointment after she had promised not to play this game again. In addition, we knew the attorney's schedule was packed and that she also had court for most of the day. We knew Sandi was looking for a fight, so we tried to be as understanding as possible with our response: "Sorry, Sandi, we cannot move the appointment tomorrow because the attorney has a full schedule. We also have no way to reach her because 9am is her first appointment."

This statement fueled what would be the biggest fight and the largest Sandi meltdown that we had yet faced. Sandi began a vicious and non-stop attack on DJ and me that started at about 11pm and did not end until Tuesday at 6pm. The barrage of horrific messages would be interrupted by sudden kind and friendly messages buried in between. It was as if a switch had been flipped in her mind. She called us every name in the book, threatened the adoption several times, demanded to talk but would not allow us to call her, and refused to stop texting. Finally I lost it, and my anger took over my body. I threw my iPhone against the wall and broke it, knowing that at least now she could not text me. She focused on DJ and fought with him until well past 1am over absolutely nothing. He would tell her he did not want to fight and was just going to bed, but she would just attack him with more threats. The last text from her read, "Why are you doing this to me? I don't have to go to any fucking appointment that I don't want to." DJ reminded her that if she did not go then the adoption could not move forward, as this was a legal requirement for an adoption. Enraged she said, "What the fuck? Now you throw money in my face? That is bullshit. That's my fucking money." DJ simply turned off his phone.

Monday morning was the first cloudy day that I could remember in over six months. The sky had turned from bright blue to dark grey. It reminded me of the fall days in the Midwest when there was fierce, cool breeze and large, dark clouds filling the sky. At first we thought things had blown over with Sandi since there were no messages from her. I was able to repair my phone by putting it back together and reinserting the SIM card. There were no messages on my phone either. At 8:25am, DJ messaged her to see if she was up. "I'm changing the appointment to later. This is too fucking early," she responded. Again we told her that she couldn't change it; the attorney's schedule was full, and we would be charged for the missed appointment. "I don't give a fuck. This is too early and too much stress on an 8 months pregnant birth mom. How could you guys do this to me? You don't ever do shit for us. You always have to get your way." Wow, this was coming from the same woman whom we turned our lives upside down to help. Monthly living expenses, relocations, phones, food, costumes, and moral support—yet we had done nothing for her. We then told her that the adoption would essentially be over if she did not go. "Fine. Fuck it. We will go but I am not happy."

The appointment was at 9am sharp, and at 9:15am Jill called me and said that she had not shown up. At the same time Sandi messaged me, "I demand another lawyer. This one is rude." I asked her how she knew that when she was not even at the office. She read the message but did not respond. "Fine. Tell her I'll be late," she finally said. Jill received a follow-up call an hour later saying that Sandi and Doug had gone to the meeting late but had successfully completed this needed step. We were thankful and thought that we could now move forward and the fighting would be over.

Being the marketing professional that I am, I always love research, so during this time I continued my quest to find out more about Sandi's last adoption. We had heard bits and pieces of the story but not any details. Since the family would not talk to us, I did the next best thing and called the adoption agency. They had banned Sandi from ever using their services again, so I assumed they would talk to me since they had nothing to lose. In some ways, I was happy that I talked to them, but in other ways, it scared the living hell out of me and sent DJ and me into a more potent state of anxiety.

For privacy reasons I will just refer to the adoptive family as Jane and John. They were the last family to adopt from Sandi and their adoption services provider I will call Stacy. This is the unaltered, factual, unembellished story of their time from the birth to their current state. This information came directly from the adoption agency and social worker:

"Jane and John were thrilled, as they had reached the end of a hard battle. That had dealt with Sandi and family for 8 months that was a living nightmare. They never thought they would have survived this long, but here they were in the hospital in Golden Valley as their baby girl was being born. For the past two months, Sandi had done everything in her power to draw attention to herself and make Jane and John unsettled. Nearly every day Sandi would call them and tell them that she was in labor. At first, Jane and John fell for it and made the four hour drive to Golden Valley, only to find out that it was all an act of drama. Sandi showed absolutely no concern for wasting the time of John, Jane, or the nursing staff. She did this for over a month, and finally they realized it was all an act and they would call the hospital to confirm the labor before driving in. Every time the doctor told them that she was not in labor.

When the false labor game stopped working for Sandi she started doing things that she believed would actually induce her labor. On one night she purposefully threw herself down her stairs to try and induce labor, and she had the nerve to tell Jane about it. When that did not work she took every herb and home remedy that she could find on the Internet in high doses, with absolutely no concern for the baby's well-being.

The time of the birth had arrived and Sandi was now in the delivery room and had been in labor for several hours when Jane and John arrived. Stacy was there as well to support and help Sandi through the process. Jane and John were now in the delivery room when the doctor proclaimed that there was a very severe complication with the baby. Sandi would need an emergency C-section immediately. She refused, and the doctor begged her to do it. "The baby will die if you do not," he yelled. "Fuck no," Sandi yelled, "you ain't doin' nothing that's gonna hurt me or cause me pain! I don't care what happens to the baby." Jane, having lost a child at birth in her past, was horrified as she was beginning to relive her past tragedy. Her husband and a nurse attended to her. Doug had taken an entire bottle of anti-anxiety medication and was now passed out on a chair in the room with his mouth hanging wide open. Several times Sandi would verbally consent to the C-section, the doctor would come back from home (it was the middle of the night), and the anesthesiologist would prepare her for surgery. She would then change her mind, send the doctors away, and cuss everyone out. After the third time, the doctor literally said, "Sandi. Your baby is going to die. I am going home." His harshness and tone were enough to make Sandi consent, the surgery was completed, and a healthy baby girl was born. As the doctor left he bumped into Jane and said, "Jane, if I were you I would get as far away as possible from anything genetically connected to this woman. Run; get away now." (This was the actual statement by the doctor and was confirmed by several sources).

Jane and John got to see her for an hour and then Sandi said that she needed rest and alone time. When they came back to visit the attendant told them, "Sandi is not accepting any guests at this time." They had signed a legal agreement that they were to be allowed in the room at any time and could see the baby as often as they wanted. Sandi was not talking to Stacy either, and a hospital worker approached her and said, "I don't think Sandi is going to follow through on this adoption. She had named her, is breastfeeding her, and has never mentioned adoption a single time." Stacy was very concerned.

The day of the hospital discharge came, and Sandi was supposed to sign the adoption papers on that day. Instead, she said she needed more time with the baby. Jane and John purchased two rooms at a local hotel, one for Sandi and family and one for them so that they could be close. Sandi and Doug drove the newborn to the hotel without a proper car seat, and the other kids didn't have booster seats. In the middle of the night, after several guests complained, the hotel manager went to Jane and John's room and knocked. "I am sorry to bother you, but we are getting many guest complaints about the people in your other room. They are smoking, and they will set the fire sprinklers off." John marched to their room and Sandi allowed him in. The room was a cloud of cigarette and marijuana smoke with the infant and kids right in the middle of it. Cigarette butts and roach clips littered the floor along with empty bottles of booze. Jane and John had ordered them pizza, and they had the entire room covered in pizza sauce and soda. The room was trashed. Knowing he could not say what he wanted to, John simply asked, "I know you guys smoke and that is fine. But can you please go outside? This is a non-smoking room." "Whatever," Sandi sarcastically replied.

The next morning John and Jane went down for breakfast at the hotel. The staff had come to know them very well and was very sympathetic toward them and their situation. "I am so sorry, guys, about what happened last night," the front desk attendant said. John and Jane thought she was referring to the trashing of the room and the drugs. "What in the world happened?" the clerk asked John and Jane. They asked what she meant, and to their shock the clerk said, "Oh, I am so sorry; I thought you knew. Sandi and family checked out and left with the baby in the middle of the night." John and Jane were devastated. In addition to the new news, the hotel was also threatening to call the police and CPS due to the drugs and alcohol. John and Jane knew that if the police or CPS were called then their entire adoption would be at risk, as CPS would more than likely take the baby. They were able to discourage the hotel from calling the police however the manager insisted on calling CPS.

The next day Sandi ignored messages from both Jane and Stacy. She was at home with "her" baby girl. There was no word from her for hours until she erratically decided to text message Jane at 1am to ask her if she wanted to come over and spend time with the baby. Jane was not about to miss an opportunity with the baby, and she rushed over to their house and stayed until 4am. Sandi then abruptly said that Jane had to leave and sent her on her way back to the hotel.

The very next morning Sandi went to a local shelter and charity that served the low-income population of Golden Valley. She told them that she had just given birth and had planned to place the baby for adoption but had now changed her mind. She was in desperate need of baby items. The charity showered her with diapers, formula, a crib, clothing, a Pack'n Play, and a car seat. She then called Stacy and asked her for a personal loan of $750: "Can you loan me $750? It will get me through until next month, and I will pay you back when I get a job." Stacy quickly replied, "Sandi, if you need to borrow money from me now, then you cannot support a newborn baby. You cannot do this to your adoptive family, and I will not loan you any money. Even Doug is begging you to stop this." "It is my fucking decision," Sandi yelled.

At this point, Stacy told Jane and John to just go home and give her time to work things out. She had promised them that she would do everything in her power to help get the consent signed. She was honestly worried about the safety of the baby given how the other kids lived. She was a former CPS worker and had worked on many complaints that rolled in on Sandi. She also knew Doug had been in and out of mental institutions for the entire year (this was news to us). She was having daily conversations with Sandi and making some progress toward getting her to realize that she could not afford another child.

What Sandi did next was something that only the sickest and most evil person on the planet could do, and she did it without hesitation. Despite knowing about John and Jane's tragic loss of their last baby, she sent a text message to Jane that read, "OMG. She is so cute and cuddly. I bet you wish you were holding her right now." The message hit Jane and John like a ton of bricks. John wanted to drive to Golden Valley and deal with Sandi and Doug on a personal level. They wanted to immediately call CPS and report Sandi. They forwarded the message to Stacy, who was horrified to read it. She begged John and Jane to not react because that was what Sandi was seeking: more drama and attention.

Stacy picked up the phone and called Sandi right away. "Sandi, what in the world are you trying to do to this family? What you did was simply evil. We are done playing games. You make up your mind right now: are you going to keep the baby or are you going to place her for adoption with Jane and John?" Sandi knew right then and there that her game was over, and she said, "I will give her to Jane and John. Tell them to come back, but I want to get a present for the baby first."

Jane and John rushed back to Golden Valley and were cautiously optimistic. Sandi signed the paperwork; the baby was now legally theirs and the contract was irrevocable. But Sandi had one last game to play before they left. She made the entire family, kids and all, go to JC Penney, where she bought the baby a locket and everyone a present. When they got to the cashier she told Jane to pay.

Hurt, traumatized for life, but home with the bouncing bundle of joy, Jane and John finally found the end of their hard road. Sandi would beg them for money, but they would not relent. Instead she would get pregnant as soon as possible so that she could earn her living again.

Jane and John had every intention of keeping their visitation agreement whole. They actually wanted an open adoption and dreamed of having a wonderful relationship with the birth mother. This dream came to an abrupt halt on their first visit back to Golden Valley. In the hotel room, Sandi and Doug both smoked cigarettes and filled the room with secondhand smoke. Sandi had no interest in the baby and sat with a scowl on her face and her arms crossed. The straw that broke the camel's back was when Doug pulled the baby by the arm hard enough to scare everyone and make the infant break into a crying fit. Jane and John took the baby home and really never looked back. They would not put their baby in that unsafe and terrible environment again.

The very last time that they ever spoke again was when Sandi asked them how the baby was doing. Jane replied, "Oh, she is doing great. As a matter of fact we just got home from the pediatrician. She has a little bit of thrush, but she is otherwise perfect." Sandi immediately flipped out and accused them of neglect. She even called the agency and said, "When that baby left my house she was in perfect health. Now she is sick because they take her all over town. This is neglect!" This was her last and final attempt to give Jane one last uppercut, and thus ended the relationship between the two families, probably forever."

Tuesday was the strangest day in the course of the adoption. While we thought the fight was over and everyone was happy, the realization that we were incorrect came in the form of an early morning blast of text messages. "I can't believe you did that to me. You guys are so mean. You can't talk to me like that and think it is ok. What is your problem? You can't treat an 8 month birth mom like this." Once again we were shocked to read this, as we thought everything was fine. We inquired what she was talking about, and she continued on her rant: "You guys always get whatever you want. You don't care about my feelings. I am still pissed about last night. Then you throw the money thing in my face? This is unacceptable." I quickly replied, "Sandi, we did not throw the issue of money in your face. We had to do what our attorney told us. Because you were refusing to go the appointment, the adoption could not move forward, and she could not authorize any future payments or fund. It was not our choice. We have to go by the law." Sandi completely ignored our message and said, "And you threw the money issue right in my face. How could you do this to me? How dare you make us have separate conversations? This is fucked up."

DJ and I tried with all our might to calm her down without success. "You are the worst couple I have ever had to work with. You are so mean. YOU NEVER DO ANYTHING NICE FOR US. Fuck this shit." Statements like that honestly made us want to tell her off and completely walk away, but we were too close to the finish line. "Sandi, we do everything you ask and more. I am sorry you are mad. We will not fight with you anymore," I said. She quickly jumped back in with, "What? I'm done. I'm done with you both. This adoption is over. I'm done with both of you. You need to come down here now and fix this. It's important." I replied, "Sandi, we told you we cannot come down until the weekend. I have work and DJ has school. We cannot come down."

"This is more important. I don't give a fuck about your jobs or school. Get down here right now and fix this," she yelled.

For eight hours Sandi relentlessly repeated the same messages to both of our phones. We were both in tears. I was unable to work, and DJ was unable to study. I was shaking and could feel my blood pressure rising. In the course of her rant, she called us every name in the book, said the adoption was over many times, and demanded we leave that very moment for Golden Valley. All we would do was tell her, "Sandi, we will not fight with you." We informed Jill and the lawyer about what was going on, and they offered us support as they said there was nothing they could do at the moment. Jill called Sandi and told her to call immediately. This pissed off Sandi even more. We ignored her while Jill text messaged her and asked her if she wanted to unmatch with us. Jill forwarded Sandi's response to us: "No. Why would I unmatch?"

The most insane part of the entire day was that in the very middle of an influx of 20 or 30 horrible text messages to us, she would say something like, "By the way, I could always save my breast milk and freeze it for you guys if you don't wanna use formula." These odd messages were just peppered into all-out blitz of insults. She would go back into the tirade and then thirty minutes later say, "Don't u think that would be nice? The milk?" Her rant continued until about 6pm when she suddenly went quiet. DJ and I were both nauseous, shaking, stressed, and unsure if we still were going to be able to adopt Amelia. When I got home all we could do was hug and hold each other, shaking and crying. We were devastated, and we really could not take any more abuse. The emotional roller coaster had become too much. On Facebook I asked my friends and family for prayers and good thoughts. DJ did the same. We were overwhelmed with the support that people threw at us. It was a very emotional day.

Around 7pm on that Tuesday night, my phone beeped, and we both thought, *Here we go again.* Reluctantly I looked at my phone, and it was indeed Sandi. "Hey guys, does Amelia have enough clothes?" *Ok, we thought, where is this coming from?* "I wanna get her something really nice!" We felt as if we had just fallen into the rabbit hole or walked into *The Twilight Zone.* We told her that the blanket that she was crocheting was more than enough and that it would be with Amelia forever. We said it was better than any gift money could buy. "No it's not. Then I'll have to make it bigger."

To cap the day off, Sandi's last message to me was, "Ya know I love you guys!" Again I was taken aback and wondering where this was coming from. Then she made a post on Facebook that said, "So excited for my whole family to be together this weekend" and she tagged DJ and me. Now my guard was up, and I thought there had to be more to the story. Literally two seconds later my phone rang, and it was Jill. "I am sorry to have to ask you this on such a terrible day, but Sandi wants a $60 advance." To be honest, I thought she was kidding. She was not. Sandi wanted an advance of $60 so she could purchase Amelia a present. This woman was no longer sane.

I called my close friend who happened to be an OBGYN and explained the erratic behavior. She explained to me that a women's body goes through many chemical and hormonal changes during a pregnancy that are really hard on the body. For Sandi to have been pregnant for six continuous years would be a very extreme case. She was likely to have hormonal and chemical imbalances in her brain. This explained some of her actions, but it did not explain her evil tendencies. My friend suggested that it was possible that she was either mentally ill or traumatized by her childhood. Either way, she said, it was no way to live or treat others, especially kids.

Earlier in the day I had left a voicemail for Stacy, the adoption service provider who had worked with Sandi in the past. I did not expect a return call. At 9pm that night she called me back, and we spoke for over an hour. She could hear the desperation in my voice. While she swore she would never work with Sandi again, out of the love in her heart she offered to help us. She said there would be a limit to her time with Sandi, but she was willing to help us and act as a pregnancy counselor and mediator. This would be a huge benefit for us since she already knew Sandi and her manipulative ways. She knew everything that happened with the last adoption, and she would easily be able to forecast Sandi's next move. She also had a relationship with Sandi, Sandi trusted her, and they knew how to work together. Stacy had the last adoption as experience under her belt, and she would be more prepared for Sandi's drama and antics.

We had a few other things going for us in that we had a strong relationship with the kids, with Sandi and Doug, and with Sandi's brother. We had met all of her sisters, and they seemed very nice. The symbolic gesture of the blanket and Sandi referring to the baby as Amelia and "your baby" were also good signs. We also had surrendered to the fact that we would have to spend the next three weekends in Golden Valley bonding with them. The wildcard in all of this would be if Sandi's crazy, meth-addicted mother showed up. We were praying that she stayed in her tent in Oregon (where she lived) and would not cause any trouble until after the baby was with us.

With everything that had happened up to this point and including the new information we received about the last adoption with Jane and John, the stress levels of DJ and I had intensified to the point that we could now feel it physically. DJ could not focus, had racing thoughts, was unable to do his schoolwork, and felt tightness and anxiety in his chest. I was even in worse shape than DJ given my work stress as well. My blood pressure was high, my hands would shake, I was unable to sleep, my hair was falling out, and I could feel the mounting anxiety in my head. We both said every day that we did not know how we would make it another four weeks. At this point it would have probably been a good idea for us to both see our doctors, but unfortunately we had no time. What we did have was the hope that in less than a month, a sweet baby girl would be in our arms and home with us as part of our new family. We banked on that thought to make it through each hard day.

# Chapter Fifteen

The giant redwoods of California are one of the most unique forms of life on our planet and are found nowhere else in the world. As a lover of the outdoors and someone who believes that nature is a higher power, I make every opportunity to explore this natural wonder. When I enter the forest, I am immediately calmed from any stress or worry in my life. My mind becomes a sponge that absorbs all that the forest has to offer. The unique smell of freshness, the new life that grows vertically from the trunks of fallen trees, the rocky creeks, and the acres of beautiful ferns all bring me to a place of serenity that I cannot describe. The cycle of life from decay to new growth to trees the size of skyscrapers is a miraculous thing to view. As I hike into the forest, a small amount of light surrounds me, and pockets of sunlight beam through the trees to the forest floor. Continuing deeper into the forest, the light disappears, the floor darkens, and the only thing you can see is the canopy of trees above you. The deeper I hike, the darker and more mysterious the forest becomes and the even more drawn to it I am. I feel like I could walk forever into a place of peace, mystery, and the unknown.

At this point we were three weeks away from the birth and I was hiking into Sandi's dark forest blindfolded, unsure, petrified, and sick. We did not know what to expect, and our lives were full of mystery. It was an extremely dark place, but we knew there was light somewhere in her forest. Somehow we knew we would stumble upon the beam of light that would bring us that coveted sense of peace and serenity. We would find our special life growing up from the dark forest of Sandi.

At home, things had become very rough. Sandi was so out of control that we were now visiting every weekend and taking days off of work and school to attend to her manipulated emergencies. At this point we had made thirteen trips to Golden Valley, which accounted for approximately 234 hours of driving, 31 nights in the hotel, $3000 in meals, and $1700 in gas. These were considered expenses not included in the adoption costs. We had not had a weekend to ourselves in months, had not had time to grocery shop in six weeks, and our weekdays were consumed by Sandi's drama. In short, our week was visiting Sandi Friday, Saturday, and Sunday, work and school on the weekdays, rinse and repeat.

Sandi was now doing everything in her power to purposefully upset us, scare us, or just plain make us angry. Inevitably due to the stress and extreme time together in the car, several fights broke out between DJ and me. If either of us said one wrong word to Sandi, she would be set off into a crazy fit of texts, verbal attacks, and more manipulation. Whoever set her off would usually be the one blamed for starting the fight, and, in turn, DJ and I would have a bad argument. Our relationship was never in jeopardy, but we were fighting more than we had ever done in the past. We would always end up making up, hugging, and reminding ourselves that it would all be over soon.

In the last twenty-one days of the adoption, our weeks usually went like this:

**Monday:** 50 to 60 texts asking for additional money. Her excuses ranged from her kids unplugging the refrigerator, to the dog dying from worms, to her washer being broken and needing to do 30 loads at the laundromat, to the kids needing school supplies. It would start in the morning and continue all day, and she would erupt at us if we did not comply. She would say, "You guys never do nothin' for me. Fuck this shit. How do you treat an eight and a half months pregnant person this way? How dare you talk to me like that? You are fucking supposed to make the last weeks easy on me." Late at night she would start the manipulation games of "Something is wrong with the baby," "I need to go to the ER," "I need a fucking breast pump NOW. Right fucking NOW," "The baby's head is super low. You guys need to get here now," "I am so sad and depressed about this adoption," and "You guys are going to be like the last two families and block me when I sign the papers."

**Tuesday:** Texts asking for money. Texts asking us to change her doctor's appointment earlier because she "needed this thing out of her." Texts about early labor. Texts saying she and the kids were starving. Texts about not being sure about the adoption. In the evenings, she would attack us personally, saying, "You are the worst couple I have ever worked with. You never do fucking anything for me." Around 11pm she would be completely fine and would just want to talk like nothing had happened.

**Wednesday:** The messages began immediately upon waking up that she needed something new and needed an advance. We would refuse. She would try every tactic she knew to no avail. Then would come the demands to come to visit sooner than Friday. We would explain that we had work and school and couldn't come any sooner. She would then say, "This is more fucking important than your work or school. Just fucking come down here so we can go the doctor's appointments." Of course, "doctor's appointments" was code for breakfast, lunch, and dinner… She would usually continue the Wednesday barrage until about 10pm.

**Thursday:** This was usually the best day. She knew she had lost about the money, and she knew we would be there the next day. On Thursdays we rarely had issues.

**Friday:** "Hey, what time are you guys leaving?" We would respond that we were leaving at 3pm. "Why so God damn late?" Later in the day, she would ask, "Hey, what time did you guys leave?" "3pm," we would say at about 4pm, one hour into the nine-hour drive. "Are ya almost here?" We would just shake our heads and not respond.

In one of the most dramatic weeks, Sandi had found a complete lemon of a car for sale on a website that she frequented. She had managed to save up a little money via her usual scams and by skimming some off the top. She asked DJ to help her negotiate with the seller of the car. DJ talked to the man, and the car had no battery, a bad transmission, one tire missing, and no title. DJ explained to her that buying a car with no title was risky and that the car did not even run. She would hear none of it, though. She finally had the man bring the car out for Doug to look at before she bought it. He took one look at the car and told the guy to get the hell off his property. DJ was on the phone with Sandi at the time, and he could hear the fight between Doug and Sandi ensue: "Doug, you are so fucking dead, you piece of white trash. I want this car. I want it now, God damn it. There ain't nothin' wrong with it." DJ listened for a while before he hung up the phone. Doug held his ground and refused to allow her to buy the worthless car.

Once Sandi got an idea into her head, she could not get it out. She would not stop until she got what she wanted. Since the car did not work out, she insisted on buying another car on the same website, this time for $400. She begged us for money, but we refused. She begged anyone she could find for money and somehow managed to piece enough together to purchase an old, retired police car with 300,000+ miles on it. It had mechanical problems, including a broken stabilizer bar, which rendered the vehicle unsafe to drive. She did not care at all and managed to convince Doug to purchase it despite this. She then turned to us to pay for the insurance and registration. Because Sandi had no driver's license, it was completely illegal for us to purchase her insurance. We had no choice but to say no.

Sandi tried for two days to get us to pay for the car and simply would not listen to us. We told her it was illegal over and over, but she would not give up. Once again, this set her off on an all-out attack on us. This time, however, we just ignored her as best as we could. She swore at us, told us we never did anything for her, told us that she was having second thoughts about the adoption, tried making up outrageous excuses of why she needed money, and threatened the adoption, yet we never fell for it. We ignored her and did not engage in the fight. While she was mad as hell at us, it worked. By later that evening, she had let up on the harassment and attacks and had forgotten the whole thing.

Through our close network of sources, we had also been able to find out a small amount of information from the first adoptive family. To this point, all we had known was that they were a married couple that had walked away from the adoption at the hospital during the delivery. We knew it had to be bad to walk away at the very end of the adoption, and we feared the story would scare us into panic. A social worker who was involved in the adoption was kind enough to tell us the basics behind what happened.

Very similar to our situation, the loving couple had spent months matched with Sandi through an adoption agency. As with us, it had started out well and everything had been great. The similarities to our story were rather remarkable, almost as if she had this entire scheme pre-planned. They visited the family, bonded with them, and dealt with Sandi's constant abuse and manipulation. They went through the same trials and tribulations that we did, and their stress levels climbed daily. Sandi manipulated them, abused them, and used any excuse possible to get additional money. She used many of the same tactics she had used on us, including faking early labor issues, concocting stories to get relocated to a new home, and lying about not having food. She texted them constantly and lied about everything in order to get more money. The couple did their best to keep their sanity all the way through the entire pregnancy. They had grown to hate Sandi, and they had also come to the conclusion that she was just a bad seed. They worried about her passing her negative traits to the baby. Despite everything, they continued down the path and spent a fortune to make it to the delivery.

Once the big day arrived and Sandi was in labor, everything changed, just like it had for Jane and John. She demanded to breastfeed the baby and would not allow them to see the child. She left the hospital with the baby and did not inform the adoptive parents. Each and every time she agreed to sign the consent forms, she would change her mind as soon as everyone arrived. She made insinuations that she was going to keep the baby and made horrible comments to the adoptive family, similar to those she had made to Jane and John. When Sandi started demanding more money and visitation rights from the adoptive family, the couple hit their "Sandi wall." Despite investing immense amounts of time, love, and money into this adoption, they had determined that they could not tolerate Sandi for another day. I am speculating, but I also firmly believe that they did not want to adopt anything associated with Sandi after seeing how wicked she was.

The couple sadly packed up all their belongings and left Golden Valley and Sandi. They insisted they would never speak to her again. In doing so, they left Sandi in a very tough situation. She would not get the two months of postpartum funds that she was counting on. In fact, she was left with nothing and would have no way to live. Regretting her decision to push the couple too far, Sandi desperately tried calling them to let them know she had changed her mind and would sign the consent. She had the lawyer and the social worker call multiple times as well. But the adoptive family had taken all they could emotionally from Sandi and refused to adopt the baby. While we may never know the details behind what Sandi had done to them, it is easy to conclude that she had done some very atrocious things. It had to have been extreme for a family to invest that much money and time and still to simply walk away. I could only imagine how painful this was for them.

Stuck without any money, any way to live, and without an adoptive family, Sandi's agency was able to find the lucky couple that adopted the baby without ever having to invest months of time in Sandi and her behavior.

According to several sources, at this time Doug wanted to leave Sandi due to her crazy behavior, and she used her mean, manipulative, and evil tactics on her own common law husband as well, telling him, "I am the only family you fucking have. You leave me and you are completely alone in this fucking world. I will leave, and you will never see the kids ever again. I will make sure you never fucking see them again!" Doug was stuck because he knew she would follow through with the threats.

Despite learning this story, DJ and I pressed on with the adoption. I had to save every day of vacation that I had in order to have some income during my leave of absence. In addition, DJ could not miss any more school, as he was already far behind. All of our trips to Golden Valley toward the end were Friday through Sunday. Every time, Sandi would get mad and demand we stay longer, and every time we explained to her about work and school. She would be on her best behavior while we were there in person until Monday rolled around.

During these final weeks, it was very obvious that Sandi and Doug were neglecting the kids even more than usual. Carrie's face and neck were covered in self-harming cuts, scrapes, and bruises. She was covered in dirt from head to toe and looked like she had not been changed or bathed in weeks. She smelled awful, and it seemed like she just didn't care about life anymore. Duncan and Camille were also in bad shape, with dirty clothes, black hands and feet, and a stench that made us gag. Sandi was also now being much more physical with the poor little kids.

She was very forceful with them and often yanked them by the arm with far too much force. She would also smack them and push them around. I will be honest: it was difficult to watch without reacting. In addition, the conditions of their home had deteriorated since our last visit. Cat feces was all over the house, stacks of dirty dishes engulfed the kitchen, and the bathroom was indescribable.

We had made it a point that we were going to keep ourselves on their level and just try and hang out as friends. DJ took Camille and Sandi to get their nails done while Doug and I stayed at the house and played video games. We actually had a lot of time to connect, and I was able to learn a lot more about his personality. I had a lot of fun with Doug during these Sandi-free visits and came to really respect him in a weird way. Sadly, I believe he is a desperate man trapped in a desperate situation. DJ also had a chance to really talk to Sandi during their time together. He let her know how her text messages during the week really impacted us, and she said, "Oh, that, ha ha. I just really get mad easy. I don't really mean anything by it." DJ simply rolled his eyes.

Having learned about the experiences the other families had faced and having talked to the social worker, we knew Sandi would be demanding money from us at the end of the adoption. She had already been hinting at how she was terrified about how she would be able to live after the baby was born. Throughout the time we were matched with Sandi, she had taken advances from her postpartum funds that had added up to $1000. That was more than half of what she would have to live on. We worried that Sandi's children would be homeless and living on the streets if we did not do something. We knew that giving her money during the delivery would be illegal, and we wanted nothing to do with that situation. Thus, we decided to launch a preemptive strike. We talked to our attorney and decided to give Sandi her full postpartum amount after the birth. This way, we could be assured that she would be ok during the two months after the birth, she would feel more secure, and we would not have to hear any more of her worries. Because their living situation had changed over the course of the adoption, Sandi's family now required more money to get by so we were able to justify the additional funds from a legal perspective. Not only was it completely legal but we felt it best for the kids.

While riding in the car I told Sandi about our plans and how we were going to help her. I thought she was going to be jumping for joy and completely excited. Instead, she was completely unimpressed and unappreciative: "Oh, really? Cool! That is one less thing I gotta worry about." As usual, there was no "thank you." I am not sure she really understood what a gift we were giving her. She would be able to live for two months with all her bills paid while she and Doug looked for work. I was flabbergasted that she did not seem to care. Nonetheless, she would not get that money if she did not follow through with the adoption, and that was the only leverage we had.

On the weekend of October 24th, Sandi had decided that she wanted to throw a birthday party for me with all the bells and whistles. While I honestly did appreciate the gesture, my birthday was the very last thing on my mind. She had ordered me a gift, food for catering, and a cake from Safeway, and she even asked DJ to take her to the dollar store to get some decorations. Sandi's brother was even involved and was extremely excited to give me a present that he had purchased for me. It was very flattering that they were thinking of me, and it even made me feel better about our chances of Sandi signing the consent papers. It also made me feel like she truly did care about us and I was very grateful.

As DJ and Sandi set off to do errands, Doug, her brother, and I stayed home with the kids and played video games. The kids were behaving horribly and even took crayons and marked up the entire exterior of my new Volt. They were all fighting, pulling each other's hair, wrestling on the ground, and the only thing Doug said was, "Knock it off. I am going to kick all of your asses." They were climbing on tables and stools to get on top of the refrigerator, where there was candy. It was truly like a circus, and the commotion in the house was unlike anything I had ever witnessed. At one point everyone noticed a terrible smell, and we realized Carrie had pooped her pants. Instead of cleaning her up, bathing her, and changing her clothes, Doug just took her underwear off and put on the same soiled pants. She then came running in wanting me to hold her. As sorry as I was, there was no way I was going to do that, and I had to keep my distance from her for the rest of the day. These kids were not only neglected, but they were abused both physically and mentally.

DJ had to chauffer Sandi around in order to get everything for the party. The first stop was to pick up the gift she had ordered, which was a Cleveland Browns candy jar. When they arrived to pick up the gift, she told DJ she had forgotten her wallet and asked to borrow some money. Next they went to buy decorations at the dollar store. After she had finished shopping and gone to the register, she looked at DJ when the payment was due. The same experience happened with the cake: she ordered it, but DJ, of course, had to pay. Finally, they stopped at Cracker Barrel to pick up the catering. She had ordered $120 of fried foods, probably enough to feed thirty people. They got the bill and Sandi walked away, leaving DJ to pay the enormous bill. In defense of DJ, there was really nothing he could do. We were two weeks away at this point, and saying anything would have caused a huge fight.

The party was actually very fun, and I was very appreciative of the presents, particularly the ones from her brother, which he actually purchased with his own money. It meant a lot to me that he cared, and when I thanked him he said, "No, thank *you* for everything you have done for my family. People usually see my family and run. You have helped us like no other." We finished by eating the cake after they sang "Happy Birthday" to me. Sandi actually looked happy and I could see that, at the moment, she truly cared for me. I was and will always be very thankful for the party that they had for me. It was a fun experience and a happy memory that I will always have of all of us together.

Last on the list of things to do was the Golden Valley haunted house. Even though DJ and I both thought the kids were far too young, Sandi would not take no for an answer. "Fuck no; I want to see them get scared shitless," she laughed. We arrived at the place, and Camille and Duncan were already scared before we even got in line. They heard the screaming from inside and were clinging to each of my legs. Sandi was laughing and could not wait to "see them terrified as fuck." We had to break into two groups, and I took Duncan while Sandi was in the other group with Camille. Carrie was completely unfazed and walked through as if she had no fears or emotions in the world. She just had a blank stare on her face. However, when she exited she pulled down her pants and urinated right there in front of everyone. The same could not be said for Camille and Duncan. Duncan started out walking by himself until the first monster jumped out at him. He burst into tears, jumped into my arms, and buried his head in my chest. He would take occasional peeks and then he would bury his face deeper into my chest while screaming and crying. At the very end, they came at us with a chainsaw, and he lost it. He was screaming in horror with tears flying from his eyes. Right behind us was Sandi, who was holding a terrified, crying Camille. When the chainsaw came out she broke free from Sandi's arms and sprinted toward the car while crying hysterically. All of us felt terrible for the kids. I consoled Duncan by rocking him and rubbing his back. Camille clung to DJ's leg screaming to please leave. Sandi was standing in the parking lot doubled over, laughing until she cried. I looked at the horror on the kids' faces and then I looked at Sandi, still laughing. It was the first time in my life that I wanted to punch a woman square in the nose. Instead I turned my back to her and carried both kids to the car.

Back home in Livermore that following Monday, Sandi started demanding money again via text. She would not relent. She called anyone who would listen and begged for money. She said she was out of food, even though she had just received her weekly funds an hour earlier. In addition, her refrigerator was full of food and leftovers from the party. We could not figure this one out, until she finally said outright, "I need a breast pump!" Of course we wanted to know why, and she said, "I need this fucking thing out of me now! I need this over with! I need that damn doctor to induce me. I can't take this anymore. I am buying a pump to induce myself." She had also called her doctor and begged him to make the C-section sooner. He had refused. She next began text messaging DJ and telling him all of the things she was going to do to induce herself: "What I heard was black licorice, sex, evening primrose oil, and breast milk pumping would do it. I'm doin all of that tonight." Amelia's life would be in the hands of Dr. Sandi, and that made us more fearful than almost anything up until this point. In our minds, she was no longer mentally stable at all, and we could only wonder what would happen next.

# Chapter Sixteen

The cool northern California fall air had now taken over, and the spells of hot weather were pretty much gone. We could always count on 70-degree days, cold and refreshing nights, and plenty of sunshine. My sporadic dreams and nightmares concerning Amelia and Sandi's kids had become a nightly ritual. I would usually have two to three dreams every night, some of which woke me up in panic and sweat. Others gave me glimpses into my future life with DJ and Amelia. Like the other families who had dealt with Sandi, the reoccurring dreams could likely be pointing to post traumatic stress disorder (PTSD), but I certainly had no time for a doctor or therapist appointment. I would have vivid and long dreams about the suffering that Carrie, Duncan, and Camille endured every day. Each dream would end with them looking directly into my eyes and asking me to help them or to "please take us to California." I had dreams of Sandi beating them terribly and throwing them in cold, damp closets for hours. I had dreams that Carrie's self-harming had progressed from cuts and scratches to deep and severe wounds on her arms and legs. I would either wake up or the dream would transcend into one of beauty and peace. Vibrant images would immerse my mind of DJ and me holding our beautiful Amelia in our arms at the hospital. Sometimes the dream would be of all of us at home on a Saturday night playing in the living room with Boomer curled up by the fireplace. Other times the dream would be of DJ and me walking Amelia in a park or taking her out to play in the grass. The dreams gave me a sense of both peace and terror. It was hard to get any normal REM sleep, and thus I was a walking zombie during the day.

On Wednesday, October 29th, our day started with crazy messages from Sandi wanting to buy a desert tortoise on a website in Golden

Valley. She messaged DJ for seven straight hours trying to convince him to buy it. She was furious that he had the audacity to *not* purchase her a turtle and then went into a usual rant about how we never did anything nice for her. "This is just something that would make an eight and half month pregnant lady happy. Jesus Christ!" she exclaimed. When DJ said he was offended at her comments, she said, "Fuck. I never asked you to buy it!" In truth she had asked him a dozen times to send her the money for it. For whatever reason, I was left alone for most of the day.

At about 2pm I had a Facebook notification pop up on my phone that Sandi's mother had tagged me in a post. Despite knowing what a drug-addicted deadbeat she was, it still hurt to actually see her words posted for the entire world to see:

"I can't believe you Sandi giving **my** baby away to two faggetts (sic)."

While Sandi did come to our defense and yelled at her mother, it still hurt to see those words and was frankly embarrassing for my friends and family to see. I could not help myself; I sent her a private message on Facebook:

"How dare you post something like that about people you do not even know? You have never even met us, but you make disgusting comments like that. This coming from the same women who had *all* of her children taken away from her by CPS? You are a drug-addicted woman living in a tent and you are judging us? I will pray for you, as you are one person whom I truly feel sorry for."

DJ was also hurt by the comments, but we agreed to just let it go, and I blocked her from any future contact after that message.

Two weeks before the big day, DJ and I headed out for what would be our last visit to Sandi and Doug. We had had a very rough week leading up to our trip due to Sandi's erratic behavior and constant request for advances, money, and other absurd items. She had done everything in her power to start fights with us all week, but we managed to use our new tactic of ignoring her, which seemed to pay off. While she continued to press us for money, we did not succumb. Nevertheless, she was relentless in her quest to have the baby early by any method she could find, and we were getting worried. She had her last appointment with the OBGYN on that Friday, and we knew if we did not go to Golden Valley she would not go to the appointment. She would not stop messaging us saying, "Fuck, I need this God damn thing out of me now!" She insisted we come a day early despite her knowing that I could not afford to take any more days off work. She used her usually manipulative means: "What's more important: YOUR baby or work? I know she is coming this weekend, so you need to get here now. Oh, can I borrow $100?"

The drive to Golden Valley had become second nature to us by this point. It barely even fazed us to make the nine-hour drive, and we had the whole trip down to a routine of normal stops and fuel-ups. We talked a lot on this trip, reminisced about the past seven months, and agreed it was a mixture of a miracle and fate that allowed us to make it this far. We were so close to having our daughter that we could almost feel it. We also knew, however, that we would have one more big obstacle to overcome, and that would be the birth. We were certain she would pull some crazy drama at the hospital, and we were bracing for it.

We arrived in Golden Valley in time to feed the family at a local fast food establishment, and it became very clear that Sandi was not in a good mood. She was grabbing the kids as if they were dolls and flinging them around while cussing at them, "Get the fuck over here before I fucking kick your little ass. Sit down right fucking now or there ain't no trick or treating for you tonight." She was actually being nice to them compared to how she was treating poor Doug, who looked like a tired man who had been run over by a freight train. "DOUG!" she would scream. "What the fuck is the matter with you? You can't do one God damn thing right. Fucking watch your fucking kids. NOW." This went on for the duration of our meal and continued into the doctor's office. Doug would just look at us with sad eyes and say, "Guys you have no idea what a hell my life is right now."

Her sole purpose for the visit to the OBGYN was to coerce him into allowing her to have the baby early. She was actually saying aloud that she hoped Amelia did not grow so he would be forced make an early C-section. She became visibly upset when the doctor told her that Amelia had grown to six pounds and three ounces. "Sandi, this baby is growing normally. You will have to wait until November 12$^{th}$," he said. Sandi was furious and went on and on about how she could not take it any longer and how she was in so much pain. She turned her anger toward the kids in the examination room, bellowing, "SIT DOWN NOW. ALL OF YOU."

After the doctor we ran several errands, during which Sandi begged us to buy her, Doug, DJ and me all costumes to wear. We refused and said that we had to watch our budget. She was again very angry with us and told us to just leave and that she would borrow the money from her brother. So we left.

We had seen Sandi have horrendous rants and treat her family poorly, but we had never seen her as explosive as she was when we arrived at her house right before trick or treating started. She was getting the kids ready and doing their makeup when we arrived. For the next hour, we heard nothing but swearing and yelling in a tone that was much more vicious than we had previously witnessed. "God fucking damn it, Carrie, sit your ass down or no candy for you. If you touch that one more fucking time you will be sorry." She treated all three kids like this, but it was Doug who bore the brunt of her attacks. He was doing nothing wrong and was trying his best to meet her every need. But wherever he went she yelled as loud as she could, "DOUG! Get the fuck over here. Fuck you. You can't do anything right. DOUG! Get your fucking kids. I am going to fucking kill you. God damn you are worthless. Oh my God, Carrie, if you fuck up that makeup you are dead." This went on for over an hour, and Doug just looked like he wanted to crawl in a hole and die. What was supposed to be a fun day for the kids had become miserable because of Sandi.

Prior to taking the kids trick or treating, Sandi wanted to stop by her grandpa's house to show him all the costumes. We followed them to his trailer home, but we were told explicitly to not follow them into the house. According to Sandi and Doug, he was a loner, a hoarder, and lived in complete filth and squalor. His small trailer home was packed with junk, dirt, garbage, and food, and there was basically a trail to get through the house. It addition, he was an animal hoarder and had dozens of cats and dogs living in the trailer, all of which defecated and urinated inside the home and was never cleaned up. We thought nothing of this, even after Grandpa came out to meet us wearing a filthy white undershirt and looking absolutely disheveled.

While we did make trick or treating, it was honestly not very much fun. Golden Valley did not have the trick or treating I was used to. Most houses were dark and were not passing out candy. All of the rednecks in town were out in full force and actually driving their kids house to house in beat up pick-up trucks. Everyone in town went to the one neighborhood where all the doctors lived since they all knew they could score full candy bars. Sandi screamed and hollered the entire time at the kids and poor Doug. No matter what he did she just screamed, cussed, and hissed. She yelled at the kids for walking too fast, for walking too slow, or for spilling their candy. She yelled at Doug for everything he did. While all the other families were having a blast, Sandi was making this special night miserable for everyone. We did our best to make the kids happy and fill their buckets, but it was not easy. Everyone was wiped out and tired by 8pm, so we called it a night. To our dismay, a night that should have been all about the kids had turned into a somber night of dealing with Sandi.

To make things worse, when we arrived at Sandi and Doug's house the next day we realized that the entire family was infested with lice. We had been holding, carrying, and handling the children the entire day prior, so we were sure we had to also be carrying the bugs. Sandi refused to allow us to purchase any lice medication and instead dyed the children's hair with cheap hair dye from the dollar store. She cut and dyed the girls' hair and gave them ridiculous hairstyles that looked like something you would see in those terrible children's beauty pageants. She insisted the dye would kill the bugs, which was completely false. What she told us next was shocking and appalling: "It really isn't that big a deal. When I was growing up I had lice for three full years until I met Doug. I was completely full of bugs, and him and his Mom combed em' out for hours." In that moment an overwhelming sense of empathy engulfed both of us. Sandi had truly lived a life that neither of us could ever have dreamed of. She was unloved, neglected and had endured years of punishing abuse. We understood why Sandi had issues from her trauma but we would never understand why she passed that along to her kids and everyone she touched. We wanted to reach out and hug her and show her love but, as always, she was being cold and distant.

Regardless of her protestations, DJ and I went to the drug store and purchased three anti-lice kits and an additional one for us. We went back to the hotel, examined each other's hair, and then did treatments on ourselves. We also quarantined all the clothing we were wearing to be washed in hot water and dried on high. *Seriously*, we thought, *what else could happen next?*

The day before we had stopped at Walmart and purchased some bottle-ready formula in preparation for the drive home after the baby was born. Sandi was with us and did not say a word about it. But then, out of the blue, she sends us an angry text, "Why did you buy that formula? I told you that you CAN'T use that on my kids. Why are you ignoring my damn advice? You never listen to me!" We were caught off-guard and simply asked her why she was bringing this up now. We also reminded her that she had informed us that we needed to buy different types of formula in order to find the right kind for Amelia. She ignored that and continued yelling at us. To avoid a fight, we just went to the store and returned the formula to make her happy. Later that day she would actually apologize and tell us that she was simply texting because she was mad.

On what would be the very last drive back from Golden Valley before Amelia's birthday, DJ received a text message from Sandi asking us if we would get the kids birthday presents. She was not shy at all about asking. All three kids had birthdays in December, and she wanted to make sure we did not forget. Because we loved the children, we had planned on getting them birthday presents regardless of her text. We figured a small toy for each kid would be very much welcomed and enjoyed. Of course, that was not good enough for Sandi, and she insisted that we get the kids each a Nintendo DSi XL ($200 each) and a game to go with it. Once again we were blown away by her greed and audacity and simply told her, "Absolutely not. We are not rich, Sandi!" She was not happy with us, but we did not give a damn this time.

On the days leading up to the birth Sandi began playing some of the same twisted head games that she had with the past family in order to get attention. The fact was, she would do anything to get additional attention on herself regardless of the repercussions. First she told us that she was in labor, posted it on Facebook, had her sister post it on

Facebook as well, and then went to the hospital. She followed up with a text to us saying that the hospital had confirmed she was in labor and we needed to leave. Of course, I called the nurse at the hospital, who indicated that Sandi was not in labor and was being sent home. She went on to note that she has known Sandi for years and was used to her games, manipulation, and time-wasting. Despite the confirmation that she was not in labor, Sandi still barraged us with messages saying, "You gotta leave now! If you don't leave you'll miss the birth. I am in LABOR!" The very next morning she texted us and said she was not in labor. Two hours later she told us that she was at her doctor's office and waiting for an emergency exam. A few minutes later she texted, "Baby is on the way. You need to leave now. I am in labor and the contractions are close!" We did not want to make her mad, so we used an excuse that I needed a doctor's note confirming that she was in labor for my leave of absence. I called the doctor, and the nurse said, "Sandi is not in labor. In fact, she is nowhere near labor. She isn't even dilated yet. You guys should not drive up here because the baby is not coming any time soon." I was puzzled and asked her if she was completely sure given Sandi's comments to me. The nurse then asked if I wanted to hear it firsthand from the doctor, so she held up the phone and called, "Doctor Booker, is Sandi in labor?" The very irritated doctor then yelled, "HELL NO. She is not in labor, and she needs to give it all a rest. Quit wasting peoples' time!" I was very shocked at his candid and terse remarks. The nurse then went on to say that they had been dealing with Sandi for years and that they had all become fed up with her games. She said the whole office was praying for us.

Sandi continued with the messages demanding we come up despite the fact that we told her what the doctor had said. She became enraged and said, "Really? So you are calling me a liar? I am in labor, Andrew, and you are going to miss the birth!" I did all I could to rationalize with her to no avail; she was pissed. Like always, however, a few hours later all was forgotten and she text messaged me, "Hey, Andrew, we're starvin' and have nothing to eat. Can u please order us some pizza and wings?" Of course the answer was "no," but the cycle of hell continued.

In the words of *Seinfeld* character George Costanza, "The sea was angry that day, my friends, like an old man trying to send back soup at a deli." In the days leading up to the birth, "the sea" was extremely angry, and things went from bad to worse very quickly. The mind games, the pure evil, and the torture that Sandi inflicted on the other families was now front and center in our lives. It started with a somewhat nonchalant text message asking me to remind her about our hospital agreement. This was the agreement that we signed regarding when the consent would be signed, our visitation rights, and how we would be able to interact with the baby. Sandi signed the agreement giving us full access and stated she would sign the consent paperwork right after the 72 hours passed. In addition she agreed with the attorney to sign the consent on November 15th, 72 hours after the C-section, on November 12th. I reminded her of the agreement and thus set off a terrifying chain of events. "What, this ain't what we agreed to. Y are u doing this so late? Y are u doing this to me, Andrew?" I took a photo of the agreement and sent it to her, but she did not respond. Instead she became angry and began yelling at me, "This is MY baby and I need to spend ME time with her. I'll sign the consent whenever I want. I am keeping her until next week!" I was blown away and completed astonished by her behavior. "Sandi," I said, "we understand you want to spend time with her, but why are you breaking the agreement already? You promised that you would not do this to us. Where will she sleep? How will you care for her in your home with no baby supplies?" Her only response was, "IDK."

Having been in their house, witnessed the lice infestation, seen the numerous animals and all the feces on the floor, seen the unsanitary conditions of the bathroom, and having watched the turtle poop all over the carpet and not be cleaned up, I had no idea how a baby could spend even an hour there. The other factor was the pitbull, who was unpredictable, and the odd behavior of Carrie who, could potentially harm the baby by accident. I called our social worker, and she immediately headed down to Golden Valley to intervene. Sandi was going completely crazy and started her usual bombardment of angry and mean messages to both DJ and I. "U guys are changing. I knew u can't be trusted. Fuck all this! U guys always get your fucking way. Wat about me? Wat about what I am going through?" We did our best not to engage in her fight, but she went on for hours, berating and attacking us. She continued with her usual messages that we had never done anything for her or her family.

I honestly could not take her or the stress she was causing me, so I took off for a therapeutic run. During that run, she texted me twenty times and blew up DJ's phone asking him why I would not talk to her. She was completely detached from reality and was in a very scary place.

When I returned from my run, I reviewed all of her horrific text messages. She went so far as to say, "What if I don't sign the consent at all, Andrew? What if I wait until the end of the week, Andrew? How would you like that? You need to drive here NOW!" I calmly reminded her that I could not leave any sooner and that I had no vacation time remaining. "Who the fuck cares? What is more important: your job or the baby?" The social worker was on her way but was still 45 minutes from Golden Valley, so we spoke on the phone. She reminded me of the consequences for everyone if Sandi did not sign the papers on Saturday. I then asked Sandi to please just listen for one moment and said, "Sandi, we are trying to protect you as well. I cannot get paid any of my salary until the consent is signed. I am going on paid family leave, and it requires that I send in the consent to get paid. If I have no income I will not have any money for myself or for your funds. If you sign Saturday, the ICPC starts immediately. Besides, you do not have any way to care for Amelia at home. Would you at least consider staying at the hotel with us?" She immediately responded, "You are such a liar! You can just use the birth certificate to get paid." I sent her a screenshot of the law, but she did not respond. Jill and the social worker also called her to tell her about the laws. She did not respond to them either. "Andrew," she bellowed, "don't you lie to me. I will keep her as long as I God damn please."

I turned to the only people I knew that could understand the situation and sought out support from Jane and John. They were extremely helpful, kind, and caring, and they offered me some words of advice. First, Jane told me to secretly speak to the head nurse and doctor when I arrived at the hospital to explain the situation. She indicated that everyone at the hospital despised Sandi, was aware of her evil ways, and tried to protect the adoptive families. The nurses and doctor could keep the baby at the hospital longer than normal to attempt to protect her from being exposed to Sandi's home. Next she told me to just be patient while there and know that Sandi would eventually sign the papers. Then she said, "And once she signs, you walk away, drive away, fly away! Come out bitter on the other side without regret, for your actions are based on hers." Lastly she gave me some comfort by showing me pictures of her baby and offered prayers for us all week. Simply put, she was an integral part of my support network, and I was very thankful for that. She was my friend and yet I had never even met her. I knew after that night that they would be part of our family forever once we had Amelia. Jane was my guardian angel, and I felt like she was with me through the entire process moving forward.

Sandi continued her texting until about 8pm and used every tactic of manipulation she could muster up. She was just awful to us, and it was very hard not to respond and tell her how we really felt about her. Somehow we managed to restrain ourselves and avoid saying anything we would regret. Shortly after this, Sandi agreed that she would sign the papers on Saturday if we would allow her to keep Amelia until Monday. We felt we had no choice and agreed. Literally ten minutes later she messaged me, "Andrew, we have no food and Amelia is starving. Can u please send a pizza, a family sized pasta, a large order of wings, and some soda? Would u just do one nice thing for me?" I was nauseous from her comments and could not believe how this woman conducted herself.

It did not take very long for Sandi to come up with her next plan of attack, which happened the very next morning. As usual it started with a text: "I am so sad. My great aunt died today." We both offered our condolences and told her that we were thinking about her and praying for the family. She continued texting us how sad she was and how she did not know what to do. I then asked her where her great aunt had lived, and that is when the next round of drama began. "She's in Indiana and I wanna go. I am going to the funeral," she stated. I had to step back and think for a moment to ensure I was getting this correct: she was about to deliver a baby in a few days and she was going to drive 30 hours to Indiana? I immediately asked her how she was going to do that being pregnant and not having a car capable of the drive. That was when she jumped all over me, "I don't fucking know. I'll rent a damn car. I just had a major family loss. What's more important: the baby or me getting to go to the funeral? Fucking A, Andrew, I don't fucking know," she said. "Ok," I responded, "but I don't know how you can do that when you can deliver at any moment. I am also not sure of the laws if you deliver in Indiana. It would likely disrupt the adoption. I also need to know if I should cancel my hotel for the weekend since you won't be there." "Why are you treating me like this? I can't believe you would do this so close." I did not know what I said that was so bad. "Cancel your fucking trip if you want to," she responded at last.

I was panicking and desperately reached out to one of her family members and offered my condolences about the death. Their response was not surprising: "I have no idea what you are talking about; nobody died." It had now become apparent that she had concocted the entire story. She just wanted to create drama. She did a great job of upsetting DJ, Jill, the social worker, and me, and she got the attention she wanted. Finally I called her bluff and said, "Ok, Sandi, I just cancelled the trip." That got her attention, and she said, "Fine, I am not going. Whatever! Don't cancel the trip."

It was crystal clear now that Sandi was trying to purposefully make these last few days as miserable as possible for everyone. I was in the middle of an important meeting with my CEO to align everything that needed to be done before I left for paid family leave. I had already wasted a lot of my time dealing with Sandi's first crisis. As I sat in the CEO's office, my phone started going off as it received countless messages in a short period. I quickly turned the phone off. When I was finished with my meeting I turned the phone back on, and I had 32 text messages from Sandi regarding her desperate need for money. I politely explained, once again, that there were no more advances allowed by law. I explained that money issues were not in my control and she would have to speak with Jill. This set her off again. "Andrew, this is important. I need money for stuff. Personal stuff. Gimme your attorney's number right now!" I then explained to her that she was *my* lawyer and therefore could not talk to Sandi. In fact, my lawyer had given me explicit instructions to never give Sandi her phone number. I tried reasoning with Sandi, and I continued to repeat that I had no control over the finances. "Yes you do," Sandi insisted. "I demand to talk to your lawyer now. It's *my* money. Don't you do this to me now.

Andrew, I don't ask for much. THIS IS MY MONEY AND YOU CAN'T NOT GIVE IT TO ME! I don't need this stress. Give it to me NOW."

Rationalizing with her was not working, and there was nothing more I could do. I called Jill and the social worker and asked them to please contact Sandi to explain the situation. Both of them called, but it did no good. Her attacks, insults, and tirade continued to all that were involved in the adoption. Eventually I turned my phone off, and DJ did the same. A few hours later we both got text messages from her, "Hey guys, how is your day goin'?" The insanity was now to the point that we could not help but be concerned about the ominous clouds ahead of us. We were nearly certain that the personal items she wanted to buy were baby essentials. We feared she had officially changed her mind.

After months of waiting, torment, torture, and a roller coaster of emotions, it was time to pack up the car and head to Golden Valley for the final time. I spent the week completing all the paperwork for my leave of absence from work and closed down all of the projects I was working on. We were nervous, and we knew Sandi would continue to cause us problems, but we were fairly confident that we were prepared for anything. We were planning on driving to Barstow, California, for one night to break up the drive.

DJ thought it would be a good idea to set Sandi's expectations that we would need to cut back on her spending since I was not going to be receiving my usual income. He politely told her that we could not afford to take them to breakfast and dinner every day and we had to reduce our spending to ensure we could pay all of our bills and hers. Any normal person would understand this predicament. The message, however, send Sandi into a complete breakdown. "Did you really just say that? We can't go to nice dinners? This is ridiculous. Why are you doing this to me now? I deserve my fuckin' meals. I am pregnant!" She continued on her rant for over an hour. She then switched methodology and turned her attention to our finances as a whole. "If you can't afford our dinners, then you can't afford a baby. You don't have enough money to give Amelia a good life." DJ and I were stunned and could not believe what we were hearing. We tried to rationalize with her and explain that we simply had to be careful with our spending, but she would not hear it.

Desperate, we reached out to Jane and John. To our amazement, Sandi had done the exact same thing to them and leveraged the baby to ensure she got her "meals on wheels." We realized then that everything was a scripted game to her and we were simply a repeat of her last adoption.

It was not long after we began our drive that Sandi began shifting gears once again. She was aware of our plans to stop in Barstow and was contemplating ideas to get us to drive all the way through to Golden Valley. We were about an hour away from the hotel when she tagged us in a post on Facebook that said, "The baby is coming tonight!" We were absolutely sure it was just another attempt for attention, but we needed to know. We messaged Sandi, but she did not respond. We called the hospital, which did not have any record of her being there. Finally, she replied to us and told us that it was definitely labor this time and that her contractions were eight minutes apart and continuing to get closer. She did not sound like she was lying and seemed to be very honest. She indicated that she was going to the hospital soon. We continued on past Barstow despite having already paid for the room and drove until we reached Golden Valley at 1:00am. We were preparing to go to the hospital when Sandi messaged us, "The contractions stopped. What time do u wanna meet for breakfast?" We did not reply and felt disgusted and exhausted.

Knowing that Sandi was not in labor and having arrived so late, we simply turned off both of our phones and went to sleep. We also did not set an alarm so that we could sleep in for the first time in months. We both slept like rocks and spent most of the morning just relaxing. We did not offer to take the family to breakfast, but we did decide to meet them for lunch. Doug was a complete emotional wreck at lunch and whispered to us that he really needed to talk to us and that it was serious.

We had to go directly from lunch to our storage unit so that we could carry all of our baby items to the room. It was the perfect opportunity to get time alone with Doug, so we asked him if he could help. Sandi was furious at the idea of Doug being alone with us and immediately lashed out at him, yelling, "God damn it Doug, don't you do this to me. Don't fuck with me right now. You can't leave me alone with all these kids when I am pregnant." For the first time ever, we witnessed Doug have a real backbone and firmly stand up for himself, replying, "Sandi, you can live for fifteen minutes without me. Just drop it. I am going to help them out." Sandi was furious and gave him the look of death.

Like a ticking time bomb, no sooner did Doug get into our car before he went into a complete emotional breakdown. I have honestly never witnessed anything like it, and both of our hearts felt for him. His uncensored eruption went as follows: "You guys are two of the nicest people I have ever met. You have helped my family like no other people have ever done. If it weren't for you we would be in a homeless shelter. But there are things you need to know. First of all, Sandi is a seriously evil bitch. She is evil to the core, and she doesn't give a shit about anyone but herself. She doesn't care about me or you. I can't believe I'm telling you this but you need to know. I can't live like this anymore, guys! I am trapped and I can't get out. I have nowhere to go, no family to turn to, nowhere to sleep if I leave, and no money to help my kids. She knows I don't have the means to leave. It fucking sucks. I don't want to be with her anymore. I don't get any say in anything. I can't even have a phone or Facebook account without her taking it over. I am not allowed to have any friends. I watch her torment my children. She has never given me a single dollar from our adoption funds. If I get any money I have to hide it in my fucking sock!"

We listened to him and supported him as his rant turned to tears. He continued, "I don't know what the fuck went wrong in her life, but dude, she is fucked up, mentally ill, and evil. But just because she is like that doesn't give her the right to constantly hurt other people. She is the reason I can't see my God damn children. I don't blame Jane or John for leaving after what she did. Her behavior cost me a relationship with my kids. I can't even get a job because she sabotages it every time. She has ruined everything in my life and now she is about to do it to you guys. Sandi is planning on signing the consent, but she is planning on *not* signing the thirty-day waiver. That means she will torture you guys for thirty days and change her mind if she wants. I wanted you to know this because I love you guys and I don't want to see you get hurt. I don't know what you can do, but I wanted you to know. She *will* give you the baby, but she will put you through pure hell until then. I also want you to know I am leaving tonight! I can't take this and I am leaving, going to the bar and getting smashed, and then coming back when I decide to come back. I will be back before the birth. Just know I love you guys, you will be great parents to Amelia, and Sandi is just one fucking evil and messed up person. She lied to you guys every day. I am so sorry!"

We tried our best to comfort him and let him know that he was a good guy, a kind person, and that he deserved better. I personally promised him that I would help him if he ever decided to leave. Because he had no phone, he even gave me a secret way to get in touch with him if I needed to via his biological brother, who lived in Golden Valley. Doug was touched and he disclosed even more about his past, "You guys have been so damn nice to me. Nobody has ever actually liked me. I grew up getting' beat everyday by my drunk dad. My brothers beat the shit out of me every day too. I never had a real home. I lived in the woods or car most of my life. Hell one summer my Mom locked me in an old freezer for three hours in the blazing sun. I would have died but one of my bros heard me screaming for help. I've been in and out of mental places because my head's all messed up. When things start going right, more bullshit happens. Just last year I went to a bar and met the wrong crowd. I was dragged out of the bar, tied to a tree, and beaten by three dudes for hours. I don't even remember anything other than waking up in the hospital and learning that I nearly died. Shit just don't ever go right for me. You guys are the only ones that ever treated me with any respect. Thank you."

Hearing about Doug's past really opened our eyes to how much pain and suffering he had endured in his young life. We wanted to help him and wanted to make things better for him but we were still handcuffed by Sandi. It was at the moment that we decided that we would do anything in our power to help Doug after the adoption. We wanted to help him and give him a real chance to get his life in order. We wanted him to be the father that we knew he could be if he had the chance. "Let's just get through this adoption and then we can do whatever we can to help Doug. Even if he has to come to California for a while then so be it. The guy needs a break," DJ said. I agreed, "I know Babe, you are 100% right. He is a good guy. We'll do what we can for him."

As soon as we pulled up to their house and got out of the car Sandi went ballistic on Doug right in front of the kids. "Fuck you. You are a piece of shit. You are no fucking father leaving your pregnant wife at home. Fuck your ass. You are no man and no father!" We were ready for the normal Doug to back down, but we were astonished when he responded, "You know what, Sandi? Fuck you! I won't take this shit anymore, and I won't take you!" He erupted at her nonstop until she was crouched over crying hysterically. Hanging in their messy garage was a punching bag. He hit that bag with the force of Mike Tyson, turned around, and ran away. He ran down the street, down the next road, and disappeared.

We called our social worker, and, bless her kind soul, she showed up immediately. First she met with us at our hotel and helped us to devise an action plan for the coming days. She was very confident that everything would work out. Next, we all went back to Sandi's house and found her sitting outside like a puppy dog waiting desperately for Doug's return. The social worker did an amazing job getting us all talking and calming the situation. She worked magic with Sandi, and by the time the evening was complete, she had Sandi convinced that signing both the consent and waiver was the right thing to do. Sandi and Doug would be meeting with the attorney three days after the birth to sign our needed paperwork. To be honest, she was a miracle worker, and we will forever be in debt to her for how much she helped us and the situation. Thus, for the time being things were back to normal, and DJ and I felt like things were finally pointed in the right direction.

The night before the planned birth of Amelia, I had one of the most memorable, emotional, and amazing dreams I have ever had. Two years prior, I had lost one of my dearest friends during an epilepsy surgery that had gone wrong. The tragic loss took from me my closest friend, my mentor, my second father, and one of the nicest men who has ever walked the Earth. The loss shook me to my core, and to this day I have not been able to completely let it go. I would, in some way or another, think about him every day. This night, however, this friend appeared to me in a surreal, vibrant, and spiritual way. In the dream, I was walking into the hospital for Amelia's birth when uncertainty surrounded me. I had a feeling of hopelessness and fear. As I walked alone down the dark hallway, it suddenly became illuminated by a white light. It was as if the brightest star had descended from the universe and provided a warm and unexplainable light. At the end of the hall was my friend, motioning me to come to him. As I approached, all of my fear and uncertainty about the adoption vanished instantaneously. He grabbed me on the shoulders, looked into my eyes, and said, "Drew, don't worry. I am watching out for you, buddy. I will take care of everything. I love you."

I woke up, immediately recalled the dream, and had a sudden sense of serenity and peace. I will never know if it was truly a dream or if it was much more that cannot be explained. It was too real to be just a dream. Nonetheless, I then knew that somehow, some way, everything would be ok. I would lean on this hope many times during the next several days.

# Chapter Seventeen

The day we had been waiting for had finally arrived, and we found ourselves at Sandi's house at 4:30am on November 12th waiting to take her to the hospital for her C-section. The moon was bright, vibrant, and nearly full as we stood in the cold, crisp fall air on her porch. The birth was scheduled for 8:00am, but the doctor wanted us there early to prep Sandi for the surgery. I was so nervous that I had turned to carrying a bottle of Pepto-Bismol with me to settle my stomach. DJ's nerves were showing as he clearly wore his emotions on his sleeve. Nevertheless, we were very excited to meet Amelia.

Surprisingly, Sandi was relatively calm when we arrived at Golden Valley Regional Medical Center and was quickly moved to a pre-delivery room to be prepared for the surgery. Sandi, Doug, DJ, two of her sisters, and I all surrounded her with support and reassured her. We were trying to be as supportive and comforting as possible.

Around 8:05am Sandi was placed on the stretcher and moved down the hall into the operating room. DJ, Doug, and I all waited by the infant nursery, which had glass windows so we could see into the room of what would be Amelia's first crib. There was a nurse inside the nursery preparing for Amelia's arrival. For a moment, all of my feelings of anger, hate, and the memories of the past seven months completely left my mind. I felt a sudden sense of calm and euphoria. I assumed that Sandi would be in the operating room for quite some time and was preparing myself for a long wait. At 8:17am I heard the most beautiful sound I have ever heard in my life. It was the high-pitched wailing of my baby girl. I could not believe it had happened that quickly, and before I knew it the operating room doors opened and my sweet girl was carted right past me. The nurse knew that we were the adoptive parents and slowed the cart for just a moment before rushing her into the nursery.

To say that she was beautiful would be a dramatic understatement. She was an angel, and I fell in love with her immediately. DJ and I both cried as she was washed, examined, poked, and prodded for about twenty minutes. We were both sobbing with joy as she was put in her diaper, hospital onesie, and a cute pink hat. We watched as she was given two shots and screamed in terror. It broke our hearts to see her in pain. DJ was so emotional that he could not stop crying and smiling at the same time. "It's just that she's so beautiful. She's so small. I just don't' know what to say. I want to laugh and cry. This is going to be my daughter some day after we get married and I adopt too. This is just amazing."

The nurse then allowed Doug to go into the nursery to see Amelia, but before he went in she brought her out to briefly meet her new daddies. We sobbed as we looked into her bright blue eyes. She had beautiful strawberry blond hair, fair pink skin, and a face that you would expect to see in a Gerber commercial. She was the most glorious and wonderful thing either of us had ever seen.

We were quickly moved to a private hospital room, and Sandi was in a relatively good mood despite the pain and drugs that she was on. We had worried that she would not adhere to the agreement that we would have full access to the baby after birth and would help care for her. We were astounded when Sandi kept every word she had promised us. During the first day, we cared for Amelia for nearly the entire day, holding her, changing her diapers, and caressing her. Sandi seemed very uninterested in the baby, and by the time evening had come she was constantly going outside to smoke cigarettes. She had insisted that all three kids come to the hospital, and most of the day there was constant chaos in the room. The kids were screaming, fighting, and running around the small room. We stayed until about 11pm and then left to go back to our hotel. It was very hard to leave our daughter, but we did not have any choice. In addition, Doug stayed at the hospital to care for Amelia that night.

The first sign of looming trouble began that night when our phones never stopped ringing and receiving text messages. We received panicked calls from both Sandi and Doug. Doug had fallen severely ill with an unknown diagnosis and had been admitted to the emergency room.

Sandi, having absolutely no empathy, was infuriated at him because he could not be in the room and was asking us to go to the ER to get him discharged. Doug was texting us asking for one of us to go to Sandi's room to help out. At 3am we left for the hospital and told her that we were on the way. She replied, "No. Go back home. I only want Doug." She would not reply to messages after that, and we had no idea what was going on.

The next sign of trouble came in the morning when Sandi posted a message on Facebook with a picture of her and Amelia and stated, "Welcome Michelle Jo Peters into the world." Sandi had told us that she would name her Amelia Laurie as we had all agreed. We were miffed as to why she would suddenly change her mind and make her own name for the baby. Our instincts made us suddenly feel very uncomfortable and nervous. We immediately left for the hospital.

Upon entering Sandi's room, she immediately asked us to go up to the third floor to check on Doug. When we arrived to room 386, we found a very sick man. Doug was hooked up to several IVs, was on monitors, and was vomiting when we entered. Despite being in pain, he was happy to see us. He had been diagnosed with pancreatitis, an unknown liver issue, and an infection. He was receiving several rounds of intravenous antibiotics and anti-nausea medications. Doug was in really bad shape, but he still wanted to talk. "Guys, Sandi is fucking angry at me because I can't be downstairs helping her. She doesn't give a damn for me. Do you see what my condition is? How could my own girlfriend not even fucking care?" He began to cry. "I need to get things off of my chest. Sandi smoked the entire pregnancy. She also makes me smoke weed every day because she doesn't like my high-energy personality. That's where all the money goes. This whole time she's also been saying shit like, 'how can two guys fucking raise a baby. It's bullshit. I don't want them to raise her.' She'd also call you guys faggots and talk about how you're goin' to hell. That one day when her Mom was talking shit, she was actually agreeing with her. She was laughing about it and thought it was funny. She was encouraging her to say shit. Honestly I am not sure what her true intentions really are." We thanked him for being honest and told him that no matter what happened he could rest assured that he would be a part of Amelia's life. It would be dishonest to say that his words did not make us even more apprehensive than we already were.

Back in Sandi's room she was demanding that we get Doug to her room regardless of his condition. We explained that he was very ill and that he could not be moved at this time. "Fuck that piece of shit. Doesn't he know how much pain I am in?" She then called him and unleashed on him like I had never seen: "You know what, Doug? I am not fucking around this time. You either get the fuck up here or you are gonna be homeless. Get up here now or your ass is kicked out and you can be alone with no house, no kids, no family, and no friends. I AM IN PAIN. Now get the fuck up here." Doug hung up on her, since there was nothing he could do. She began texting him for hours and berating him in all possible ways. She even went up to his room and screamed at him in front of doctors, nurses, and other patients.

Next she turned to us and demanded we go get her kids and bring back food for her. "I am fucking starving. I need two twenty piece nuggets, food for the kids, and a large soda." DJ stayed with her to help with the baby while I went and picked up the kids and food. When I arrived back, she left DJ and me with Amelia and went with the kids outside to smoke. She was gone for several hours.

In the room, DJ and I were able to bond with Amelia. We held her, kissed her, and comforted her as much as we could. She was starving, and Sandi had been gone so long that the hospital social worker informed us that we had to give the baby a bottle since she had not nursed in over three hours. The staff was getting concerned about Sandi's aloof behavior. The head nurse then came in and informed us that because of their concern, they had arranged a room for us in the hospital to stay with Amelia. We were more than happy to accept the offer. We also feared that the hospital might call CPS, which would really make the fragile situation more intense.

Sandi finally arrived back up in the room and smelled like an ashtray. She was not in a talking mood and asked us to take the kids home, where her brother was waiting to babysit them. DJ took the kids home while I sat in the hospital room with Sandi and our social worker. She quickly fell asleep while I held Amelia in my arms. Doug was text messaging me to inform me that his condition had worsened and he was now so sick that the doctors were very concerned about him. When Sandi woke up I gave her an update on Doug's condition, and it sent her into a tailspin. "All right, that's fucking it. I am done with this shit. I want to go home." She stormed out of the room to go outside to smoke. Our social worker followed her. She was not supposed to leave for another 24 hours, and the doctor had not cleared her or the baby to leave.

We stayed in the room and cared for Amelia as drama unfolded throughout the hospital. Sandi went to Doug's room and again screamed at him and berated him. She then limped her way to the outside of the hospital, got into her car, and told the social worker that she was going to leave against medical advice. I was informed of the situation and was asked to go outside to try to talk to her. When I arrived, I found her crying and smoking while talking to our social worker. "I can't do this anymore. I want to go home and be with my kids and family. Fuck Doug. This is crazy. He doesn't fucking know the pain I am in."

Because Sandi was in so much pain, it took her a long time to get back to the room, so I took the time to inform the hospital staff of the situation. They were appalled at her behavior and informed me that they were calling social services. They also said that if Sandi left against medical advice, Amelia would become the property of CPS and the adoption would be disrupted. It was all now in our hands to convince her that she simply could not leave. DJ and I were both crying and could not believe her lack of care or concern.

As Sandi limped her way back to her wing, she was told about the situation. "Call my fucking doctor and tell him to discharge me now. This is fucking crazy!" The staff informed her that it was 1 am and no doctor would discharge her at this time. They also informed her that social services had been called and the hospital social worker was on her way. For reasons unknown to me, Sandi completely changed her tune. "Never mind, I will just stay here. Fuck it. Drew can watch the damn baby tonight. Tell her not to come." Regardless of her desires, the social worker was already on the way and would have to talk to Sandi. When she arrived she informed Sandi of the repercussions of leaving the hospital that night and promised her that she would be released the next morning. This seemed to calm Sandi down, and she went back to the room.

DJ and I took the baby in the rolling bassinet and brought Amelia to our hospital room. I slept on the hospital bed while DJ slept on the pullout sofa. It was a rough night as the registered nurse on duty came into our room every two hours to check the baby and to wake us up to feed her. While we got nearly no sleep, we did not mind, and we enjoyed the time with our daughter. Sandi did not come to see Amelia at all that night. In fact, at 8am when we awoke, we went to her room and she was outside smoking.

When she returned, she immediately started to work on her discharge while DJ and I had to watch mandatory videos on SIDS and shaken baby syndrome. It did not take long before she and the baby were cleared to go home. The next step was her desire to get Doug out of the hospital as well. She marched into his room and told him it was time to go. Doug was vomiting and looked like complete hell. The doctor came in and informed us that they still did not know what was wrong with his pancreas or liver and if he left, he would be in danger. "If you leave, you will likely be back here in worse shape in no time at all," he told Doug. Sandi kept yelling at Doug until he snapped, ripped out his IVs, and stood up, declaring, "Let's fucking go, Sandi!"

We all traveled back to her home, and we took Amelia because they did not have a working car seat. We entered the home, which was in the worst shape I had ever seen it in. The house was so dirty that you could not walk. Garbage, old food, feces, and dirty clothing covered the extremely dirty carpet. There was over a foot of trash and dirty laundry covering the entire home. The cushions from the couch were ripped apart to where cotton was all over the room. The kitchen floor was covered in old food, and dirty dishes were thrown in all places. The bathroom was completely soiled and had human excrement on the floor. We nervously asked Sandi where the baby would sleep, and she said, "She'll just sleep on the couch with the other kids."

We could not believe what we were hearing. We had just watched the SIDs video about how infants should never sleep anywhere but alone in a crib or bassinet and should never sleep on a soft surface. We text messaged our social worker, and she agreed to bring a used swing/sleeper. Doug was passed out on the floor due to his illness, and Sandi was changing Amelia on the grotesquely dirty carpet. We had no idea how we would deal with this for at least another 24 hours before she would be able to sign the adoption paperwork. We were literally sick with worry and concern. We felt hopeless and helpless.

We stayed until very late so that we could ensure Amelia would make it through the night. I had put together the bassinet so that I was sure she would have a safe place to sleep. To add additional worry, Sandi was uninterested in nursing Amelia and we had to beg her to do it. Who would be doing this while we were gone? The other problem was the fact that Carrie had no idea how to be gentle with infants. No matter how many times we tried to educate her, she would hit Amelia hard in the face or accidently scratch her. We woke Doug up and begged him to try his best to watch out for the baby. He promised he would do his best. We left the house and headed back to our hotel room, worried and scared but hopeful that tomorrow would be the day that Amelia became legally ours. As we left, we could hear Sandi screaming and cursing at the kids. It would not be long before she became physical as usual.

It was impossible to sleep that night, and both of us tossed and turned while pondering the coming day. Would Sandi play evil mind games as she did with the last families, or would our extreme efforts to bond with her ultimately pay off? We honestly did not know and stayed up all night imagining every possible scenario. We hoped that it would be a smooth day, but we also were very aware of who we were dealing with. The signing was scheduled for 11am on Saturday the 15th of November.

With no sleep and no appetite, we left the hotel and met at Sandi's house at 10am. Doug was feeling better, our social worker was already there, talking to and counseling Sandi, and the kids were watching cartoons. Sandi asked several times if we could change the appointment to a later time, but we all informed her that this was not possible since the attorney was only coming in on a Saturday for her. We were pleasantly surprised when Doug told Sandi that it was time to go and she did not put up a fight. On schedule, we all departed for the attorney's office.

The attorney's office was actually a house that had been converted into an office, with a big dirt front yard and a large front porch. Sandi, Doug, and the social worker all went into the office to sign their portion of the documents while DJ and I played with and watched the kids. They were in the office for over an hour when we finally saw the door open. Doug made a beeline for his car, where he put his head on the steering wheel and cried. DJ and I went over to him, gave him a big hug, and thanked him for signing the papers. Sandi then came out, and she was crying and being helped to the car by the social worker. We also hugged her and thanked her again. She was crying hysterically and told us, "I can never do this again! I hate this fucking attorney. I never want to see her again!" She was in pain and we did feel very sorry for her. We could see the pain in her eyes and, for once, she was showing us true emotions. We did everything in our power to comfort her at the time.

Because I was adopting as a single parent, the only person left to sign was me. I entered the office, signed my few documents, and within about fifteen minutes the procedure was completed. As far as we knew, I was now the proud parent of Amelia Laurie Branham. Instantly it was like a 500-pound backpack had been removed from my body, and I felt peace for the first time in nearly eight months. I was a proud father, and Amelia was the light of my life.

After all that Sandi had done to me, DJ, Amelia, her kids, and my family, I was done with her and wanted to leave Golden Valley as soon as humanly possible. I still intended to honor my visitation agreement, but I needed to get far away from Sandi and her life for a long time. Adoption law required that we stay in Arizona, so we went to our hotel, quickly packed the car as if we were evacuating from a tsunami, and got on the highway heading west. In our minds, we were free and would never step foot in Golden Valley, Arizona, again. As we drove away, we cried with joy and happiness as we thought our long nightmare was finally over.

About an hour away, we stopped in Lake Havasu, Arizona, and got a quaint hotel that was right on the water. We set up Amelia's crib, unpacked, and had an amazing night for the first time as our small family. We finally posted pictures on Facebook, called all of our friends and family, took videos, and text messaged pictures to everyone we were close to. It was not only closure for DJ and me, but it was closure for everyone who cared about us. We got over 200 "likes" and nearly 100 comments on our first Facebook post. The immense amount of stress from the past months hit us all at once, and before we knew it, our new family was asleep. We were finally free.

As the indescribable amounts of stress left our bodies, it took a toll on us physically. We slept like we had never slept before despite having to get up to feed and change the baby. When the phone began ringing at 9am we did not hear it. When I finally came back to consciousness, I looked at the phone and had missed several calls from my adoption attorney. We did not think anything of the calls but instead assumed it was regarding the Arizona and California ICPC process. We began getting Amelia ready for the day, changing her diaper and feeding her, when the phone rang again. Once again it was my attorney.

"Drew, are you sitting down? I am afraid I have some bad news. One of the documents was filled out incorrectly, which means all the papers have to be filled out again. I am so sorry. You will all need to meet the attorney again today at 2pm."

I was speechless, and DJ could tell by the look on my face that something was terribly wrong. I told him the news and he began to sob. I held him in my arms and cried with him. Given the events of the past day, we had no idea if we could convince Sandi and Doug to sign again.

We got ourselves together and ramped up our spirits. We knew we had one more game of chess left in us, and we would do whatever it took to get this done. Reenergized, we told Sandi that a few documents were missing and we would be coming over soon. We drove as fast as we safely could back to Golden Valley and pulled up to their house. Doug immediately greeted us and told us not to worry; they would sign the papers. Once again, we had a temporary sense of peace. We brought Amelia inside the disgusting home, and Doug immediately picked her up and showed his love for her. He kissed her, caressed her, and told her how much he loved her. Sandi sat with her arms crossed and no emotion.

At 1:30pm we all knew it was time, once again, to leave for the attorney's office. Doug was ready and wanted to get it over with quickly. Sandi started crying again and said she needed more time. Again, we told her that the attorney was coming in on a Sunday and that we were not able to change the time. Doug got the kids ready, got everyone into the car, and said Sandi would be out in a few minutes. We waited in the driveway for twenty-five minutes, but there was no sign of Sandi. Doug would go into the house, they would have a screaming match, and he would come out and let us know she was coming. What we did not know at the time was that she was up to some of her usual sinister behavior. Our social worker was also at her house, and several times she had to leave to get away from Sandi, which was very much not like her. When we had a moment to grab her, she had a look of death on her face and would not say much. She only said that she was "very concerned."

After waiting for an hour, Doug came back out and said that Sandi wanted all of us to go to the attorney to sign the documents and that she would come in fifteen minutes. We were afraid that we were so late that the attorney would leave, so we had no choice but to go right away. There was a sense of panic and uncertainty in the air as we drove to her office. We had no idea whether or not this was going to become a very serious problem and potential obstacle for the adoption. We were extremely scared and confused.

At the office, Doug marched in and signed all of his papers without any hesitation. The attorney and notary witnessed the signatures, and his part was done. There was no sign of Sandi at all. In fact, she had now told Doug and the social worker that she would not be coming at all and had changed her mind about the adoption. Before I could even react, my phone rang.

"Is this Andrew?" a voice inquired. "This is Debbie, Sandi's landlord. I don't know how to tell you this, but I care about you guys and I want to ensure this adoption goes through. Sandi just called me and told me she was keeping the baby and wanted to know if I would give her a break on the rent!" She was crying as she told me this devastating news. I was speechless as she continued, "I also wanted you to know that I stood up for you guys! I told her that if she backed out of the adoption I would take the rent check from your attorney, rip it up, and evict her immediately. I could not be a part of her disrupting the adoption. I told her that she cannot hurt people like this...I did my best. I am sorry to tell you this, but I hope it helps. God bless."

The shock I felt in my heart was like a nuclear bomb. Rather than falling apart, I remembered the chess game and the hope that the dream about my friend had given me. DJ and I had come so far, and I knew we could do anything. We knew we would find a solution one way or another. It was quite possible that this landlord whom we did not even know had saved out adoption via her conversation with Sandi. We would later send her flowers and thank her personally.

The attorney suggested we all go to Sandi's house together so that we could talk to her in person. Within five minutes we all pulled up to the house, and Sandi was outside smoking on the porch. Doug escorted the attorney into the garage because, knowing she was also a social worker, he did not want her anywhere near the disgusting home. Doug and our social worker went inside the house with Sandi to talk to her, and a few minutes later they called me into the house while DJ was distracting the kids. I walked inside and found Sandi on the couch crying. She asked, "Do you promise, Andrew, to keep your promise and let me see her?"

"Yes," I replied, "I have every intention of keeping my visitation agreement with you, Sandi. I would not break that unless you did something really bad."

She then looked at me and said the magic words: "Ok, I will sign. Let's go."

I was an emotional wreck at this very moment. My thoughts and feelings were extremely mixed and I was very appreciative that Sandi was going to sign. Despite all my anger, hatred, and fear; I was still grateful beyond words for her to give me a chance to be a father. I felt compassion for Sandi as it seemed like she was ready give up the fight. At that moment I felt like she was going to put a permanent end to the games, the manipulation, and the fraud. Unfortunately, as soon as I would feel the empathy I would quickly remember all that she had done to us.

With that, we did not waste any time so as not to give her another opportunity to change her mind. We all walked into the garage, Sandi re-signed her documents in front of the attorney, and the notary notarized them all. We had everything we needed once and for all. Rather than leaving, we decided to stay and allow them to spend some time with Amelia. Despite our true feelings for Sandi, she had done her part, and we felt we owed her at least one more visit. She was also very visibly upset and emotional and we saw a sliver of love in her eyes. My mind raced with thoughts of all the abuse that she had endured throughout her life, the lack of love from her parents, and her mental illness. I thought back to the day we matched and how excited we were to have an open-adoption and a new extended family. She truly was a woman in pain and, inside we felt sorrow for her.

We stayed for several hours as Doug and the family held and played with Amelia. Sandi, however, simply sat on the couch with her arms crossed, a scowl on her face, and stared at her phone. "So I get my postpartum funds now, right?" she asked. As always, we informed her that we could not talk about financial issues and that she could call Jill any time she wanted. She wasted no time and called Jill requesting $1000 of her postpartum funds. After this, she seemed to get angry, and we could feel the tension building in the air. She went out on the porch and began chain smoking, and DJ went out to talk to her. A few minutes later I was asked to come out to talk to her with DJ.

"Andrew, did you tell my sister-in-law Kendra that I am a bad person?" she asked. The evening before, Doug's sister had asked me how things were going, and I had told her the truth.

"You know what, Sandi? I did. You are *not* a good person. In fact, you are a terrible person. What you did to us for nearly eight months was complete torture. It was evil. You are evil! Honestly I don't know how you live with yourself."

She quickly shot back, "Oh, so now you fucking want to say something? What? What did I do that was so wrong?"

It was as if a switch was flipped in my brain and the months of withholding my thoughts and opinions were released like a nuclear bomb. It was now time for a tag-team effort from both DJ and me. We told her about the manipulation, her taking advantage of our kindness, the fraud with the relocation, the fake illnesses, the fake pregnancy issues, lying about the baby's sex, stealing DJ's aunt's money, forcing us to come down every weekend despite my work and DJ's school, lying about being in labor, and all the other bullshit she had pulled. She was speechless. I continued, "And by the way, Sandi, we know you smoked the entire pregnancy, we know what you did to the last adoptive couples, we know you used our money on drugs, we know you forced Doug to smoke weed, we know you used us for money when you didn't need it, we know you used fake medical drama to hurt us, we know you lied to make us come and visit, we know you called your landlord today and tried to change your mind, we know you changed your mind today after all this time, and we know you lied to us 99.9% of the time. All you ever cared about was money. You treat Doug like he isn't even a person, and I will not comment on your parenting skills. For God's sake, we opened our hearts to you and your family and all you did was hurt us. Every single day."

DJ was now completely irate and he too was ready to vent, "Not only did you completely purposefully destroy our lives for seven months, but you also disregarded my school and our family. You interrupted me during my final exams. You didn't care. You disrupted me in the middle of classes. You didn't care. You would send me 100 text messages a day begging for money when I was already overwhelmed with school. Yet you didn't care. All you wanted was money. All you ever cared about was money. All you ever will care about is money. You are heartless! The way you treat your kids. You should be in jail. No child deserves to be treated how you treat them. What in the hell is wrong with you? You are horrible Sandi and you don't care!"

Pandora's box was now open. She denied everything, went into the house, and slammed the door. There was really nothing she could say. Everything we had said was 100% true. We went back in, and she began yelling at us. Doug jumped in to defend us. He finally said, "It is best if you guys probably leave now. Take Amelia far away from all of this." We did not hesitate; we grabbed our belongings and jetted out the front door.

As difficult as it is to admit, this emotional release was truly liberating. It is impossible to describe how good it felt to finally unload that emotional-constipation. For seven months, we endured manipulation, greed, pathological lying, fraud, and acts of pure evil. We had witnessed Sandi hurt three loving children both physically and emotionally. We had learned the horrors experienced by two other families. Yet for those seven months we had to bite our lips. There were so many times that we had come so close to exploding on Sandi but we somehow found the willpower to withhold it for the sake of Amelia. We had to literally bite our tongues for months while we endured horrific abuse. Thus, when we unloaded on Sandi on her porch it felt as though a hundred 50-pound bags of sand were lifted off of both of our shoulders. We felt free. We felt real again. We felt some of the anxiety leave our souls. We also felt some guilt as we knew Sandi was a sick person. In our eyes, a mentally stable person could not behave as she had and we had to try our best to find empathy toward her. As usual, we experienced a rollercoaster of emotions ranging from anger, to hate, to sympathy and sadness.

On the way home, Sandi began texting us asking how she could make things right. I told her that she could start by apologizing for everything she had done to us and to begin treating her kids and Doug with more respect and love. She was also texting DJ, who quickly realized that the balance of power was shifting into our direction. He actually texted her to never call or text him again and he blocked her number from calling or messaging his phone. He was feeling both a sense of relief and a sense of anger as he relived the memories of the past. By the time we had arrived back in Lake Havasu, she had apologized countless times for nearly everything. She said she wanted to be a better person. We knew it was all a lie, told her we would talk to her tomorrow, and I too blocked her from my phone.

We expected that we would be approved by both Arizona and California in the morning and would soon be on our way home. We had a wonderful night in the hotel with Amelia and spent hours holding her, rocking her, and bonding with her. We went to bed early after the long and emotional day.

Nine in the morning, on Monday the phone rang, and it was my adoption attorney. DJ and I looked at each other, petrified with fear. I answered, and the somber sound of her voice made me know right away that it was not going to be good.

"Andrew, I don't know how to tell you this, but there is a mistake on two of the forms. The adoption still is not legal. I don't know what to say other than I am sorry. This has never happened to me before."

I simply hung up the phone, and we held each other and cried once again. Why us? It was like God was forcing us to have a relationship with Sandi. We did not think there was any way in Hell that Sandi would sign any more papers. She would also likely change her mind again. This was the adoption from Hell, and things continued to pile up. Every time we thought it was over someone dropped a bombshell on us. Feelings of hopelessness, dread, and fear engulfed both of us. How was it even possible for this to happen again? Was Sandi making mistakes on purpose to delay the adoption? She was smart, but we did not think she was smart enough to come up with a scam this complicated. The fact of the matter was that our attorney was simply not experienced enough with California adoptions. She was not familiar with the paperwork and thus was making critical mistakes. It was not her fault as she was not an expert in California law, however she was the only option available to us. She felt horrible and apologized profusely. We made certain that we told her that it was not her fault.

I was very down but DJ was positive and insisted that we find one more burst of energy to get this done. "Come on Drew, we can do this. Pick yourself up and let's go outsmart her one more time!" We mustered up any strength we could find, packed up the car, and headed back to Golden Valley. We had one last chess match to play, and we knew we had to win. Our game plan started out by texting Sandi, "We are heading to Golden Valley to visit. We are giving you one last chance to be a better person. Now is the time to show us. We have two more papers that need to be signed. If you really want to show us that you have changed, then now is the time." She immediately text messaged us back and said she was fine with it and would happily sign the papers again.

This time we came prepared with the attorney and the notary, and we ensured that all the paperwork was perfect. We walked into her filthy house and presented her with the documents. It was a damn miracle that she signed with no issues. In what could have been a horrible mistake, I believe my being honest with Sandi about my feelings was what made the difference. She knew that I thought she was a bad person, and she wanted to try and prove me wrong by signing the papers without any drama.

Sandi invited us to stay for dinner and offered to cook us a homemade meal so that we could avoid eating out for one day. We did not want to eat in that dirty and unsanitary house, but we agreed just to be kind to her and the family. As usual, she did not pay any attention to Amelia whatsoever and only stared at her phone while yelling at everyone. She had yanked Carrie and Duncan's arms so hard that both were on the ground whimpering. When Carrie started crying she gave her a hard slap on the face. She then dragged her to a separate room. Duncan got up to follow his sister, and Sandi kicked him as hard as she could right in his stomach. He fell backwards and scraped his back on the table, leaving three welts along his spine. "Enough, Sandi," I yelled as I went to hold Duncan, who was crying hysterically. DJ went into the back room to hold and comfort Carrie.

We realized that nothing had changed with her when she started to bring up her favorite subject: "Hey, where's my money? I need my postpartum funds now. I really need my money. Call your damn lawyer and get me my money." As was always the case, we explained to her that we were not able to discuss money and that she had to call Jill. "That's not fair. I signed the fucking papers. Give me my money. I need my money. We are going to move to Utah or Wyoming this week." I was sad to hear her say this because we knew then that not only would she never change, but that she had no love for Amelia. To her, Amelia was simply a short-term paycheck. It was also sad that she believed she could relocate to a new city with no jobs, no connections, and only $2000. She would not last a week, but we knew she had already made up her mind.

Surprisingly, Sandi's dinner was amazing. Why? It was amazing because Sandi never got off of her phone or the couch, and I had to cook everything, serve everyone, and then clean up the entire mess. She never even offered to help, saying she was in too much pain. I made chicken parmesan, garlic bread, and angel hair pasta, which everyone devoured. DJ was not feeling up to playing the game any longer. He was no longer even pretending to like Sandi as he sat in the corner not speaking to anyone except the kids. Upon leaving her house, we never received a "thank you" from anyone, and Sandi never touched or looked at Amelia. Her last words that night were, "I need my money. Get me my money."

Despite Sandi's lack of interest and angry demeanor, we both wondered if there was some pain hidden deep within her. We knew she had wounds from her past, but we also knew there had to be pain for her placing yet another child for adoption. While she had never showed us much more than manipulation and anger, we knew that she had to be masking her feelings. We hoped that she loved Amelia. We hoped that someday she would find her way and get the help she needed. It was very clear that something had made her this way and we did feel for her at times.

We were now in the homestretch of the adoption, but we were not counting on anything going right at this point. Any time our phones rang we froze in fear. We now simply needed to wait for Arizona and California ICPC to clear, which indicates the paperwork was approved and we would be free to go home. According to both Jill and our attorney, this was simply a formality and would only take a day or two. Neither Jill nor the attorney had ever had any issues or problems with this process. Thus we simply had to wait at the hotel for clearance to leave.

Two days went by, and we had not received any word from ICPC Arizona. Finally, Jill called us on Wednesday and told us there was an issue. "Well, Andrew, the roller coaster of the worst adoption case in American history continues. There is a hold on your ICPC paperwork because there is an open CPS case against Sandi. We do not know the implications of this or how long the delay will be. They will not provide any answers other than someone called CPS on the family. We just have to wait and be patient. I am really hoping that this is not anything serious." By this point, nothing shocked me, but once again there was a shadow of doubt over my adoption. How could so much go wrong?

I immediately called my legal team and others in Golden Valley and Arizona who had helped me in the past. After several hours of calls, I found out that someone had anonymously called CPS and told them about Sandi's abuse of the children and the conditions of the home, and the anonymous person had even complained that she was "selling babies." Obviously we were not the people who had called CPS, but it did not take long before Sandi was contacted and told that a social worker would be coming out. She was frantically cleaning while also barraging our phones with text messages and accusations. We had still not heard any information from ICPC, and we were becoming very worried. At about 4:00pm we were told that the issue was not related to Amelia and therefore would not be a serious issue. We were told that the clearance should come the next day.

After one more restless night and afternoon, to our delight at 4:00pm on Thursday we were approved by Arizona ICPC and preliminarily approved by California. By 5:00pm we had been officially approved by California, and we were free to go home. We had decided that we would stay one additional day to keep our promise to Sandi to allow her to see Amelia before we left town. To be honest, we did not do this for Sandi. We did it because our consciences were eating at our hearts. We wanted to see the kids one last time, we wanted Doug to hold Amelia, and we wanted closure. We knew that Sandi did not deserve a visit, but we wanted to take the high road before we left. Many in our circle of family and friends did not understand this, but it was our decision and ours alone. We would keep our word and allow one last visit.

To this day we do not know who called CPS. We know it was not anyone who was associated with me. I had planned on calling CPS once we were home in California to ensure the safety of the kids, whom I had come to love. Our theory is that the landlord called CPS because she was so disgusted with Sandi trying to change her mind. She knew the condition of the house, the kids, and she was aware of Sandi's past. The only other explanation was that Doug had called. Why would he call CPS on himself, though? The answer is actually quite remarkable if it is true. Doug had left Sandi on Wednesday and had not yet returned home. In fact, he left the car at Sandi's sister's home with the keys and her welfare food card on the seat. No one had heard from him since. Several people who wanted to help Doug had told him that calling CPS would help him by giving him a clean break from Sandi. If this happened, the kids would be temporarily taken away and then the attorney would offer to help him gain custody of the children for free. She offered Doug her legal services without any charge because everyone was so concerned for him. We all wanted to help him out of the abusive relationship. We will never know who called, but I would like to think it was Doug trying to better his and the kids' lives. The sad part was that CPS was not doing their job properly, and they called Sandi warning her of the imminent visit. She would have time to clean the house, bathe the kids, and make her disgusting home look like it was perfect. Regardless, I had every intention of letting CPS know every detail of the past seven months as soon as the time was right. I could not personally save these kids, but I was bound and determined to do anything and everything possible to help them.

The day before we were to go home to Livermore, we learned that Doug had attempted suicide and was in the hospital. We learned that this would be at least the fourth time that he had attempted to take his own life. He had left his home to go put in job applications when everything that was on his mind caught up with him. We believe that he had pondered Sandi's treatment of him, his feeling of being a failure, and his fear that his life would never improve. It was also possible that he was clinically depressed and had never been treated for it.

By this time, DJ and I had grown quite fond of Doug, and we could honestly feel his pain and torment. We immediately left Lake Havasu for Golden Valley to make one last visit with the family. Prior to our arrival, we had notified Sandi's sisters that we would be coming for our last visit, and they agreed to meet us at her house. We really did not have any interest in seeing Sandi, and our hatred for her was still fresh. That being said, it was important to see the children one more time. As we played with the kids and smothered them with love, Sandi said her goodbyes to Amelia, as did the sisters. Sandi told her that she loved her and gave her a small kiss on the forehead. Around the same time Doug called and asked us to hurry to the hospital so he could say goodbye to us and to Amelia. He was about to be taken by ambulance to the mental hospital.

DJ stayed at the home to watch the children while I took Sandi and Amelia to see Doug before he left. During the car ride, Sandi made a lackluster attempt to apologize to me, saying, "Andrew, I don't want you to hate me forever. I want things to be back to normal. I am sorry for lying, for manipulating you, for lying about the labor and relocation, and for making up lies about the pregnancy. I am also sorry about the whole changing my mind thing. I am sorry I cost you so much money. I really don't know what's wrong with me." For a split second I felt sorry for her. Then she did what she always did to make her true colors show: "Do you think you can help us with some money? I mean, like, help us with living expenses for a few more months?"

I looked at Sandi, almost exploded, and then simply said, "Sandi, you are getting our legal postpartum funds. Other than that, you will never see another dime from me or my family."

At the hospital I found Doug curled up in a hospital bed shaking with fear. He smiled when he saw me and reached for Amelia. He looked at her in the eyes, kissed her several times, and said, "I love you so much, Amelia. I will always love you. Daddy loves you more than anything in the world. You be a good baby for Andrew and DJ. I will miss you always." He kissed her several more times as he cried. He told both Sandi and me that he would need to get actual help this time and would not be able to be discharged for a while. "I have to really get help this time. I am hearing voices. I walked into the hospital last night and told them to please help me or I was going to blow off my head."

Sandi then coldly said, "You will be discharged in 72 hours; I will make sure of that. I will call the hospital myself."

Doug gave me a look of helplessness, and we both knew that nothing would ever change with her. I felt a very deep sympathy toward him and hoped he would be alright.

Before I left, Doug said to me, "I love you, bro... Can I ask you a question? Are you and DJ really my friends? I really don't have any friends."

Without hesitation I said, "Doug, you are definitely our friend, and we will never stop helping you if we can. I love you! You are like the brother I never had."

Doug turned around and cried. It was an unlikely friendship that had formed between Doug, DJ, and I. It was a friendship built with a strong bond that held us together. It was a friendship that I honestly hoped would last forever.

It was now time to go and close the book on this chapter of our lives. I brought Sandi home, DJ and I said a long goodbye to the kids, we gave Sandi a cold hug, and then we packed the car up for the ride back to Lake Havasu. As we pulled away, we looked at the house that we had spent so much time in. For a moment, we realized that we had spent a great deal of time in a home that we would have never stepped foot in a year ago. We had acclimated to the smell of dog and cat feces, a house infested with lice, months of dirty dishes piled up, a year's worth of dirty laundry littering the floor, garbage strewn throughout the house, and children who were so dirty that their smell took our breath away. What we could never acclimate to was the treatment and abuse that the kids suffered every day.

Despite all of the negative experiences we had with Sandi, we were extremely thankful to her for giving us what we could never have on our own. We were and would always be grateful to her for ultimately doing a selfless act. On the outside, she was using adoptions as a means to gain financial benefit. On this inside, she knew that she could not care for another child when she could not even care for her own. Our anger and resentment were strong and probably always will be but we will always be thankful to her for giving us the chance to be loving fathers.

We drove down their street for what would likely be the last time. We silently reminisced about the past 206 days and all the turmoil that Sandi had brought into our lives. While we had never given up during this entire time, we also never dreamed of the day that we would drive down their street for the very last time. We remembered the dozens of times we had pulled up to their house and dreaded getting out of the car to face Sandi. Our mixed emotions would likely haunt us for a lifetime. For reasons I cannot explain, I suddenly felt a deep sense of empathy toward Sandi. I thought about her childhood where she was raised with almost no love, little attention, and years of abuse. Simply put, she had had a horrible life for 24 years and she was continuing that as a result of the trauma in her childhood. It will never excuse her behavior and the abuse of her children, but at that moment my heart hurt for her.

We both intended to keep every promise we had made to Doug and the kids. We knew deep inside, however, that we would probably never allow Sandi to be big a part of Amelia's life. We knew there was always the possibility that time would heal our wounds, Sandi would change for the better, and we could someday have the relationship we had dreamed about back in May. Maybe even Amelia would someday get to know her birth mother. We knew that chance was slim. That being said, our job was to be great parents and that started by sheltering Amelia from people like Sandi. Someday we would have to explain to her about her mom, and we knew it would be the most difficult discussion we would ever have. We prayed for Doug's speedy recovery and the safety of the three children. We prayed Sandi would change or get the help she needed.

I had one last piece of unfinished business to attend to, and it was with a great deal of guilt that I managed to pick up my phone and call CPS. I felt a horrendous sense of guilt because I knew I was probably going to be the reason that the family would be split up. I felt obligated to call so as to save these innocent children from a life of neglect and abuse. I spent upwards of twenty minutes on the phone filing the complaint. As I explained the story to the social worker I knew I had done the right thing. Sandi has escaped CPS for years, but I did not think she could avoid or manipulate them this time. DJ and several others were also going to file complaints during the coming week. It was all of our hope that CPS could somehow find a way to help these loving and sweet children and maybe give them a real chance at a bright future. I went so far as to give them all my information in the event that the kids were placed into a foster program. While I could never afford to help all three, I would be willing to help at least one if they could not place them as a family.

Failure is something that every human on our planet experiences on a frequent basis. Most of us accept our failures, learn from them, embrace them, and become stronger and better people as a result. We turn our failures into something positive. Sandi chose failure as a lifestyle. She chose not to better her life. She chose to be cruel and abusive to her family. She chose to torture others who tried to love her. Sandi embraced failure as her mantra, and we did not think that would ever change. Many people say that there are no truly bad people. I am not so sure about that, but I am sure that Sandi will forever haunt my memories. I hope people will continue to pray for her as I will. I only want the best for her and her future. In time we will forgive her. In time, we will try to ensure that she gets to see Amelia if she gets the help that she so badly needs.

On November 22, 2014, at 7:04pm, we reached the summit of the Altamont Pass that overlooked the bright lights of the Livermore valley. When we reached that peak, joy and happiness filled our hearts. We looked at Amelia, who was soundly sleeping in her car seat, and realized just how lucky we were to have such a blessing in our lives. The amount of love that we felt for this ten-day-old baby girl was beyond words. There was a reason that we fought for 206 days to bring her home. There was a reason we were put through such a rigorous test. She was the light of our lives, and we will be forever grateful to all of those who helped us along our turbulent journey. She helped us understand so much about life, goodness, and unconditional love. For the rest of our lives, we would dedicate everything in us to ensure that Amelia was the most loved little girl in the world. She was what made the whole ordeal worth it.

We continued down 580 West and soon reached our exit. As we did, the vivid, haunting memories of the past instantly evaporated from our minds. We turned onto our street, pressed the garage door opener, and pulled into the garage. This was the day we had been awaiting so many months for. Together we held Amelia, opened the door, and found Boomer eagerly waiting to welcome us home. In our living room, we laid down a blanket and set Amelia down. Boomer slowly circled her, sniffed her, and then gave her a little kiss on the head. DJ and I held hands and observed the beautiful scene. This was our beautiful family, and we were very proud daddies. The battle of our lives was over; however, our journey as a happy family was just beginning.

## Helpful advice for those considering open-adoption

Our adoption was a very extreme case where nearly everything that could go wrong did. Yet, here we stand months later with our amazing family and the love of our lives, Amelia. Our long and difficult fight was grueling but it was clearly worth every moment of stress and anxiety. If we had to do it all over again we would not hesitate for a moment.

While our adoption was "the most difficult" in American history, yours will likely be a much different story. Please do not let our case discourage you from adoption, fostering, or surrogacy. As with most adoptions, your experience will most likely be a smooth process where you find love and long lasting relationships with your birth mother. The end result will be your dreams coming true and a bundle of joy in your home. Adoption is truly a blessing that will bring joy and happiness to thousands of families every year.

That being said, as a result of our intense adoption experience we have learned many lessons that we feel could be of assistance to those families exploring the idea of adoption (or those currently in the process). The following tips should be a guide to help you proactively think through some possible issues, complications, and solutions. It is our hope that the problems we encountered will serve as learnings for others in the adoption process. You may also feel free to ask us any questions on our Facebook page: *drewanddjadoption.*

> **Be prepared and proactive!** Whether you are adopting as a couple, as a single, or a same sex couple, the best advice I can give you is to be extremely prepared. In fact, be overprepared. The best thing you can do to improve your chances of a timely match will be to proactively clear many of the obstacles before you even sign with an agency or facilitator. As a starting point, you should be completely prepared for the difficult financial aspect of adoption. Total expenses are

different for every adoptive couple, but you should be prepared to spend between $15,000 and $50,000 dollars. The range is very broad, given that legal expenses, agency expenses, and birth mother expenses vary greatly. Set a budget that you are comfortable with and stay within that range as you are vetting the process. If you find that you simply cannot afford an adoption, do not be too distraught as there are many ways to help your situation. Some solutions that you may want to explore include: low interest adoption loans, employee adoption benefits, loans from family, and fund raising events. There are websites and articles that are dedicated to helping prospective adoptive couples with fund raising.

Once your **finances are in order**, the next step should be to get your home study completed. On the surface this seems like a very easy process but the fact is that it is not only time consuming but it is tedious and expensive. The process is lengthy and can take some couples months to complete. If you are passionate and extremely dedicated like I was, you can complete it quickly. For some, however, they simply do not have the time available to complete the process fast and it will likely take two to three months. Getting the process done prior to starting the adoption process will set you apart from other couples who have not begun. That alone will increase your chances of a timely match. Every home study is different, but you will most likely need to take parenting classes, adult and infant first aid, and adult and infant CPR. In additon to the courses there will be required readings, in-home social service visits, finger printing and criminal background clearances, a plethora of paperwork, and letters of reference from up to ten people. That is only a part of the home study process and there is much more involved. In short, get it done and your process will not only be faster but you will be less stressed.

**Select an agency or facilitator.** Once you have secured your finances, set a budget, and have a completed, approved, and signed home study – you are now ready for the next big step. There are essentially three choices for domestic adoption; agency adoption, foster to adopt, and facilitator adoption. My expertise is in agency and facilitator (independent) adoption and thus cannot comment on fostering. There are advantages and disadvantages to using an agency and a facilitator. For agencies, you often deal with large corporations with hundreds or even thousands of waiting adoptive families. The advantages of using an agency are that they have massive marketing budgets, they work with many birth mothers at once, and they offer classes, courses, and seminars to prepare you for the process. The disadvantages are that there are so many people in the 'waiting families' pool that your wait times to be matched will almost surely be significantly longer. Most agencies that we interviewed suggested waiting times of over a year and sometimes as long as two years. In some instances, we met couples that were never matched and had to find a new agency (this would be very costly).

Adoption facilitators are not agencies. They are independent professionals that find birth mothers and match them with adoptive parents. They usually charge a hefty fee for their services but often only work with a small number of clients at once. Each professional works differently, but in general they will help you find a birth mother that is right for you and see the process through all the way to the end. The advantages of a facilitator are that you get personalized attention, you can decide which birth mother you want to attempt to match with, and the size of the 'waiting families' pool is significantly smaller. In my opinion and experience, your chances of being matched quickly are greatly improved with a facilitator. The disadvantages of a facilitator are that it is often more expensive and you have to do some of the work yourself (hiring adoption attorneys, social workers, etc).

My personal opinion is that if you are not in a hurry you should use an agency as they have all the resources to see you through from start to finish. In addition you will likely pay lower fees. The only caveat is clearly that you must be prepared to wait. If you are interested in matching quickly and bringing home your baby sooner rather than later, then you should use an independent adoption facilitator.

Regardless of which option you chose, the most important piece of advice I can offer is to thoroughly vet them before making a commitment. With today's modern technology you can find reviews and testimonials on nearly anything…adoption included. Read the reviews and testimonials to learn more about the agency in question. When you find an agency or facilitator that you think you are comfortable with, take the time to do your homework. Make a list of questions and concerns that you have and set up a conference call to discuss each one. If an agency does not have the time to do this, then they likely do not have the time for your adoption. Ask to speak with clients that have adopted with them in the past. Use these opportunities to learn exactly how the agency or facilitator handled every aspect of the adoption from start to finish. If you are uncomfortable with any of the information or answers that you receive, then you should probably continue your search. A good agency or facilitator will be happy to answer all of your questions and concerns.

**Talk to her!** Your lucky day has arrived. Not only have you found an agency that you love but you have been matched with a birth mom. Your first inclination is to sign the papers and get going. Wrong! This is really where we made our biggest mistakes. We allowed the thrill and excitement of being matched to overshadow our judgment. In hindsight, we should have asked more questions, done more research, and made more of an attempt to get to know our birth mother before proceeding. You are about to embark on a six to nine month journey with a woman you do not know. Ideally, your relationship will continue with her for the rest of your life. It is imperative that you do as much homework on her as you can. Read her medical files and background information, then read them again, and finally read them one more time. Ask the agency about any concerns or questions you may have. Most likely she is a wonderful person and will be a great birth mother, but you owe it to yourself to do as much detective work as you possibly can.

Once you have completed the background information I would suggest you take it one step further. Ask the agency if they can provide two to three character references that you can call or email. Talk to people that know her and find out as much information about her as you can. If she is unwilling to allow this, it is quite possible that there is something about her that she does not want you to know.

At this point if everything seems legitimate and you are comfortable, ask your agency to arrange a conference call with her. Use this time to ask her any remaining questions or concerns that you may have. This is not the time to be timid or modest. Ask her anything that your heart desires so that you can walk away very comfortable that you know her as best as you can. If you live within driving distance of her or you do not mind flying, ask the agency to arrange a pre-match visitation. The visit should be no more than a few hours. You can take her to lunch or dinner and simply have a live, face to face discussion. If she has a family, you can use this opportunity to meet them and to see how she interacts with others. While this step may be unnecessary and expensive (travel costs), it will do wonders to put your mind at ease knowing that you have matched with a person that you will be comfortable with. Again, this person will likely be a part of your life and your child's life for many years to come.

**Set Boundaries.** So at this point you are comfortable with your finances, have a concise budget, you found an agency that you are pleased with, and you have been matched with a birth mother that you are certain is right for you. Congratulations. By now, you have established a relationship with your birth mother and you are comfortable having normal and intimate conversations with her. This is the perfect time to set expectations and boundaries for the remainder of the pregnancy and post-pregnancy. Establish a plan for what your communications and visitations will be like, moving forward. Many experts recommend having a set weekly call to simply talk and to get to know one another. Agree to a set number of visitations that you are comfortable with and that are financially feasible. It is important to set boundaries on how often you should communicate on the whole. For us and many other families, text messaging proved to be a big problem. If you are not comfortable receiving frequent text messages, you should set a boundary for phone calls only. Often times birth mothers have more time than you do and the messaging can quickly become out of control. By having a set weekly call and prearranged visits you can eliminate the need for text messages all together.

Money and finances are an issue that very few people are comfortable talking about and there is good reason for it. If there is one boundary that should be put in place above all others it is regarding money. DJ and I clearly failed at this and it caused us massive headaches and stress as a result. Working with your agency, establish a clear boundary that you cannot talk about finances with your birth mother under any circumstances. Money should never be discussed at any point. If the subject of money or finances comes up, it should always be directed toward the agency or facilitator. The easiest way to do this is to set the boundary early and often. There will likely be times when your birth mother requests additional funds or expenses. This should always be done through the agency and never directly between the adoptive family and birth mother. Not only does having these conversations open up a can of worms, but it can also be illegal under some adoption laws. When in doubt, always defer those questions to your agency. In addition, set a budget with your agency and stick to it. Do not veer off course for any reason other than a legitimate emergency. Everytime you 'give in' or provide financial support above and beyond the agreement, you are setting yourself up for more problems down the road. Your golden rule should be to never, ever talk about money, gifts, or finances.

It is also very imperative that you have early discussions about doctor visits, the time at the hospital during the birth, and the post placement agreement. Do you want to attend some of the doctor visits and ultrasounds? Now is the time to have that discussion so there are no surprises. Attending the OBGYN appointments is also a way for you to bond with your birth mother. Work with your agency to create a hosptial plan for when the baby is born. Will she allow you to be present at the birth? Do you want to be present? Will you be allowed to be in the room with her after the delivery? Will you be authorized to help with the care of the baby in the hospital? Will the birth mother be nursing the baby for the first few days? What is the timeline for her to sign the consent papers after the baby is born? These are all touchy subjects that must be discussed in detail and in writing to ensure all parties are aligned from the start. Your agency can help you with the official paperwork that comes along with some of these questions.

**Bond.** Now the hard work is behind you and you have a great relationship with your birth mother and family. Use the remaining time to bond with her and her family. She will soon be a part of your extended family and bonding now will help set you on the course for a problem-free relationship. Use your weekly calls to share pictures, talk about your week, listen to each other, and provide love and support. Use your visitations to get to know her and her family better. The visits will allow you to trust her and for her to trust you. Take her and her family out to an occasional lunch or dinner when you are in town. Do something fun as a group such as going to the zoo, playing at a park, or simply having coffee and talking. Plan the visits around doctor appointments if she has allowed you to attend. Use this precious time to build your mutual relationship so that by the time the baby is ready to come, you are all one big and happy family.

**Review the plan.** One month prior to the delivery date you should take the time to work with your agency and birth mother to review the plan one last time. Everyone should be aligned at this point but it never hurts to revisit the established plan. Discuss the day of delivery, the delivery itself, the hospital stay, the baby care plan, breast feeding, bottle feeding, the hospital release, and the plan for the day she will sign the consent paperwork. Having this discussion long before the delivery date will ensure that there are no major surprises.

**Final Advice.** A close relationship with your birth mother is not the only relationship that needs your attention. You should have a very close relationship with your agency or facilitator. It is key that you remain in constant contact and always keep one another up to date on everything. You will also want to hire the very best adoption attorney and social worker if needed. Your adoption is literally in the hands of the adoption attorney that you choose. You want to be 100% certain that he or she knows the laws inside and out. If you are adopting in a state other than your own, he or she must know the adoption laws in both states. As you did with the agencies, research your attorney before you hire them. Read reviews, have consultations, ask questions, and ask for client testimonials. Ask your agency or facilitator for a referral to an attorney that they know and trust. It is important to find an attorney that fits your budget, but you must also find one that has expertise in adoption and your states. This is one area where you do not want to 'pinch pennies'.

Finally, if your state requires you to hire a social worker for your birth mother, be sure to also do your homework for this. This person plays a pivotal role in many adoptions and you want to be sure you have a caring and understanding licensed social worker.

In general, these tips only cover the major areas of the adoption and specifically areas where we made mistakes. If you follow these guidelines, you will have a much smoother and less stressful adoption than we did. Hopefully you will establish a loving and caring relationship with your birth mother that will last for the remainder of your life and your child's life. The process of adoption is long and complicated and you want to be sure that you are fully prepared for the journey. Being prepared will make your life and the life of your birth mother much more problem-free, thus leaving time for bonding and fun.

We wish you the very best! Please do not hesitate to reach out if you have any questions. No question will be ignored and no question is dumb.

# *Update:*

Amelia has now been home with us for two months and our lives are nothing but happiness, joy, and excitement. The stress of Sandi has evaporated and the huge weight of her existence has been lifted from our lives. We have no contact with Sandi other than mailing or texting an occasional picture. We completely ignore her texts and her continued ploys for money and power.

Amelia is nothing but a joy to be around. She is our angel and is one of the calmest and happiest babies I have ever had the pleasure to be around. We were blessed with the rare baby that sleeps through the night, rarely cries, and is always smiling. She has brought pure pleasure to both of us and our families. We love her more than words can describe.

CPS has been to Sandi's home several times per week since we left and no fewer than six reports were filed against her. On a positive note, it has forced her to make the living conditions better for the children. While I know she is not doing it out of love; the fact of the matter is that she is being forced to clean up her act. As I type this, sadly the children are still in her home but CPS is working diligently to ensure their safety. They have forced her to enroll all three children in school, which makes us extremely happy. Not only will they have an opportunity for a public education, but they will also now be able to learn to socialize with other children. They will be able to make friends. They will have loving and caring teachers to ensure that they are safe and not abused.

Sandi has also been provided with free childcare so that she would have no excuse for getting a job. She was forced to put in job applications and actually found work at a local hotel. We are very pleased that at least some progress has been made.

As was planned, Doug left Sandi and immediately received help by a group that provides assistance to people of domestic violence. Sandi had punched Doug in the throat shortly after we left and the police were called. Doug managed to find the courage to seek the help he needed and he was attempting to start a new life. As difficult as it was, he too filed a report with CPS and was 100% honest with them about everything. Doug was receiving counseling, treatment for alcohol and drugs, and therapy. We had hoped that he would get sober, find a job and eventually be able to get custody of the children. Unfortunately, we had learned that Doug has several more mental health issues, began drinking again, and had been in and out of psychiatric hospitals in Las Vegas. We have since lost touch with him all together.

On December 17th, we hosted a unique reunion of all the adopted sisters. Both of the other families that had adopted from Sandi came to our home and the sisters all got to meet for the very first time. It was an amazing event and something so rare that it could have been on a television show. Three adoptive families, three different cities, and three biological sisters meeting for the very first time. We had a wonderful time and our extended family was blessed with a new branch to our adoptive family tree. It was a day we will never forget and hopefully the beginning of a long and happy relationship between the three families. For the remainder of her life, Amelia will have two biological sisters with whom she can have a loving and close relationship.

CPSIA information can be obtained at www.ICGtesting.com
Printed in the USA
BVOW05s2207301015

424527BV00002B/45/P